HOW I BUILT MY PC FROM SCRATCH

EVERYTHING BASIC YOU NEED TO KNOW ON BUILDING YOUR OWN AMD PC FOR GAMING & VIDEO EDITING

Dr RJ Nair

+For Deepti+

+CONTENTS+

HOW TO READ THIS BOOK

o The only thing you must do here is to just start, the remaining will fall into place.

o This book is divided into two sections. Even though the demarcation is not distinct, the two sections here are, Theory knowledge and practical knowledge.

o Theory knowledge will give you all the basic knowledge for you to proceed into becoming the best PC builder.

o The practical knowledge section comprises of hardware involved in building PC.

o If you are a beginner in the world of building your own PC, I suggest you complete both sections.

o The theory knowledge will ensure the beginners to have a basic knowledge about the selection and working of various components of PC.

o This will invariably avoid a lot of mistakes the beginners make during the process of PC building.

o Theory knowledge will help you in selecting the most valuable PC components available in the market in your quest to build your own PC.

o But if you have all the basic knowledge and want to just dive into building your own PC, Practical knowledge is all you need to proceed.

o Even though I don't recommend it, I never went around to read all the basics of PC building. This section was later exclusively written for beginners to have a basic knowledge as this can invariably avoid any mistakes during PC building.

o Most motherboard manual comes with basic instruction and guidelines. If you read them carefully, this is the only thing that is required to put the components together to build a PC. But there are always unforeseen circumstances that can arise if your basic knowledge is not good.

o I have created separate sections so that even if you don't have that basic knowledge but still in a hurry to build a PC. You can now directly dive into section two, Practical knowledge. This section of the chapters is especially highlighted as 'Yellow' under the contents of the book. I have included everything basic required to build your own PC under this section of chapters.

o I have also included a different budget-wise handpicked selection of PC components in this book, which will help you in selecting the PC components without the hassle of checking for their compatibility with each other.

o In case if you want to tweak your selection of components for your PC build with some other replacements, more expensive or more budget-friendly, all you have to do is to go to the 'PCPARTPICKER' website, select your PC component of choice, click add. Select all the components and add them to the list. This will make sure that you are selecting only compatible components.

o Since the components are already Pre-selected for you here in the practical knowledge section, highlighted as yellow under the contents of the book, you can skip the theory knowledge section to save time. This is only an option and not a suggestion.

o The theory knowledge section is the non-highlighted part of the contents of the book. This section will give you a strong background in building your own PC.

o This section will help you in selecting the various components required to build a PC, their compatibility, their performance, their required field of use, etc.

o I have also included a special chapter: Most common mistakes, which will cover all the likely mistakes that can happen to you when you build your own PC. This section along with the practical knowledge section as mentioned before includes all the basic knowledge required to build a beginner to intermediate level PC.

o The green highlighted chapters in the contents indicate the top components currently available in the market

o Any errors in the book, please contact me in my email: deeraknair7721@gmail.com

o This is my first edition. Henceforth I will be adding more details to keep it updated. Good luck!

INTRODUCTION

o I'm a medical doctor by profession. I did have some basic knowledge about PC. During my undergraduate years when I was left with very few breaks from studying, which I filled with learning hobbies like Video editing. This was like a breath of fresh air to me. I always had a plan to create educational videos, creating and editing them, so on and so forth.

o This process took me to a different side of things I was not accustomed to. But I did enjoy it very much.

o Learning about video editing was challenging and fun, also it led me to create a mini studio at my place, learning about photography, videography, etc.

o Video editing using Adobe Premiere Pro requires a well efficient high-end PC or laptop.

o A high-end laptop with the necessary configuration to support the video editing process in adobe premiere pro can be very expensive and comes with limited features with no room for expansion.

o This is when my interest in a desktop PC peaked, especially a custom build one. Here you have more room for upgrade.

o There is always a Budget-friendly choice for you unlike a laptop or Prebuilt PC for the same configuration as the self-build PC.

o The first lesson I learned in this process is to get the best motherboard in the market as it gives you more than enough room for future expansion or upgrade. This is very important as other components are attached to the motherboard. These components can easily be removed from the motherboard and replaced easily. But not the same case when it comes to the motherboard. It's a tedious process when it comes to motherboard replacement.

o I always believe Gaming, Video editing, and PC building should go hand in hand.

o Most of the choices of Prebuilt PCs available in the market are all gaming PCs except for a few. But these can be very expensive too.

- I did also include all the basic knowledge required to build yourself a nice basic to intermediate level gaming PC too. And the configuration and the requirements to build the best gaming PC based on your budget, profession or requirement.

- This book is the gateway to the world of building your own PC for Gaming and video editing.

PC building can be so much fun, at the same time it is filled with difficulty and challenges too, a Little by little hard work and full-on passion will take you to the world of artistic creativity. At the end of the day building PC is like creating life itself, breathing, moving machines, that talk and communicate with you in many ways, makes our life easier. The satisfaction you get from this is beyond words. So, don't deny yourself from this amazing experience and start building one right now. You will also notice that this has opened a world of possibilities.

MY FIRST PC BUILD

o Here I would like to share my experience and photos of my first PC build.

o I did a lot of research before diving myself into the beautiful art of PC building.

o I'm sharing here all the knowledge I learned necessary to build a beginner to intermediate level PCs.

o Advance level PC Build, I consider to be extreme gaming PCs with their water-cooling systems. This is a bit more complicated. Maybe one of these days I might release a book for advance builders.

o Building PC requires a keen sense of observation and patience.

o If this is your first build, spend some time with your PC components, just before assembling them.

o Take enough ESD precautions. Some even consider it not necessary. But you are working with the sensitive circuit board which require much care. Needless to say, they are expensive too.

o If you follow this book, word to word, I promise, you will find it much easier than you anticipated and the satisfaction after, has no words to express.

o I kept staring at the PC, couldn't take my eyes off, it's the first most beautiful thing I have ever created. I was so proud of myself.

o I believe this is an art on its own. And my passion is all for it.

Good luck and thank you or taking this journey with me.

PICTURE BELOW SHOWS THE FIRSTEVER PC I BUILD FROM SCRATCH (Without PSU & Cables attached)

(Figure 1A)

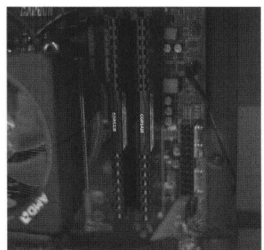

 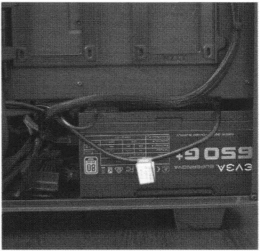

BEST TIPS IN SELECTING COMPONENTS
&
BUILD
PC

BEST VIDEO EDITING PC

o A specialized and optimized Computer for Video Editing can save you time, a lot of frustration and in the long run, lots of money.

VIDEO EDITING AND COMPUTER HARDWARE

o If we want to build the best Computer for Video Editing, the first step is to analyze what Hardware your Video Editing Software uses the most. there are so many different Video Editing Applications out there, but I will focus on my got to video editing software. It is a very popular Video Editing Software, that many professionals and also amateurs edit in. Lots of other Video Editing Apps use the Hardware in very similar ways.

o There are a lot of steps of video editing (WORKFLOW) you go through, before a perfectly formed video that you have created, these steps include:

o Load Footage into my Project
o Add video, B-roll, Music, clips sequences into the timeline and rough cuts with this footage.
o Playback timeline clips a lot of times along with editing.
o Add Transitions, Effects, Titles.
o Add Sound Effects and Music.
o Color Grading.
o *Video rendering* - Video rendering can be one of the most hardware-demanding processes for a computer, especially when it's done in real-time.
o Exporting

The most important steps that we need to focus as much as possible to build our best Computer for Video Editing

o The software reads the data in the form of video and audio after it's been uploaded into the software.

o The editing software DECODES this footage.

o The software then manipulates this video based on the various effects and corrections we apply to the footage.

o This footage is then stored in RAM so that there is easy access to this footage for playback in real-time.

o During the process of RENDERING, software encodes the footage from the timeline to your desired codec.

o This encoded data is now stored in the storage drive.

READING & LOADING OF FOOTAGE

o The speed of transfer and reading of your footage depends on your **storage device** and the **transfer bus**.

o (A) The 3 most used storage options are:

o (i) **HARD DISK (HDD)** - Even though it has great cost/GBs, it is the slowest of the 3 when it comes to sequential read and write speed. It is a great device to back up your data which doesn't require frequent access. The lifespan is around 5 years, some achieve more. It's good to have multiple copies of your data if the budget is not an issue. Refer to my 'RAID' chapter to know about the different methods to back up your data footage. A good HDD to consider is the BARRACUDA series from SEAGATE and WESTERN DIGITAL'S BLUE or RED series. These HDDs come in sizes up to 14TB, though the best price/GB mark lies somewhere around 8TB.

o (ii) **Solid State Drive (SSD)** - They are faster than HDD drives. SSDs are 4 times faster than HDD. A 7200 RPM Hard Drive - average read/write speed is 80-160MB/second, SATA 3 SSD - read/write speed up to 550MB/second, NVMe SSD - read/write speed up to 3500MB/second. *I would choose to store and use the video footage from the NVMe SSD during my editing in adobe premiere pro since its sequential read and write speed is over high up in the chart*. Even if you choose the SATA SSD because of its price or some other reasons, I wouldn't recommend it to be your storage drive for the editing. The performance of SATA SSD is slightly better than HDD. But practically will never be able to achieve a better significant speed because of the bottlenecking. The full potential of SATA SSD can't be reached because of the SATA interface. Even though SATA SSD and NVMe SSD both are flash memory unlike HDD which has a mechanical disk, NVMe is a new interface protocol technology that uses PCI express (PCIe) to transfer data to and from the SSD drives. This makes it much faster and reliable than SATA SSD and HDD.

NOTE

- **BUS:** A bus is simply a circuit that connects one part of the motherboard to another. The more data a bus can handle at one time, the faster it allows information to travel. The speed of the bus, measured in megahertz (MHz), refers to how much data can move across the bus simultaneously. Think of a bus as the electronic highway on which data travels within a computer, from one component to another. It's the conduit used by your entire system to communicate with your CPU. A bus is a collection of wires and connectors through which the data is transmitted. When used about personal computers, the term bus usually refers to what is commonly called the local bus (on older systems) or system bus (on newer systems). This bus is considered the first bus on the electronic highway and it connects the CPU to the main memory (RAM) on the motherboard.

- All buses consist of two parts -- an address bus and a data bus. The data bus transfers actual data whereas the address bus transfers information about the data and where it should go. The address bus is used to identify particular locations (addresses) in the main memory. The width of the address bus (that is, the number of wires) determines how many unique memory locations can be addressed. Modern PCs and Macs have as many as 36 address lines, which enables them theoretically to access 64 GB of main memory. However, the actual amount of memory that can be accessed is usually much less than this theoretical limit due to chipset and motherboard limitations. The size of a bus, known as its width, is important because it determines how much data can be transmitted at one time. The bus-size indicates the number of wires in the bus. For example, a 32-bit bus has 32 wires or connectors that transmit 32 bits simultaneously (referred to as in parallel). It would be considered "32-bits wide." A 16-bit bus has 16 wires or connectors that can transmit 16 bits of data in parallel. You would say it is "16-bits wide."

- ○ **Bus Speed:** Every bus has a clock speed measured in MHz This measurement represents the speed in which information and data can move across the bus on the motherboard. A fast bus allows data to be transferred faster, which makes applications run faster. Bus speed is one of the factors which determines the speed of your CPU.

DECODING THE FOOTAGE

- ○ Almost every Footage is encoded in some way usually mainly to save space. it has to be decoded before playback and viewing.

- ○ Decoding is a process that is usually done by the Processor (CPU). Unfortunately, no CPU is best for all types of Footage 'Codecs' or Video File types.

- ○ You will have to choose the CPU based on the type of footage you choose to work with. Example: AMD THREADRIPPER is the best CPU to handle 'RED camera footage'. To be specific, the 2990WX model.

- ○ If you are using other image sequences, CPU with higher core-clock is preferred for these types of footages. Clock speed is measured in GHz (gigahertz), a higher number means a faster clock speed. To run your apps, your CPU must continually complete calculations, if you have a higher clock speed, you can compute these calculations quicker and applications will run faster and smoother as a result of this.
- ○ H.264, DNxHD /HR or ProRes Footage seems to be easy enough to decode, that almost all CPUs perform more or less the same here.

- ○ The Decoding part in these Footage types usually is not the bottleneck in slow playback.

- ○ Playing this footage is only halfway through, what about adding new effects or transitions, etc.

FOOTAGE MANIPULATION - EFFECTS, TRANSITIONS, COLOR GRADING, TRIMMING & ADDING TITLES

o If your edits intensive with lots of effects, transitions, color grading, then you will want a maximum Core-Clock CPU.

o The effects are calculated in a hierarchical order. Most can't be outsourced to other cores. A single core will be doing all the calculations of effects in that single frame. For example: If you applied the following effects, like fade, blur, brightness and glow to a part of the footage. A single core of the CPU will take up the job of editing them rather than four CPU mores doing the same job at the same time. This is because the effects are connected. The other frames can start working on the effects of other frames of the footage. Time remapping is an exception where they aren't just dependent on each other on a per-frame basis but in between frames also.

o Like discussed before, the type of footage matters.

o No one CPU that has lots of cores AND a very high core clock to handle all types of footage. This is because the CPU has to stay with a specific thermal and power limits.

o Having a high-clocked CPU is good in handling Effects heavy Projects.

o **A fairly high clocking CPU with lots of cores is a good place to start.**

STORING CACHED FOOTAGE IN RAM

o This is automatically done by the editing software.

o The moment you press any button to playback your timeline, remove your timeline, add or remove any effects, the Software will, (i) Read the Footage (ii) Calculate the Effects on the Footage are calculated (iii) Store the Result in your System Memory (RAM). This process is known as CACHE. This is stored in RAM for the CPU to access the data in the form of footage and directions to be done to the footage.

o Next time you want to view a frame or a sequence, adobe premiere pro or other video editing software doesn't have to calculate everything again but can read the already calculated result from RAM, which is much faster.

o When you playback the footage, the video editing software looks ahead and calculates the frames to come. Sometimes frames are calculated right away. Editing software in a way buffers ahead of the footage yet to come so that there is no interruption in your real-time viewing of the footage.

RANDOM ACCESS MEMORY (RAM)

o RAM is VERY fast, even if you get the worst kind of RAM and it would still be fast enough for almost any of your editing.

o It is still very important to get enough memory for RAM. If there is not enough RAM in your PC, the software will store the excess cached memory in the other drives, which can make the editing process much slower. From this, it is clear that the RAM should have enough memory to store the cached data.

o Reading, calculating and caching will be done multiple times during the process of your video editing sessions.

PROJECT RENDERED TO VIDEO FILE

o RENDERING TO VIDEO FILE is similar to the above process which includes reading the footage —> Calculating the various effects on the footage —> Storing the resulting frames into the storage device. If the Timeline has already been cached, all the Video Editing Software has to do is read the cached Frames from RAM and save them to the Video File. Apart from this, there is one more process called *ENCODING*.

o Encoding - This is an important stage that happens during the rendering process. The video produced without encoding is an uncompressed file. During rendering the sequence from the timeline is encoded, meaning it is compressed into a specific codec, specific for the device you are planning to play the video in. H.264, H.265, WMV9, ProRes, DNxHD, Sorenson, Cinepak are some of the popular codecs out there.

○ Different codecs use different methods to compress the video file. Some skip 2 frames, the difference is negligible and helps in the compression instead of saving all the frames in its entirety. Some codecs reduce color and contrast to save more space. This process is done to compress the file with maximum care not to lose the quality.

○ To summarize the Video Rendering Process and the hardware involved:

○ (i) Reading Footage (SSD)
○ (ii) Calculate / Apply Effects in your Timeline (CPU, GPU)
○ (iii) Store the Frames in RAM (RAM)
○ (iv) Read Frames from RAM (RAM)
○ (v) Encode Frames (CPU)
○ (vi) Pack frames and Audio into a Video file (CPU)
○ (vii) Save resulting Video on Disk (SSD)

○ SSD can usually be ruled out as a bottleneck during the process of rendering because of its decent speed unless the file involved in rendering is a large uncompressed file or EXR file format.

○ The RAM should always be large enough to fit the frames that are being rendered preventing the slowing of the rendering process.

○ The CPU will be responsible for the performance in encoding your frames during rendering.

○ For Rendering out your video projects, having **higher core-counts** is the way to go. But there seems to be an optimum around 16 / 18 Cores and a slightly higher Core-Clock than having double the Cores with a lower Core-Clock. This means if you have a CPU with high core counts and high core-clock, you are at a higher advantage rather than having CPU with higher core count and lower core-clock.

HOW MUCH RAM DO YOU NEED FOR VIDEO EDITING?

- (i) 8GB of RAM: Editing smaller than 1080p projects. You will also have to close down other programs that are using up lots of your RAM in the background.

- (ii) 16GB of RAM: Editing 1080p - 4K 8bit Projects, with minor usage of background Programs.

- (iii) 32GB of RAM: Good for any type of editing with heavy use of background hogs, such as editing large images in Photoshop.

- (iv) 64GB or more: Editing 8K footage in 10bit or more along with having several RAM-hogging Programs open at once such as After effects.

- *FUTURE PROOFING:* It is always ideal to choose a RAM with a slightly higher memory than required as this will leave enough space or upgrading your system. This applies to other PC components as well.

BEST COMPUTER HARDWARE FOR VIDEO EDITING

THE PROCESSOR:

- (i) Best performing INTEL CPU for Video Editing: Intel i9 9980XE (https://amzn.to/39siphB)

- (ii) Best performing AMD CPU for Video Editing: AMD Threadripper 2950X (https://amzn.to/32WMmUC)

- (iii) Best CPU for Video Editing under 500$: AMD Ryzen 9 3900X (https://amzn.to/2IiJnfw)

- Of course, the high core and high core-clock CPU will be the number one choice here like the INTEL CORE i9 9980XE, 18 CORE from Intel and AMD THREADRIPPER 2950X, 16 CORES. These CPUs are very expensive.

- The budget-friendly choice here will be: (i) AMD Ryzen 9 3900X (https://amzn.to/3aswHyI) & (ii) Intel i9 9900K (https://amzn.to/3cyacds). These CPUs still can seem to be very expensive to some but it is a good investment.

- You can also choose from the list above (picture), what CPU can you afford based on performance and budget.

If you are handling RED video footage, AMD THREADRIPPER 2990WX and 2950X are the best choice.

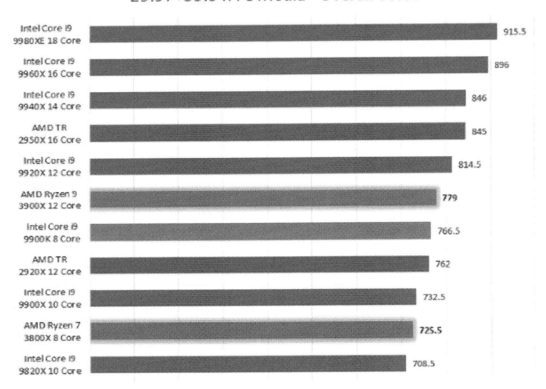

Puget Systems Premiere Pro Benchmark V0.2b

29.97+59.94FPS Media - Overall Score

CPU	Score
Intel Core i9 9980XE 18 Core	915.5
Intel Core i9 9960X 16 Core	896
Intel Core i9 9940X 14 Core	846
AMD TR 2950X 16 Core	845
Intel Core i9 9920X 12 Core	814.5
AMD Ryzen 9 3900X 12 Core	779
Intel Core i9 9900K 8 Core	766.5
AMD TR 2920X 12 Core	762
Intel Core i9 9900X 10 Core	732.5
AMD Ryzen 7 3800X 8 Core	725.5
Intel Core i9 9820X 10 Core	708.5

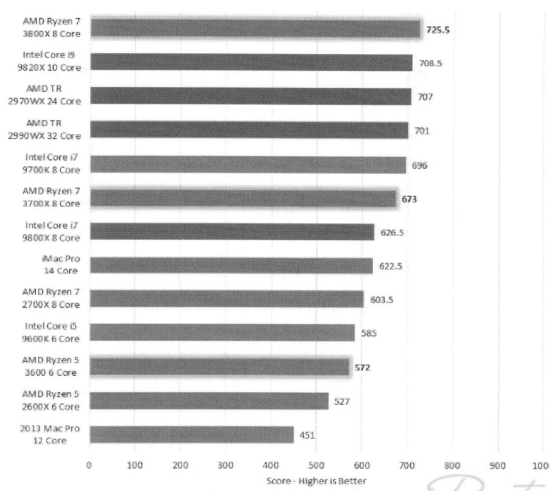

CPU	Score
AMD Ryzen 7 3800X 8 Core	725.5
Intel Core i9 9820X 10 Core	708.5
AMD TR 2970WX 24 Core	707
AMD TR 2990WX 32 Core	701
Intel Core i7 9700K 8 Core	696
AMD Ryzen 7 3700X 8 Core	673
Intel Core i7 9800X 8 Core	626.5
iMac Pro 14 Core	622.5
AMD Ryzen 7 2700X 8 Core	603.5
Intel Core i5 9600K 6 Core	585
AMD Ryzen 5 3600 6 Core	572
AMD Ryzen 5 2600X 6 Core	527
2013 Mac Pro 12 Core	451

Score - Higher is Better

PC Specs: RTX 2080 TI, 64-128GB of RAM, Samsung 960 Pro 1TB,
Software: Windows 10 Pro (1903), Premiere Pro CC 2019 (ver. 13.1.2), Puget Systems Pr Benchmark V0.2 BETA

BEST STORAGE FOR VIDEO EDITING

o **NVMe SSD** should be your number one choice for running your operating system (OS) and the video editing software.

o Instead of running the THREE TIER SYSTEM (Refer to the 'ADOBE PREMIERE PRO SYSTEM REQUIREMENTS FOR VIDEO EDITING' chapter), you can go for **TWO TIER SYSTEM**, where NVMe SSD to run your OS & Video editing software. All the footage required can be saved into the NVMe SSD till the editing is done. After which, all the footage including the project file can be moved to the backup storage, HDD. Media cache files and scratch files can also be stored in the NVMe SSD and can later be moved to the backup storage after completion of the project.

BEST RAM FOR VIDEO EDITING

o Video editing doesn't depend on the performance of the RAM but having enough of it.

o Any DDR4 RAM will be more than enough for video editing but be sure to have enough of it.

o I would set *16GB* memory as the base level to work with footages that are <2K. But if you are working with large footage, quality greater than 2K, I would prefer to use *32GB* or more. *64GB* will be great for 10bit footage, RED Camera videos, 4K, and 8K footages.

o **CAS LATENCY:** Column Access Strobe (CAS) latency, or CL, is the delay time between the moment a memory controller tells the memory module to access a particular memory column on a RAM module, and the moment the data from the given array location is available on the module's output pins. In short, Time between the CPU asking for data and RAM releasing it. In synchronous DRAM, the interval is specified in clock cycles.

o **LATENCY PARADOX** – To calculate a module's latency, multiply *clock cycle duration* by the *total number of clock cycles*. These numbers will be noted in official engineering documentation on a module's datasheet.

Latency is often misunderstood because on product flyers and spec comparisons, it's noted in CAS Latency (CL), which is only half of the latency equation. Because CL ratings indicate only the total number of clock cycles, they don't have anything to do with the duration of each clock cycle, and thus, they shouldn't be extrapolated as the sole indicator of latency performance. By looking at a module's latency in terms of nanoseconds, you can best judge if one module is, in fact, more responsive than another.

LATENCY CALCULATION: The two variables that determine a module's latency: (i) The total number of clock cycles the data must go through (measured in CAS Latency, or CL, on data sheets) (ii) The duration of each clock cycle (measured in nanoseconds) Combining these two variables gives us the latency equation: *latency $^{(ns)}$ = clock cycle time $^{(ns)}$ x number of clock cycles*.

Technology	Module Speed (MT/s)	Clock Cycle Time (ns)		CAS Latency		Latency (ns)
SDR	100	8.00	✖	3	=	24.00
SDR	133	7.50	✖	3	=	22.50
DDR	333	6.00	✖	2.5	=	15.00
DDR	400	5.00	✖	3	=	15.00
DDR2	667	3.00	✖	5	=	15.00
DDR2	800	2.50	✖	6	=	15.00
DDR3	1333	1.50	✖	9	=	13.50
DDR3	1600	1.25	✖	11	=	13.75
DDR4	1866	1.07	✖	13	=	13.93
DDR4	2133	0.94	✖	15	=	14.06
DDR4	2400	0.83	✖	17	=	14.17
DDR4	2666	0.75	✖	19	=	14.25
DDR4	2933	0.68	✖	21	=	14.32
DDR4	3200	0.62	✖	22	=	13.75

o In the history of memory technology, as speeds have increased, which means clock cycle times have decreased, the CAS latency values have also increased, however, because of the faster clock cycle the true latency as measured in nanoseconds has remained roughly the same. By optimizing the balance between the **maximum speed your processor is capable of** and **the lowest latency memory available** within your budget, you can achieve a higher level of performance using newer, faster, and more efficient memory.

o Based on in-depth engineering analysis and extensive testing the answer to this classic question, speed or latency? is BOTH! Speed and latency both play a critical role in system performance, so when looking to upgrade we recommend: **Step 1:** Identify the highest memory speed supported by both your processor and motherboard (including overclocking profiles). **Step 2:** Select the lowest latency memory (latency $^{(ns)}$ = clock cycle time $^{(ns)}$ x number of clock cycles) that fits within your budget at that speed, remembering that a superior (i.e. lower) latency means superior system performance.

o If you like to optimize your RAM as much as possible, the rule is as follows: (i) Look for High Clock Speeds, for example, 3200Mhz is better than 2400Mhz (ii) Look for Low CL Latency (in nanoseconds) based on the formula. (iii) Go for a higher number of Channels, so Quad Channel would be better than Single or Dual Channel. Usually, the amount of RAM Sticks defines the Channel Width. 4 RAM Modules = Quad Channel RAM (2 = Dual, 1 = Single), but this can vary on different systems.

BEST GPU FOR VIDEO EDITING

o We don't talk much about Graphics Cards when it comes to Video Editing. The reason being, that GPUs still don't have a huge impact on any kind of Performance improvement when Editing Videos. Some occasional Effects that might be GPU-Accelerated but as you can see in the Benchmark overview (picture below), the only real difference you can see is that AMD GPUs seem to be performing not as good as the Nvidia, at least in

Premiere Pro. Also please refer to the chapter," ADOBE PREMIERE PRO SYSTEM REQUIREMENTS FOR VIDEO EDITING" for more details on GPU vs Video editing. (Picture courtesy: Puget Systems)

○ Always confirm your system requirements for the type of Video Editing Software you choose.

○ Most of the time Nvidia GPUs are superior.

○ AMD's GPUs Nvidia GTX or RTX GPUs have a better price to performance ratio to Nvidia Quadro GPUs.

○ Having a multi-GPU Setup does not benefit you in Video Editing.

If you are GPU Rendering in 3D, Multi-GPU setups will scale almost linearly. I recommend an Nvidia RTX 2070 (https://amzn.to/38u8AON), as this is a fairly strong GPU, that ranks top in price/performance in a multitude of Benchmarks across many different use cases. Anything above the mentioned GPU can be very expensive but there is not much difference in the performance level for the increase in price. Then again, this is not for the budget PC. Look at the benchmark performance in the above picture and select the GPU based on your budget.

Premiere Pro CC 2018 Benchmark
Overall Score

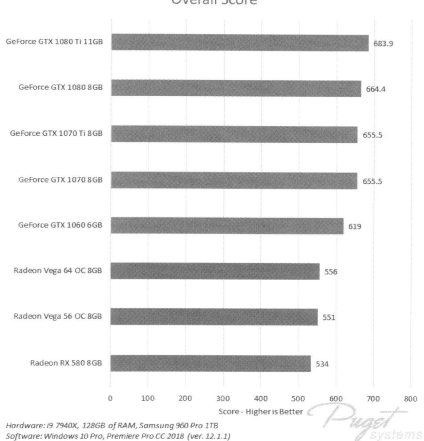

	Score
GeForce GTX 1080 Ti 11GB	683.9
GeForce GTX 1080 8GB	664.4
GeForce GTX 1070 Ti 8GB	655.5
GeForce GTX 1070 8GB	655.5
GeForce GTX 1060 6GB	619
Radeon Vega 64 OC 8GB	556
Radeon Vega 56 OC 8GB	551
Radeon RX 580 8GB	534

Score - Higher is Better

Hardware: i9 7940X, 128GB of RAM, Samsung 960 Pro 1TB
Software: Windows 10 Pro, Premiere Pro CC 2018 (ver. 12.1.1)

10BIT VIDEO

o Rec. 2020 is an ITU (International Telecommunication Union) recommendation, first introduced in 2012, that sets out the standards for UHDTV (UHD 4K and UHD 8K). Included in these standards is the Rec. 2020 Color Space which is an RGB color space that has a color gamut that is wider than almost all other RGB color spaces. It was defined in 2012 as a standard for a bit depth of 10 or 12 bits for 4k and 8k TVs.

o Monitors usually have two types of popular color Bit depths, 8bit and 10bit. These bit depths are understood as bits per channel, meaning with 8 bits you will have 256 color steps per channel (R, G and B). Together they make up to 24bits per color, or 1*6.7 Million Colorsrange*, that we are mostly accustomed to. You can appreciate this as color support in the monitor specs. 10bit Monitors can output 10bits per channel, so 1024 color steps per channel. This makes 30bits per color and totals a *1 Billion Color-range*. This shows that the 1 billion colors are much better than just measly 16.7 Million colors. But the problem with this is your other Hardware and Software along with your monitor has to support this too.

o You will need a Graphics Card that supports 10bit. Quadro or Radeon Pro Workstation GPUs are the choices for this. Also, your work will have to be in at least 10 bits too. If you are working on a JPG Image, MP4 Movie or Render your Animation to a png-sequence, these formats store color in 8bits per channel This meaning that your 10bits per channel Monitor will not show any additional Bit depth in your work. Unless you work on Canon RAW, RED 10bit or EXR Sequences, you will be able to see the higher color range, that a 10bit Monitor will grant you. Especially in Gradients, or Vignetted uniform Backgrounds, you can quickly spot if a Monitor is making good use of its 10bit capability.

o If your work is dependent on driving 10bit displays, having a Quadro is recommended, as GTX / RTX Cards will only output 8Bit to a monitor. But there is another way to drive 10Bit Monitors by using Decklink Card.

o **DECKLINK CARDS** - If you are inclined to use the GTX/RTX for your standard workflow and monitor then you can use

this adapter to have a 10bit output, provided your
monitor supports the project frame rates. These Cards
are made for HDMI / SDI in 10Bit. They are great for
recording 4K or even 8K, 10Bit Video in Real-Time. So,
the combination of your GTX/RTX GPU and the decklink
cards (PCIe supported) will save you some money.
Checkout: https://amzn.to/2IkG7QZ

BEST MOTHERBOARD FOR VIDEO EDITING

o The Motherboard in itself doesn't directly affect the
performance of the video editing. It acts as a perfect
host for other important PC components that enhance the
video editing process. The motherboard should also be
compatible with these components.

o Once the perfect CPU for your video editing is done,
selecting a motherboard depends on the type of CPU
socket. AM4 socket for Ryzen series, except
Threadripper which uses the TR4 SOCKET. When it comes
to Intel, LGA 1151 for an i7 8700K or i9 9900K CPU and
a 2066 Socket for any type of i9-X type of Intel CPUs
such as the i9 9980XE or i9 7890XE.

o Almost every ATX standard sized motherboard has enough
PCIe Slots for your GPU and additional Card. There are
enough SATA Connectors for your drives and usually come
with 5-7 USB Ports for anything external you might need
to plug-in.

o Motherboards now available in the market come with M.2
slots for NVMe M.2 SSDs. Most have 2 or more of the M.2
slots now. Your motherboard manual should also mention
the number of M.2 slots that can be used after the GPU
installation.

o BEWARE: M.2 cards sometimes share lanes with SATA
Ports. If you have too many of them running at a time
for example, if you have 7 SATA SSDs hooked up at the
same time to your PC, then your M.2 Slot will run at
lower speeds or might not work at all, on some
motherboards. This is one of those rare instances. But
it's worth noting.

BEST PC CASES FOR VIDEO EDITING

- This is the first thing people see when they see your PC. It should be aesthetically pleasing.

- There are a lot of features that come with the new generation PC cases. They should be able to accommodate all the components selected for the video editing. I have mentioned these details in my chapter about cases.

- Some important criteria to keep in mind while selecting a case are to make sure the motherboard, ATX type being most common is compatible with the ATX cases.

- Select a PC Case that is professional and minimalistic looking and has some noise dampening features as well.

- Do check out my chapter on PC Cases for more details.

WHY BUILD YOUR OWN?

- You save a lot of money by getting different individual parts without involving any middleman or company.

- You can get exactly any kind of parts or part combinations you want or your PC.

- You learn a lot about how a Computer works.

- You can upgrade your Computer yourself now.

- With all the extra Computer knowledge you gained through research and learning can be used to fix problems that might arise later on.

- Assembling a Computer is easy, it is just plugging different compatible PC components into each other.

- It is fun and satisfying.

It is an accomplishment highlighting your creative side.

BUDGET BASED PREBUILT PC CONFIGURATION

HERE ARE SOME OF THE BEST PREBUILT PC CONFIGURATION BASED ON BUDGET:
ALWAYS ADD ALL THE COMPONENTS IN PCPARTPICKER.COM TO CONFIRM COMPATIBILITY,

BEST AMD COMPUTER FOR VIDEO EDITING
BUDGET ~800
TOTAL COST: $833
TOTAL WATTAGE: 334W

1) COMPONENT: <u>CPU</u> AMD RYZEN 5 1600
WATTAGE (Max): 65W
COST: $215/₹8,499
PURCHASE LINK: https://amzn.to/2PRUrEq

2) COMPONENT: MOTHERBOARD
ASROCK B450M-HDV
WATTAGE (Max): 60W
COST: $78/₹6,699
PURCHASE LINK: https://amzn.to/2Is2h3z

3) COMPONENT: <u>GPU</u>
SAPPHIRE RADEON PULSE RX 570
WATTAGE (Max): 180W
COST: $119/₹15,499
PURCHASE LINK: https://amzn.to/2TJBdSH

4) COMPONENT: MEMORY RAM
Corsair Vengeance LPX DDR4-3200 CL16, 16GB
(2 x 8GB)
WATTAGE (Max): 14W
COST: $73/₹10,080
PURCHASE LINK: https://amzn.to/2VOrIUT

5) COMPONENT: SATA SSD STORAGE

CRUCIAL BX500 480GB 3D NAND SATA 2.5-INCH SSD

WATTAGE (Max): 10W

COST: $59/₹5,200

PURCHASE LINK: https://amzn.to/38HNyfw

6) COMPONENT: HDD STORAGE
WESTERN DIGITAL 1TB BLUE, 3.5"
WATTAGE (Max): 15W
COST: $45/₹3,180
PURCHASE LINK: https://amzn.to/2wzvK98

7) COMPONENT: <u>HDD STORAGE</u>
WESTERN DIGITAL 1TB BLUE, 3.5"
WATTAGE (Max): ~
COST: $89/₹4,945
PURCHASE LINK: <u>https://amzn.to/32YpZ0J</u>

8) COMPONENT: **PC CASE** COOLER MASTER Q300L
WATTAGE (Max): ~
COST: $45/₹4,190
PURCHASE LINK: https://amzn.to/2TLA78S

9) OPERATING SYSTEM (OS):
MICROSOFT WINDOWS 10 HOME (64-BIT)
COST: $110/₹10,973
PURCHASE LINK: Microsoft

BEST AMD COMPUTER FOR VIDEO EDITING
BUDGET $1400
TOTAL COST: $1385
TOTAL WATTAGE: 334W

1) COMPONENT: <u>CPU</u>
AMD RYZEN 5 3600X
(Comes with Wraith Spire CPU cooler)
WATTAGE (Max): 95W
COST: $215/₹18,948
PURCHASE LINK: https://amzn.to/2IlLwqO

2) COMPONENT: <u>MOTHERBOARD</u>
GIGABYTE X570 AORUS ELITE ATX AM4
WATTAGE (Max): 70W
COST: $202/₹20,670
PURCHASE LINK: https://amzn.to/2PTjreN

3) COMPONENT: GPU

NVIDIA GTX 1660TI 6GB - GIGABYTE WINDFORCE

WATTAGE (Max): 120W

COST: $290/₹26,390

PURCHASE LINK: https://amzn.to/2PRaoLj

4) COMPONENT: MEMORY RAM

Corsair Vengeance LPX DDR4-3200 CL16, 16GB (2 x 8GB)

WATTAGE (Max): 14W

COST: $73/₹10,080

PURCHASE LINK: https://amzn.to/2vJPEhx

5) COMPONENT: NVME SSD STORAGE
SAMSUNG 970 EVO PLUS 500GB M.2 SSD
WATTAGE (Max): 10W
COST: $110/₹9,999
PURCHASE LINK: https://amzn.to/3ayt9es

6) COMPONENT: SATA SSD STORAGE
SAMSUNG 860 EVO 1TB 2.5" SSD
WATTAGE (Max): 10W
COST: $150/₹12,999
PURCHASE LINK: https://amzn.to/2POw1M3

7) COMPONENT: HDD STORAGE
WESTERN DIGITAL 4TB BLUE, 3.5"
WATTAGE (Max): 15W
COST: $88/₹9,079
PURCHASE LINK: https://amzn.to/2THGbiT

8) COMPONENT: POWER SUPPLY (PSU)

CORSAIR RMX SERIES PLATINUM RM850X 850W POWER SUPPLY

WATTAGE (Max): ~

COST: $89/₹14,499

PURCHASE LINK: https://amzn.to/39GH81L

9) COMPONENT: PC CASE
FRACTAL DESIGN DEFINE XL R2 TITANIUM BIG TOWER CASE
WATTAGE (Max): ~
COST: $70/₹6,445
PURCHASE LINK:
https://world.ubuy.com/?goto=search/index/vie
w/product/B00AZQTMZ8?inf=37bc2f75bf1bcfe8450a
1a41c200364c&utm_source=uglow

10) OPERATING SYSTEM (OS)
MICROSOFT WINDOWS 10 HOME (64-BIT)
COST: $110/₹10,973
PURCHASE LINK: Microsoft

BEST AMD COMPUTER FOR VIDEO EDITING
BUDGET $2500
TOTAL COST: $2556
TOTAL WATTAGE: 424W

1) COMPONENT: CPU
INTEL i9 9900K 3.6GHZ 8-CORE PROCESSOR
WATTAGE (Max): 95W
COST: $505/₹60,070
PURCHASE LINK: https://amzn.to/2TuQBDM

2) COMPONENT: CPU COOLER
BE QUIET! DARK ROCK PRO 4 50.5 CFM CPU COOLER
WATTAGE (Max): 10W
COST: $86/₹14,799
PURCHASE LINK: https://amzn.to/39sQVZh

3) COMPONENT: <u>MOTHERBOARD</u>
ASUS PRIME Z390-A ATX 1151
WATTAGE (Max): 70W
COST: $172/₹21,199
PURCHASE LINK: https://amzn.to/3cAYQ8D

4) COMPONENT: GPU
MSI GAMING NVIDIA RTX 2070 8GB
WATTAGE (Max): 185W
COST: $805/₹79,199
PURCHASE LINK: https://amzn.to/2xg8opw

5) COMPONENT: MEMORY RAM
Corsair Vengeance LPX DDR4-3200 CL16, 32GB
(2 x 16GB)
WATTAGE (Max): 29W
COST: $140/₹13,798
PURCHASE LINK: https://amzn.to/2TsgSlZ

6) COMPONENT: NVME SSD STORAGE
SAMSUNG 970 EVO PLUS 1TB M.2 SSD
WATTAGE (Max): 10W
COST: $169/₹19,240
PURCHASE LINK: https://amzn.to/2wxsiMo

7) COMPONENT: <u>SATA SSD STORAGE</u>
CRUCIAL MX500 2TB 2.5" SSD
WATTAGE (Max): 10W
COST: $230/₹20,460
PURCHASE LINK: https://amzn.to/39GbCRB

8) COMPONENT: HDD STORAGE
SEAGATE BARRACUDA COMPUTE 4TB, 3.5"
WATTAGE (Max): 15W
COST: $90/₹8,699
PURCHASE LINK: https://amzn.to/2VLRhpL

9) COMPONENT: POWER SUPPLY (PSU)
SEASONIC FOCUS PLUS GOLD 650W ATX 2.4 POWER SUPPLY
WATTAGE (Max): ~
COST: $105/₹26,669
PURCHASE LINK: https://amzn.to/38ySyDu

10) COMPONENT: PC CASE
FRACTAL DESIGN DEFINE XL R2 TITANIUM BIG TOWER CASE
WATTAGE (Max): ~
COST: $144/₹12,422

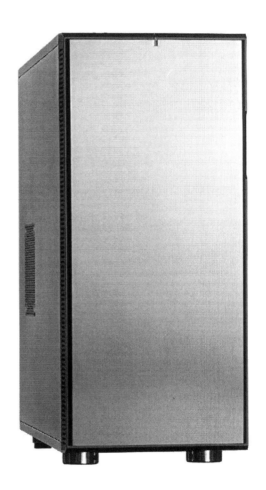

PURCHASE LINK: https://amzn.to/2J8jXlg
11) OPERATING SYSTEM (OS): MICROSOFT WINDOWS 10 HOME
(64-BIT)
COST: $110/₹10,973
PURCHASE LINK: Microsoft

BEST AMD COMPUTER FOR VIDEO EDITING
BUDGET $3000
TOTAL COST: $3028
TOTAL WATTAGE: 538W

1) COMPONENT: CPU
AMD THREADRIPPER 2950X 3.5GHZ 16-CORE PROCESSOR
WATTAGE (Max): 180W
COST: $665/₹79,900
PURCHASE LINK: https://amzn.to/2POaHXa

2) COMPONENT: CPU COOLER
BE QUIET! DARK ROCK PRO 4 TR4
WATTAGE (Max): 10W
COST: $89/₹14,299
PURCHASE LINK: https://amzn.to/2Q7DAOr

3) COMPONENT: MOTHERBOARD
GIGABYTE X399 DESIGNARE EX ATX TR4
WATTAGE (Max): 70W
COST: $390/₹39,999
PURCHASE LINK: https://amzn.to/2InIlip

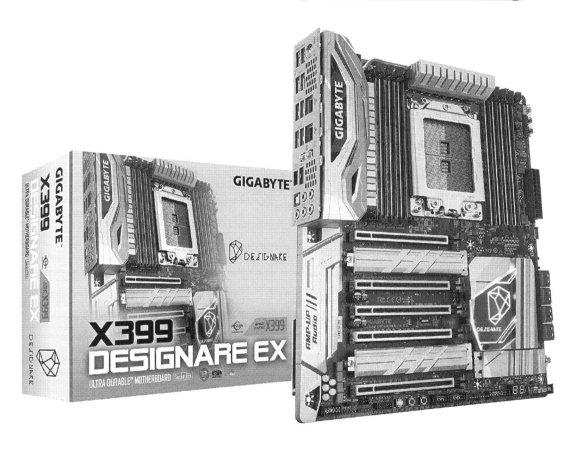

5) COMPONENT: GPU
MSI GAMING NVIDIA RTX 2070 8GB
WATTAGE (Max): 185W
COST: $805/₹79,199
PURCHASE LINK: https://amzn.to/2xg8opw

6) COMPONENT: MEMORY RAM
Corsair Vengeance LPX DDR4-3200 CL16, 64GB (4 x 16GB)
WATTAGE (Max): 58W
COST: $278/₹27,596
PURCHASE LINK: https://amzn.to/2TsgSlZ

7) COMPONENT: NVME SSD STORAGE
SAMSUNG 970 EVO PLUS 1TB M.2 SSD
WATTAGE (Max): 10W
COST: $169/₹19,240
PURCHASE LINK: https://amzn.to/2wxsiMo

8) COMPONENT: **SATA SSD STORAGE**
SAMSUNG 860 EVO 1TB 2.5" SSD
WATTAGE (Max): 10W
COST: $150/₹12,999
PURCHASE LINK: https://amzn.to/2POw1M3

9) COMPONENT: HDD STORAGE
WESTERN DIGITAL 4TB BLUE, 3.5"
WATTAGE (Max): 15W
COST: $88/₹9,079
PURCHASE LINK: https://amzn.to/2vMIlWz

10) COMPONENT: POWER SUPPLY (PSU)
CORSAIR RMX SERIES PLATINUM RM850X 850W POWER SUPPLY
WATTAGE (Max): ~
COST: $140/₹14,499
PURCHASE LINK: https://amzn.to/39p5MDT

11) COMPONENT: PC CASE
FRACTAL DESIGN DEFINE XL R2 TITANIUM BIG TOWER CASE
WATTAGE (Max): ~
COST: $144/₹12,422
PURCHASE LINK: https://amzn.to/2J8jXlg

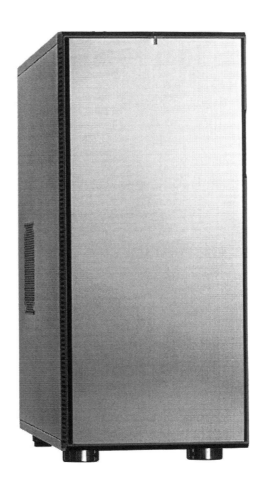

12) OPERATING SYSTEM (OS) MICROSOFT WINDOWS 10 HOME (64-BIT)
COST: $110/₹10,973
PURCHASE LINK: Microsoft

BEST AMD COMPUTER FOR VIDEO EDITING
BUDGET $6000+
TOTAL WATTAGE: 653W

1) COMPONENT: CPU
INTEL I9 9980XE 3.0GHZ 18-CORE PROCESSOR
WATTAGE (Max): 165W
COST: $3500/₹1,09,990
PURCHASE LINK: https://amzn.to/39t7jZL

2) COMPONENT: CPU COOLER
BE QUIET! DARK ROCK PRO 4 2066
WATTAGE (Max): 250W
COST: $87/₹14,799
PURCHASE LINK: https://amzn.to/2VQUMLu

3) COMPONENT: MOTHERBOARD
MSI PERFORMANCE GAMING INTEL X299 LGA 2066
DDR4 USB 3.1 SLI ATX MOTHERBOARD (X299 GAMING PRO CARBON)
WATTAGE (Max): 75W
COST: $356/₹31,100
PURCHASE LINK: https://amzn.to/2IyULEj

4) COMPONENT: <u>GPU</u>

ASUS TURBO NVIDIA RTX 2080 TI 11GB

WATTAGE (Max): 260W

COST: $1458/₹1,10,000

PURCHASE LINK: https://amzn.to/2uXFBoM
(OR)
<u>https://mdcomputers.in/asus-geforce-turbo-rtx2080ti-11g.html</u>

5) COMPONENT: MEMORY RAM
Corsair Vengeance LPX DDR4-3200 CL16, 64GB (4 x 16GB)
WATTAGE (Max): 56W
COST: $278/₹27,596
PURCHASE LINK: https://amzn.to/2TsgSlZ

6) COMPONENT: NVME SSD STORAGE
SAMSUNG 970 EVO PLUS 2TB M.2 SSD
WATTAGE (Max): 20W
COST: $400/₹34,091
PURCHASE LINK: https://amzn.to/3bigpZD

7) COMPONENT: <u>SATA SSD STORAGE</u>
SAMSUNG 860 PRO 4TB 2.5" SSD
WATTAGE (Max): 20W
COST: $875/₹54,749
PURCHASE LINK: https://amzn.to/2wuE6zg

8) COMPONENT: HDD STORAGE
SEAGATE IRONWOLF PRO 10TB INTERNAL HARD DRIVE
WATTAGE (Max): 7.8W
COST: $312/₹35,789
PURCHASE LINK: https://amzn.to/3aGIsl6

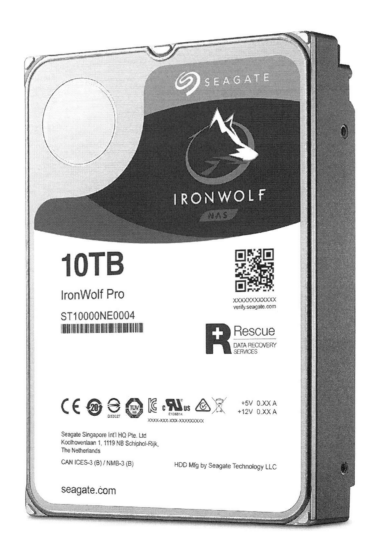

9) COMPONENT: <u>PC CASE</u> THERMALTAKE CORE V71
WATTAGE (Max): ~
COST: $180/₹15,757
PURCHASE LINK:

https://world.ubuy.com/?goto=search/index/view/
product/B074ZLQZ8F?inf=37Bc2f75bf1bcfe8450a1a41c200364c&utm
source=aglow

10) OPERATING SYSTEM (OS) MICROSOFT WINDOWS 10 HOME (64-BIT)
COST: $110/₹10,973
PURCHASE LINK: Microsoft

PREBUILT VS CUSTOM BUILD PC

o One of the most important and confusing parts is whether to buy a PREBUILT PC or enjoy yourself building one. IF you are a beginner, it needs dedication. Plus, it's a lot of fun.

o There is a target audience for both, and they can coexist in the competitive market for sure.

COST AND PERFORMANCE

o When you build your own custom PC from scratch, you are only paying for the components you purchase. The companies that are selling PREBUILT PCs are looking to make a profit along with extra labor and testing charge. This is reflected in the product as well, for example: If you invested a certain amount of money to build your PC, where you were able to afford the best RTX 2080 Ti GPU. On the flip side, if you use the same amount of money to buy a PREBUILT PC, You will never be able to afford this GPU. You might even have to go a level shorter and but the cheaper version of the same model, RTX 2080. Here clearly a custom build PC is the winner.

TIME AND CONVENIENCE

o There are benefits from paying the premium on a PREBUILT PC.

o It takes a long time to build a PC, from selecting the PC components, making sure all the components are compatible with each other, ordering them, waiting for the products to be delivered and building them, Installing the operating system and correct if any errors while building. But PREBUILT PCs are just a click or a drive away. You can edit your videos and gaming on it on the same day. They even come with windows pre-installed. All you need to do is plug in the peripheral and you are good to go.

o Another reason to go with the PREBUILT PC has to do with the effort. Not everyone is tech-savvy. To many the prospect of having to properly put together all the expensive pieces by yourself is rather daunting especially seeing not all PC components are compatible with each other. So, if you want good gaming or video editing PC now and don't want to bother finding all the best prices for each component and fitting them all together, PREBUILT PC is the way to go for you.

o You will also want to get rid of all the bloatware that will be waiting for you in your PREBUILT PC. Bloatware is the unnecessary software that is installed on new machines by the manufacturer or retailer. Software companies pay to have their product included (normally a cut-down sampler or trial) thus providing an additional revenue stream for the manufacturer. It is a form of advertising for them and the PC you buy is a monetizing vehicle. When you build your own, you are starting from scratch and you install what you want to install. However, you can achieve the same by wiping a new off-the-shelf PC and reinstalling the operating system or uninstalling the bloatware. This may prove to be cheaper and less time consuming, but it is a personal choice. I prefer building my own simply because I enjoy doing it. It used to be significantly cheaper, but savings are not that substantial these days.

CUSTOMIZATION

o Customizability is a big plus point for gamers out there, not only in terms of function but form as well. High-end PREBUILT PCs are rather easy on the eyes, but chances are they will never look exactly the way you would want your ideal PC to look like. You might end with RGB light which might look appealing initially but later turns out to be annoying. There is no changing now unless you are a PC builder.

o Buyers do have more options today when it comes to PREBUILT PC than ever before, but these options are mostly concerned with RAM and storage capacities or bumping the CPU or GPU up a notch.

o The choices of the motherboard, however, are set in stone, as is the cooling solution and the power supply unit.

o The power supply can be the biggest problem. I wouldn't suggest you buy a PC from a seller who is not willing to disclose the exact specifications of all the components in the case. Some specification sheet from certain sellers won't disclose many details about the power supply except that they are running in AC. They won't give any specifications of the power supply. It is important to know exactly what PSU you are purchasing. As this is supplying all the components in the PC, it is ideal to go for the best PSU and look for the seller who is selling them. All this hassle can be avoided in a custom build PC.

REPAIRS AND CUSTOMER SUPPORTS

○ You will need to take into account what you will be doing if something goes bad when building your own PC. You are the one in charge of all the problem-solving. I'm not trying to scare you ROM the beautiful world of PC BUILDING. But this is the reality, the good and the bad part. But the experience will leave you speechless. There are lots of online resources at your disposal that can make it much easier for you.

○ If you buy a PREBUILT PC, you can always count on the manufacturer to handle all the repairs and provide customer support. The downside here is that under warranty you will have to ship the PC back to the vendor should any hardware issues arise. This is unlike some big branded PCs or laptops where the service is done at home under warranty. This service solely depends on the vendor and manufacturer. Having this service at your beck and call is important. This also means going without your PC a week or more.

WARRANTY

○ Warranty is another important part worth noting.

○ When you buy a PREBUILT PC, the whole PC comes with a single warranty. These types of warranties are not very impressive. In most cases, these warranties will only last for 1 year. In other cases, you can extend the warranty up to 3 years by paying extra. This can be very expensive. This will add to the price of the PREBUILT PC you are planning to purchase.

○ With CUSTOM BUILD PC, you are getting a separate warranty for each component. Most pieces of hardware like CPUs and GPUs are covered by a 3-year warranty. Some warranties can even last longer, for example, EVGA power supplies offer a warranty of 10 years.

○ So, if you want your PC components to be protected under warranty, custom build PC is the way to go.

○ Nevertheless, if you are buying your products from reputable brands whether it is a prebuilt or custom build, you would want it to last longer and rely less on the warranties.

PERIPHERALS

- ○ Most prebuilt PCs come bundled together with certain peripherals. At the least it will include a keyboard and a mouse, it could be so much more. But these peripherals are usually of poor quality and built. Make no mistake, you are being charged for these peripherals which brings the overall cost-effectiveness more in favor of custom-built PCs.
- ○ So, if you are planning to go for the prebuilt PCs that don't force peripherals on you whatsoever. There are exceptions to this rule but very rare.

Since you are reading this, I'm guessing you are leaning more towards building your own PC. So, congratulations on your fruitful endeavor.

ADOBE PREMIERE PRO SYSTEM REQUIREMENTS FOR VIDEO EDITING

CPU

- o This acts as the brain of the PC. Nothing happens in the PC without the direct or indirect involvement of your CPU.

- o For Premiere Pro, CPU involvement is seen more in the system responsiveness like timeline playback, scrubbing through footage, rendering and exporting, etc.

- o To get the best performance out of CPU, it is recommended to have a multi-core processor for the Premiere Pro to have the best performance. Which means you need to have a minimum of 2 cores. Higher the processing core, better the performance. You need a processor post - AUGUST, 2015. 8 Core/16 thread CPU cores are the ideal number of cores/threads for video editing.

- o AMD CPU is slightly better for RED camera videos whereas Intel is slightly better with the rest of the other camera videos.

- o If you are planning to go for serious video editing, Adobe Premiere Pro recommends going for CPU cores not less than 6 processing cores (12 Threads).

- o As you are spending more money to buy a CPU with more cores, aim to buy CPU with *higher CLOCK SPEED* too. It's the speed of the CPU measured in the unit GHz, always mentioned in the title of all the CPU names.

- o Major competitors - AMD VS INTEL

GPU

- o Also called The Graphics Processing Unit, Graphics Card drives all the individual pixels from your computer to the displays.

- o Plug your monitor into your Graphics card and not your motherboard for the best performance.

- o A lot of the video-based calculation takes place through the Graphics Card. Effects & applications are accelerated by a high-quality graphics card.

- o **VRAM** - Like CPU is selected by their number of cores, GPU is selected based on their VRAM. For 1080p videos, a minimum of 4GB VRAM is enough and for 4K VIDEOS a minimum of 6GB VRAM is required.

- o Major competitors - AMD VS NVIDIA

- o I bought the ***MSI RX 580 Armor 8G OC Gaming Radeon RX 580 GDDR5 8GB Crossfire VR Ready FinFET DirectX 12 Graphics Card***. This graphics card has 8GB VRAM. I'm not a professional Video Editor. Most of my video editing is for my YouTube channel and this graphics card is more than enough.

RAM

- o The more RAM you have, the more leverage you are giving your computer to ***MULTI-TASK***.

- o This helps to ***handle multiple operations*** at once. This can be compared to a SMALL DESK VS LARGE DESK. The small desk has less space to keep things and do things with. Bigger the desk, larger the space to do more activity.

- o The minimum recommended memory is 8GB for video editing. Less than that Will render the PC useless. 16GB is highly recommended for 1080p. And ***32 GB*** if you are working with ***4K footage***.64GB for very complicated projects.

- o Always buy DDR4 memory RAM at the time of writing this book.

- o There is always less chance of making a mistake if you choose to buy from reputable brands like CORSAIR, GSKILL, HYPE RX, etc.

STORAGE

- o This term can be used for both space and speed of the storage device. A device with higher speed and a lot of storage is the criteria to look for in the device.

- o It is best to choose an M.2 NVMe SSD storage device for speed especially. Samsung 970 EVO Plus 500GB PCIe NVMe

M.2 (2280) Internal Solid State Drive (SSD) (MZ-V7S500) is the ideal choice.

○ Keep the entire device dedicated for the video editing. Any extra storage can be done in a separate drive, SSD or HDD. Preferably SSD. But if the cost is an issue, there are high-speed budget HDD available in the market.

○ A minimum of 8GB is required to install and run Premiere Pro correctly.

○ **IMPORTANT:** In a perfect environment - **A THREE TIER SYSTEM** is ideal. **TIER ONE:** A M.2 NVMe SSD for your operating system to run WINDOWS 10 and Adobe Premiere Pro program. **TIER TWO:** A really fast SSD or M.2 NVMe SSD for your premiere pro PROJECT FILES and the video footage and media. Thus, the different works are segregated so that the programs run at its best. This will ensure a snappy experience when you are scrubbing through your video footage in premiere pro and play your footage, playback in real-time. **TIER THREE:** A third SSD for *SCRATCH DATA & MEDIA CACHE files*. These are short cut files premiere pro use to speed up the process of displaying your video so that there is zero latency. This allows minimum to none bottlenecking in the performance. Example: SSD for running the operating system and premiere pro:

○ Samsung 970 EVO Plus 500GB PCIe NVMe M.2 Internal Solid State Drive (SSD). For all the projects: Samsung 860 EVO 1TB SATA 2.5" Internal Solid State Drive (SSD). For scratch data and media cache: Samsung 860 EVO 250GB SATA 2.5" Internal Solid State Drive (SSD).

○ **MEDIA CACHE FILES** - When importing video and audio into Adobe Premiere Pro, it processes versions of these files that it can readily access for faster performance. These are referred to as "media cache" files. These are stored in the Media Cache Files folder.

○ **SCRATCH FILES** - When you edit a project, Adobe Premiere Pro uses disk space to store scratch files for your project. These include captured video and audio, conformed audio, and preview files. By default, scratch files are stored where you save the project.

○ **A BACKUP STORAGE** - A slower optical HDD is enough for this to store all the finished project videos. I have a WD 4TB external drive for this purpose.

○ A RAID SETUP can be created among 4 x 4TB HDD drives, two as original and the other two as copies. In case if any drive fails, there is still a copy of your original video intact.

○ Store the ORIGINAL DATA in a fireproof SAFE.

OPERATING SYSTEM

○ Microsoft Windows 10 HOME/PRO 64-BIT is the preferred operating system to work the
Premiere Pro smoothly.

WHAT IS A MOTHERBOARD?

o The motherboard is the main component of the computer. It is often referred to as the 'MAINBOARD' or 'MOBO'. It is a large circuit board that fits into the computer CASE and where all the components of the computer connect to.

o **CPU** connects to the CPU socket. In AMD motherboard it's mentioned as AM4 SOCKETS. It's the name of the type of CPU socket. The compatible CPU also mentions about the AM4 sockets.

o **MEMORY SLOTS** hold the primary memory DIMMA modules known as RAM are inserted.

o BUS SLOTS - also known as the EXPANSION SLOTS/PCIe slots/SATA INTERFACES, these are used to attach various components, to add more capability to the computer Example: Video Card, Sound Card, Network Card, etc.

o **SATA CONNECTORS** - This is where the data cable from your storage devices like HDD, SSD, etc are plugged on. The Motherboard will have several of these on it.

o **M.2 SLOTS** - modern motherboards have these M.2 slots to attach the M.2 SATA SSD & M.2 NVME SSD.

o **PLATFORM CONTROLLER HUB (PCH)** - Modern motherboards come with PCH. This is the latest chipset architecture (seen on Intel motherboards). Replaced the older northbridge chipset & southbridge chipset seen on the older versions of Intel motherboard.

o CHIPSET - AMD comes with AMD CHIPSET.

o **I/O (Input/Output) INTERFACES** - These are located on the rear I/O panel of the motherboard. This has several USB ports. Some motherboards are also equipped with a Video adapter known as INTEGRATED VIDEO. This is a single unit. Older motherboards used to have separated one. It has an HDMI port for this. These adapters are not very powerful hence used for eight applications but when used for extensive Graphics applications like Video editing or Gaming, they can fall short. So, it is advised to connect your monitor to the HDMI port of your Graphics card. NETWORK INTERFACE CARD with Port can also be seen, which is designed to connect the Ethernet cable with an RJ45 connector to connect the computer for the Internet. INTEGRATED SOUND CARD - This process the audio through the computer speakers.

FORM FACTOR - Motherboard comes in different shapes & sizes, this is known as a form factor. ATX (Advanced Technology Extended) is the most common form factor used today. Created in 1995. This is the DE facto standard motherboard form factor for PCs today. A full-sized ATX motherboard measures around 12 x 9.6 inches. **ATX COMPATIBILITY** - this form factor is one of the many factors used to verify the compatibility between all the components of the PC Example: Between motherboard and the CASE etc. **MICRO ATX** - this is the other form of motherboard ATX form factor. It is smaller than the ATX FORM FACTOR motherboards and measures to about 9.6 x 9.6 inches, which makes it a square design motherboard as compared to the rectangular-shaped ATX motherboards. These motherboards are cheaper than ATX motherboards and were designed to fit in smaller computer cases. They have fewer features and consume lesser power than the standard ATX boards.

MOTHERBOARD: TIPS ON HOW TO CHOOSE THE BEST ONE?

o The first decision you will need to make when choosing a motherboard is whether you want to go with the AMD or Intel for your CPU. Once you have chosen the appropriate CPU.

o The next step in choosing components is to select the motherboard to build a PC. Now using the PCPARTPICKER website go to the list of components listed below like CPU, power supply, CASE, graphics card, RAM. Select each component and make sure your selected components for the PC building is listed. If you are a beginner to the PC building world, then this is the easier method to compare the compatibility between the different components in the PC. Cross verify the compatibility of each of these components. I use my motherboard as a link to other components and thereby choosing them.

o If you are not the beginner, then compatibility should come easy to you. You will be well versed in the factors contributing to the compatibility. Nevertheless, it is still wise to check compatibility.

o Investing in an expensive motherboard doesn't always guarantee the best motherboard.

o Focus on *features* that the manufacturer has spent money developing and tailored for your use case.

o **CHIPSET** – Determines whether you have access to some of the more advanced features like multi-GPU support or the storage oriented **StoreMI Technology.** This also decided if your motherboard supports overclocking. Also, the number of ports, connectors, and slots the motherboard can have.

o **AMD StoreMI TECHNOLOGY** – is included with every motherboard that features an AMD X399, 400-series, 500-series or TRX40 chipset. SSDs are fast, but expensive, and offer minimal capacity. Mechanical hard drives boast large capacity for a low price but are much slower than an SSD. AMD StoreMI technology "combines" these two types of storage into a single drive and automatically moves the data you access the most to the SSD, so you get the best of both worlds: SSD responsiveness, and mechanical hard disk capacity with its low price.

o **_CHIPSET COMPATIBILITY_** – If you have an incompatible chipset with your CPU, your PC won't start, and you will have to start from scratch. Compare your components in PCPARTPICKER.COM. Your motherboard should be compatible with your CPU.

o AMD is a bit more consistent when it comes to chipset compatibility.

o Buy AMD compatible motherboards.

o MSI Performance Gaming AMD Ryzen 1st and 2nd Gen AM4 M.2 USB 3 Crossfire ATX Motherboard (B450 Gaming PRO Carbon AC) – Here the B450, B stands for the type of chipset.

o Make sure the motherboard comes WI a decent sound boost, USB Type C and **Steel reinforced PCIe slots**.

o A very good compatible CPU for the above motherboard is AMD RYZEN 7 2700X with 16 threads, perfect for 4K video editing.

o B450 is best for the Ryzen 7 series of CPUs. This motherboard comes with most of the features like Sound boost, multiple M.2 slots with HEATSINK for one, reinforced PCIe slots, **a better power distribution array** which is very important for overclocking (OC). You might get an extra MHz out of overclocking. Ryzen can be a little stubborn past 4GHz, WIFI capability, USB Type C port.

o Always go for a higher-end MOTHERBOARD if you are planning to buy a higher-end CPU.

o Ryzen CPUs are all good for OVERCLOCKING which the Intel doesn't offer [Ranging from Ryzen 3 1200 to Ryzen 7].

o Motherboard selection here is all about features, make sure the motherboard comes with OC capability.

o AMD Ryzen 5 1600 is one of the best MID-RANGE CPUs out there. The compatible motherboard for that will be ASROCK AB350 GAMING K4 MOTHERBOARD [OR] MSI B350 GAMING PLUS MOTHERBOARD. This gives you a nice bang for the buck.

o AMD CPUs are perfect for overclocking especially the Ryzen series of CPUs.

o Make sure to check the type of form factor it is, for example, ATX FORM FACTOR meaning it will be compatible with the ATX Mid-Tower CASE.

o Now look for the type of CPU SOCKET. I bought the **AM4 type CPU SOCKET**, which is compatible with my AMD RYZEN 7 2700X. The CPU also will mention the type of socket it has, in this case, **AM4 SOCKET**. This indicates their compatibility. (Refer picture below)

o AMD THREAD RIPPER uses the **TR4 SOCKET.**

o LAG 1151 sockets for Intel processors.

o Select the motherboard that supports both M.2 AND NVMe. The motherboard I selected, MSI Performance Gaming AMD Ryzen 1st and 2nd Gen AM4 M.2 USB 3 DDR4 HDMI Display Port Wi-Fi Crossfire ATX Motherboard (B450 Gaming PRO Carbon AC), even though mentions M.2 slot, supports NVMe.

o If you are planning to purchase M.2 NVMe SSD, make sure your motherboard has M.2 slots that support them.

o If you have 2 M.2 slots on your motherboard, make sure which is the ideal M.2 slot for your M.2 NVMe SSD card. Check the motherboard manual for the details. In my motherboard, I had to choose the M.2_1 slot, which is the first M.2 slot that comes with the HEATSINK. I had to choose this because of 2 reasons: (i) This slot is provided with the HEATSINK as NVMe drives heat-up pretty quickly (ii) Once the GPU (GRAPHICS PROCESSING UNIT) is installed the M.2_2, which is the second M.2 slot provided in the motherboard can't be used as mentioned in the motherboard manual. **Please read them well before building your PC.**

o The key differences between M.2 AND NVMe are detailed in a chapter ahead. Do check them out.

o If you are planning of using multiple graphics cards, sound cards, M.2 NVMe + M.2 SATA SSD PCIe x4 Adapter (for older PC with a motherboard that doesn't offer M.2

slots), etc make sure your motherboard comes with the necessary PCIe slots.

o The processor also depends on the number of PCIe lanes that can be used on the motherboard. Make sure to check the maximum supported number of lanes that the CPU can handle. It is mentioned in the CPU specification. If not, check wikichip.org and look for the details of your chip. The AMD Ryzen 7 2700X I bought includes 20 PCIe lanes - 16 for a discrete graphics processor and 4 for storage (NVMe or 2 ports SATA Express).

o Make sure your motherboard comes with enough DIMM slots for your RAM. It usually has 4 DIMM slots: DIMMA1, DIMMA2, DIMMB1, and DIMMB2. (Refer picture below)

o Also, check for the maximum amount of supported RAM under motherboard memory support in the motherboard datasheet which can be downloaded from the manufacturer website. Below is the datasheet of my motherboard I bought for building my VIDEO EDITING PC.

o **DUAL CHANNEL/QUAD CHANNEL MEMORY SUPPORT** - this means your motherboard either works best in dual or quad-channel. Dual-channel means motherboard works best with 2 RAM cards inserted (refer to the picture below). The motherboard I purchased (data sheet below) is DUAL CHANNEL. I attached 2 x CORSAIR Vengeance LPX 16GB (1x16GB) DDR4 3200MHZ C16 Desktop RAM Memory Module in the DIMMA2 and DIMMB2 slots. It doesn't necessarily mean you can't attach in all four slots to increase capacity. In Quad-channel you will have to insert one RAM into every 4 slots provided on the motherboard.

o Make sure your motherboard has enough SATA ports for your HDDs, SSDs and optical drives.

o The Case is always chosen after the form factor of the motherboard. Here it is ATX. So, go for ATX. Look for the motherboard form factor (Refer to the picture below).

o Make sure to purchase the motherboard that compliments the color scheme of your case as well as your other components.

o You can use the NEWEGG website comparison feature. Here you can select and compare multiple motherboards at the same time.

o One of the major considerations when choosing a motherboard comes down to the types of connections available on the back I/O panel. For most people, the number of USB ports is going to be the most relevant number here. With high-end motherboards that more focused on VIDEO EDITING and GAMING generally have more options.

o Make sure to pay extra attention to any other audio support the ports support too.

o When purchasing a motherboard, you will have to decide on what extra features are you willing to pay for, which you like to have in your motherboard. Many modern motherboards sport customizable RGB lighting and some are specially designed to be more liquid cooling friendly. Some have built-in WIFI. While others have special cooling features better suited for GAMING and OVERCLOCKING.

o Motherboard product pages or datasheets will give you a rundown of all the notable features.

Make sure to purchase a motherboard that is appropriate for your needs and can go along with your needs, so I suggest getting the motherboard that is the best bang for your buck.

The picture next page shows the datasheet of the motherboard I selected to build my PC:
Image Source: MSI

SPECIFICATION

Model Name	B450 GAMING PRO CARBON AC
CPU Support	Supports AMD® RYZEN™ 1st and 2nd Generation/ Ryzen™ with Radeon™ Vega Graphics Processors for Socket AM4
CPU Socket	AM4
Chipset	AMD® B450 Chipset
Graphics Interface	1 x PCI-E 3.0 x16 slot + 1 x PCI-E 2.0 x16 slot Supports 2-way CrossFire
Display Interface	DisplayPort, HDMI – Requires Processor Graphics
Memory Support	4 DIMMs, Dual Channel DDR4 3466+ (OC)
Expansion Slots	3 x PCI-E x1 slots
Storage	2 x M.2 slots 6 x SATA 6Gb/s
USB ports	2 x USB 3.1 (Gen2, A+C) + 4 x USB 3.1 (Gen1) + 6 x USB 2.0
LAN	Intel® 211AT Gigabit LAN
WiFi / BT	Intel® DualBand Wireless-AC 9260, Bluetooth 5.0
Audio	8-Channel(7.1) HD Audio with Audio Boost 4
Form Factor	ATX

FEATURE

MYSTIC LIGHT and SYNC

Personalize your PC with 16.8 million colors / 17 effects, controlled in one click!

AMD Turbo USB 3.1 Gen2

Powered by AMD, ensure an uninterrupted connection with more stability and fastest USB speeds.

Turbo M.2

Running at PCI-E Gen3 x4 maximizes performance for NVMe based SSDs.

Extended Heatsink Design

MSI extended PWM heatsink and enhanced circuit design ensures even high-end processors to run in full speed.

Flash BIOS Button

Simply use a USB key to flash any BIOS within seconds, without installing a CPU, memory or graphics card.

Audio Boost 4

Isolated audio with a high quality audio processor for the most immersive gaming experience.

Core Boost

With premium layout and fully digital power design to support more cores and provide better performance.

DDR4 Boost

Advanced technology to deliver pure data signals for the best gaming performance and stability.

CONNECTIONS

1. PS/2 Combo Port
2. Display/Port
3. Wi-Fi / Bluetooth
4. LAN
5. HD Audio Connectors
6. Flash BIOS Button

7. USB 2.0
8. HDMI
9. USB 3.1 Gen1
10. USB 3.1 Gen2 Type-A + C
11. Optical S/PDIF OUT

BEST AMD MOTHERBOARD 2020

If you are planning to buy a motherboard right now but you want to leave your choices for easy upgradability, this ADM motherboards the safest investment choice.

MINI-ITX MOTHERBOARDS
TO BUILD THE MOST COMPACT AIMING PC
(Not the most affordable motherboards)

1) MOTHERBOARD: MSI B450I GAMING PLUS AC
WATTAGE (Max): 50W
COST: $129/₹15,000
PURCHASE LINK: https://amzn.to/39HkRkn
FEATURES
Supports DDR4-3466
TURBO M.2 StoreMI technology
Audio boost
XMP Memory boost
VR ready

2) MOTHERBOARD:
ASUS ROG STRIX X470-I GAMING
WATTAGE (Max): 65W
COST: $211/₹33,550
PURCHASE LINK: https://amzn.to/2I2yBtT
FEATURES:
RGB lighting technology
M.2 with HEATSINK
Overclocking ready
AMD RYZEN 3000 desktop ready

MICRO-ATX MOTHERBOARDS
(most affordable)
Balanced Price with Features
Budget Gaming PC

1) MOTHERBOARD: MSI B450M PRO-M2

WATTAGE (Max): 60W

COST: $84/₹6,150

PURCHASE LINK: https://amzn.to/38bYLom

FEATURES
Supports DDR4-3466(OC) Memory.
Audio Boost.
PCI-E Steel Slot.
Turbo M.2: Delivering Speeds Up to 32GB/s

ATX MOTHERBOARD
ATX motherboards with advanced chipset can be expensive
(For high-end PC Build)

1) MOTHERBOARD: ASUS ROG STRIX B450-F
WATTAGE (Max): 65W
COST: $129/₹13,145
PURCHASE LINK: https://amzn.to/2I4CXjU
FEATURES:
Dual-channel DDR4 3200MHz (OC).
Aura Sync RGB: Synchronize LED lighting.
Dual M.2 and USB 3.1 Gen 2 Type-A connectors.
Gaming audio: SupremeFX S1220A teams with Sonic Studio III.
AMD RYZEN 3000 DESKTOP READY.

2) MOTHERBOARD: ASUS ROG STRIX X470-F
WATTAGE (Max): 65W
COST: $170/₹19,800
PURCHASE LINK: https://amzn.to/2PD0Vaq
FEATURES:
Dual-channel DDR4 3200MHz (OC).
Aura Sync RGB: Synchronize LED lighting.
Dual M.2 and USB 3.1 Gen 2 Type-A connectors.
Gaming audio: SupremeFX S1220A teams with Sonic Studio III.
AMD RYZEN 3000 DESKTOP READY
5-Way Optimization: Automated system-wide tuning,
providing overclocking and cooling profiles that are tailor
made for your rig.

CPU SPECIFICATION

o It is the brains of every PC.

o It is second only to GPU in terms of the overall impact gameplay performance.

o It is one of the most important pieces of hardware and the most difficult to select, to choose the right one for you because of the varying specifications.

o **MANUFACTURER** - AMD or Intel? There is a war going on and you have to pick a side, the blue team or the red team? With the rise of RYZEN CPU, AMD is now shoulder to shoulder with Intel in terms of technology and advancements. They even managed to overshadow Intel, because of their CPU's price to performance ratio. AMD is now regarded as the choice for budget-friendly mid-range gaming options.

o **PRODUCT LINE** - AMD has several series of CPUs that differ in terms of intended use. AMD has the Ryzen CPU, which are aimed for the gamers, Athlon & A-Series intended for simple home and office use, AMD THREADRIPPERS is generally aimed for workstations & servers.

o **RYZEN 3** - the more budget options. They are used by gamers on a budget. They are the weakest of the bunch.

o **RYZEN 5** - they are more powerful mid-range solutions that are great for gaming and they hold well with some professional software as well. This is the performance range I recommend for most users.

o **RYZEN 7** - They are only necessary if you are planning on running the CPU heavy program. They are usually over-kill for most Gaming PC. But they feel right at home in the most high-end builds. They are great for video editing since RYZEN 7 has a total of 8 threads in the CPU. The more the threads, the better is the performance with video editing software. When it comes to video editing, CPU matters a lot, like how it is important to have the best GPU for Gaming. In gaming, CPU comes second to GPU.

o **RYZEN 9** - you don't need them. They are workstation CPUs and you won't benefit from having them over a Ryzen 7 unless you're building the most hardcore multi-GPU VR gaming PC ever.

○ **SOCKET TYPE** - Now to look for the motherboard compatibility, this always starts with the socket type. A Socket is an interface CPU uses to connect to the motherboard. Different sockets have different pin configurations and can even differ in size. So, you need to make sure your motherboard and CPU are compatible, otherwise, you won't be able to physically fit the CPU on to the motherboard. At the time of writing this book, all RYZEN CPU uses the same **AM4 SOCKETS** except AMD RYZEN THREADRIPPER which uses the **TR4 SOCKET**. So, it is important to check and confirm the compatibility between both the motherboard and CPU.

○ **MOTHERBOARD CHIPSET** - The second motherboard related spec you need to take into consideration is the motherboard chipset. As we know that the CPU interfaces with the motherboard via the socket, but it *uses the chipset to communicate with the other components*. In short, the chipset is a system of circuits that connects all the different parts of the motherboard and determines which features are and aren't available. For example, the number of USB ports, RAM slots, SATA connectors, and PCI express slots is all dictated by the CHIPSET and the same goes for the extra features. Just by looking at the chipset you could ascertain whether the motherboard supports **CPU overclocking**, multi-GPU setups, AMD StoreMI technology and so on. So, if you have great expectations for your custom PC and are ready to meet those expectations, then you should carefully consider what chipset offers the best and most relevant features relevant for you.

○ **CORES** - CORE COUNT is easily the one spec manufacturers like to flaunt around the most when advertising their CPUs. In essence, CORE is a processor, which means there are multiple processors packed into one. The more cores you have, the better your PC will be at multitasking. Before the multi-core era of processors, A single-core processor was only able to do one task at a time. Having a multi-core processor help in the worlds of video editing. In the gaming world, it helps to a certain extend. **HEX-CORE PROCESSORS (6-CORES)** Have shown themselves to be the most optimal choice in terms of both price and performance. **QUAD-CORE CPU (4-CORES)** can still run most if not all games but depending on the type of game you are playing; they can end up o hampering the performance of the game quite significantly. OCTA-CORE CPU doesn't improve the gameplay experience all that much compared to HEX-CORE CPU. If you are building a high-end PC then they are a great choice but otherwise, you won't regret opting for a HEX-CORE CPU like one of the many RYZEN 5 series out there.

o **THREADS** - We can't talk about cores without mentioning the threads. Hyperthreading is the technology AMD use to allow a single physical core to function as two local cores. This means if the specs sheet shows that if a CPU has 8-cores, it will have double the number of cores, meaning the CPU has 16 threads. If the specs under CORE shows that the CPU is 8/16, it has 8 physical cores and 16 logical cores. Logical cores and threads are the same. In essence, these technologies essentially double a CPU's core count by allowing each core to tackle two tasks simultaneously, which comes very useful when it comes to video editing. However, threads are not all that important for gaming. This is because a single-core performance is more important than multitasking as far as gaming is concerned. Having access to more cores either physical or logical isn't a bad thing but it just doesn't trump single-core performance. For example: When paired with an RTX 2080, the RYZEN 9 3900X CPU which has 12 cores and 24 threads performs either on par with or worse than the i7 9700 K CPU with 8 cores and no hyperthreading whatsoever and i7 is $200 cheaper. Yes, cores are good but when your focus is gaming, then you don't need anything more than a HEX-CORE or an OCTA-CORE CPU.

o **CLOCK SPEED AND OVERCLOCKING** - Clock speed is a spec that shows you how many instructions the CPU can process. Clock speeds are measured in HERTZ. One hertz corresponds to one cycle per second. So, if a CPU has a clock speed of 4GHz that means it can handle 4 billion instructions per second. This means that raising the clock speed automatically entails better performance. This is called OVERCLOCKING. Any program can benefit from overclocking which is why it's popular among gamers. When looking at a spec sheet for any CPU, you will see two numbers related to it, the base frequency at which the CPU operates out of the box and the maximum frequency that the CPU can achieve through overclocking. However, you will need a fairly powerful cooling solution if you want to take the clock speed to the maximum. The important fact to know is that not all CPU can be overclocked and not all motherboards support this feature. So, if you want to overclock, you will need a CPU that can handle this and a motherboard with a chipset that allows it. All AMD CPUs are **UNLOCKED** meaning they can be overclocked at your leisure. Intel CPU's have a higher maximum frequency for overclocking, which makes the gamers gravitate towards it. But AMD CPUs tend to have the benefit of coming with better stock coolers so if you are not planning to do any overclocking or just want to overclock your CPU a bit, they are by far the most cost-effective choice. **IMPORTANT:** It is important to remember that clock speed is not the only spec that determines the overall performance there are many other variables here that affect this like the CPU architecture and core count, some are even beyond your control, as some games prefer certain CPU architecture and there is nothing you can do about it.

○ **CACHE** - If there is one tech that gives the new builders a headache it's CACHE. Mostly because they give more attention to it than they should. If gaming is all that you are concerned about then it's not a very important feature for it. A CPU CACHE is a high-speed memory cache assigned to the CPU to make future retrieval of data and instructions faster. It functions as a means of high-speed temporary storage. Since its integrated into the CPU itself, it's even faster. It's really important for VIDEO EDITING as it helps in multitasking just like the multiple cores. Video editing requires a lot of multitasking, hence a reliable feature. Read the next cheaper to know what CACHE is. For gamers, this is one of the last features in their list of priorities.

○ **THERMAL POWER DESIGN (TPD)** - This spec indicates how much power processor needs to function properly. It's useful for determining what kind of wattage you will need for your power supply unit. TPD is also helpful because it tells you what temperature you can expect

○ the CPU to be at when running normal software. But this doesn't indicate the maximum temperature it can generate or the maximum power draw. It indicates how power-efficient CPU is and how hot you should expect it to run.

○ **INTEGRATED GRAPHICS (FOR INTEL CPUs)** – Integrated graphics are graphics processing units that are integrated into the CPU, allowing the PC to operate and even run games without the need for a dedicated graphics card. They don't even come close to the performance of the dedicated graphics card but if you are on an extremely low budget, they are a serviceable alternative.

○ **APU (AMD'S ACCELERATED PROCESSING UNIT)** – They are different from integrated graphics, but the function is the same. As far as gameplay performance is concerned AMD APUs blow integrated graphics out of the park and this isn't hyperbole. You can expect the AMD APUs to achieve anywhere between 50-100% higher frame rates than the Intel CPUs with integrated graphics. That is a significant boost frame rate boost especially at this level of performance where even a gap of ten frames can make the difference between playable and choppy. Both the integrated graphics and APU is only useful if the GPU fails.

WHAT IS CPU CACHE?

o A computer has 2 different types of memory. (i) One type is used in RAM modules, which is,

o DRAM (Dynamic RAM) - It uses capacitors to store data. These capacitors have to be constantly refreshed with electricity for them to store data.

o CPU CACHE SRAM - This is another type of memory that doesn't have to be constantly refreshed. SRAM stands for static RAM. SRAM is what is used in CPU CACHE. Since it doesn't have to be constantly refreshed it is faster and more expensive compared to DRAM.

o CPU CACHE is CPU's internal memory and its job is to store copies of data and instructions from RAM, that's waiting to be used by the CPU. CPU CACHE holds common data it thinks the CPU is going to access frequently because when the CPU needs to access certain data it always checks the faster CACHE MEMORY first to see if the data it needs is there. If the data is not there, then the CPU will have to access the slower primary memory, RAM to get the data it needs.

o CACHE MEMORY is very important because if the CPU can access the data from the faster CACHE MEMORY, faster the computer will perform. So basically, CACHE MEMORY will make the PC run faster at a cheaper price.

o A computer can run without the cache memory, but it will be a lot slower because even though the RAM is becoming faster, it still can't feed the data to the CPU fast enough. The modern CPU has gotten so fast, most of the time it is doing nothing while waiting around for more data, this creates a bottleneck. This is the same reason why CPU CACHE was created so that it can act as a middleman between the CPU and RAM to assist in feeding the CPU with data it needs a lot faster, which reduces bottlenecks.

o CPU CACHE comes in 3 different levels: (i) **LEVEL 1 CACHE (L1 CACHE)** - also known as PRIMARY CACHE which is located on the processor itself. It runs at the same speed as the processor. It is the fastest CACHE on the computer (ii) **LEVEL 2 CACHE (L2 CACHE)** - also known as EXTERNAL CACHE, it is used to catch recent data accesses from the processor that was not caught by the level 1 cache. If the CPU couldn't find the data it needs in the LEVEL 1 CACHE, it then searches the LEVEL 2 CACHE for the data (iii) **LEVEL 3 CACHE (L3 CACHE)** – If the CPU still can't find the data it needs in the LEVEL 2 CACHE, IT SEARCHES THE LEVEL 3 CACHE. CPU uses this to catch the recent data accesses from the processor that were not caught by the LEVEL 2 CACHE. If the LEVEL 3 CACHE doesn't have the data it requires, it will then have to go to the much slower primary RAM to get the data it needs.

In earlier computers, LEVEL 2 CACHE was located separately on the motherboard. In modern CPUs, LEVEL 2 CACHE is located on the processor but is not as fast as the LEVEL 1 CACHE. LEVEL 3 CACHE is also located on the processor. It is larger than the LEVEL 2 CACHE but not faster. L2 CACHE is often referred to as a shared cache because its memory is shared among all the cores of the CPU. Each core of the CPU has an L1 & L2 CACHES and L3 CACHES is shared by all cores.

CPU: WHICH RYZEN CPU SHOULD YOU PICK?

BEST MID-RANGE CPU: AMD RYZEN 5 3600

- o Normally I would start with the best budget pick and work our way up but this time I'm kicking this off with the best mid-range CPU assuming this is the one most of the beginners, Video editors and Gamers are interested in.

- o AMD RYZEN 5 3600 - We have a CPU operating at a base clock speed of 3.6GHz to a max speed of 4.2GHz. It is a 6-core processor with 12 threads.

- o This CPU outperforms AMD RYZEN 7 2700 in GAMING.

- o It has the new ZEN 2 architecture.

- o It is PCIe GEN 4 READY.

- o AMD RYZEN 5 3600X is $45 extra with additional features. Hence AMD RYZEN 5 3600 is more cost-efficient compared to this.

- o If you have in your budget to purchase AMD RYZEN 3400G you won't regret it because of its superior processing power.

BEST HIGH-END CPU: AMD RYZEN 7 3700X VS AMD RYZEN 7 3800X

- o Here the price margin is much higher between the models. Performance discrepancy is not worthwhile.

- o AMD RYZEN 7 3700X has a base clock speed of 3.6GHz and a maximum boost of 4.4GHz. AMD RYZEN 7 3800X has 3.9GHz & 4.5GHz.

- o So, paying $70 for a slightly better base clock speed is not worthwhile.

- o If you planning to buy a 3rd GEN RYZEN 7, then 3700X is without a doubt the right choice.

BEST BUDGET CPU: AMD RYZEN 5 2600

- o If you are planning to build a budget gaming PC, you shouldn't be disheartened by the fact that we still don't have any ZEN 2 3rd Gen RYZEN 3s. But all the

○ previous GEN CPUs are on a crazy discount now. If AMD RYZEN 3600 is a high-end CPU for mid-range money, then the AMD RYZEN 5 2600 is a mid-range CPU, you can get on budget right now. This is a 6-core, 12 thread CPU with a base clocking speed of 3.4GHz and a maximum boost of about 3.9GHz.

○ This CPU doesn't have new ZEN 2 architecture. For the budget solution, this is a pretty good CPU.

○ For an extra $20, you can go or the AMD RYZEN 2600X, which will take the maximum boost speed to about 4.2GHz.

○ It comes with WRAITH SPIRE COOLER FAN.

BEST APU: 2nd GEN (AMD RYZEN 5 2400G & AMD RYZEN 3 2200G), 3rd GEN (AMD RYZEN 5 3400G & AMD RYZEN 3 3200G)

○ Not all budget PCs are interested in CPU that can't even render frames on their own.

○ This means you need a dedicated graphics card to make use of the AMD RYZEN 5 2600.

○ So, if you are looking for a 2 in 1 combo that can service both a CPU and GPU then you may just want to turn your attention to the new 3rd GEN AMD RYZEN 5 2400G.

○ Both the AMD RYZEN 5 2400G & AMD RYZEN 3 2200G APUs don't have the ZEN 2 architecture. It is mentioned on the box.

○ These APUs use ZEN+ architecture.

○ For all intents and purposes, their 2nd GEN CPUs snuck their way into 3rd GEN like AMD RYZEN 5 3400G. As long as you know what type of PC you are building, it's not a big deal.

○ This shows that not all 3rd GEN CPUs have ZEN 2 architecture. So, make sure before purchasing, if you are looking for ZEN 2 architecture.

- Their performance - you won't find a better APU at this point. They both received a clock speed bump so that 3200G has a maximum speed of 4GHz and the 3400G can go all the way up to 4.4GHz.

- The AMD RYZEN 5 3400G has a wraith spire cooler which is a nice upgrade.

To give a better feel for the performance - Both 3rd GEN & 2nd GEN RYZEN APUs could run Fortnite game at 60fps. But if you must lower the resolution down to 720p to obtain this with the 2nd GEN CPU whereas the 3rd GEN CPU reaches the performance in 1080p.

BEST RYZEN CHOICES FOR 2020 ARE:

- Always make sure if your CPU is ZEN 2 architecture. Zen is the codename for a computer processor micro-architecture from AMD and was first used with their Ryzen series of CPUs in February 2017. ZEN 2 is the latest CPU architecture.

1) CPU: AMD RYZEN 9 3900X 12-CORE, 24 THREAD
WATTAGE (Max): 105W
COST: $470/₹44,600
PURCHASE LINK: https://amzn.to/2VBtatA

2) CPU: AMD RYZEN 7 3800X 8-CORE, 16 THREAD
WATTAGE (Max): 95W
COST: $340/₹32,200
PURCHASE LINK: https://amzn.to/2I4QTKY

3) CPU: AMD RYZEN 7 3700X 8-CORE, 16 THREAD
WATTAGE (Max): 65W
COST: $300/₹29,090

PURCHASE LINK: https://amzn.to/2HZUxps

4) CPU: AMD RYZEN 7 2700X 8-CORE, 16 THREAD
WATTAGE (Max): 95W
COST: $170/₹19,350
PURCHASE LINK: https://amzn.to/393ilVf

5) CPU: AMD RYZEN 5 3600X 6-CORE, 12 THREAD
WATTAGE (Max): 95W
COST: $215/₹18,599
PURCHASE LINK: https://amzn.to/2veRcAc

6) CPU: AMD RYZEN 5 3600 6-CORE, 12 THREAD
WATTAGE (Max): 65W
COST: $175/₹16,100
PURCHASE LINK: https://amzn.to/2T72ob1

7) CPU: AMD RYZEN 5 2600 6-CORE, 12 THREAD/65W
WATTAGE (Max): 65W
COST: $120/₹13,100
PURCHASE LINK: https://amzn.to/38aJtQS

8) CPU: AMD RYZEN 5 2400G 4-CORE, 8 THREAD/
WATTAGE (Max): 65W
COST: $174/₹9,638
PURCHASE LINK: https://amzn.to/2Tm0jHb

9) CPU: AMD RYZEN 3 2200G 4-CORE, 4 THREAD
WATTAGE (Max): 65W
COST: $108/₹7,150
PURCHASE LINK: https://amzn.to/2I4VhJW

10) CPU: AMD RYZEN 5 3400G 4-CORE, 8 THREAD

WATTAGE (Max): 65W
COST: $171/₹13,080
PURCHASE LINK: https://amzn.to/3adw2B2

11) CPU: AMD RYZEN 3 3200G 4-CORE, 4 THREAD
WATTAGE (Max): 65W
COST: $92/₹8,229
PURCHASE LINK: https://amzn.to/2I6a9rA

**THIS IS THE SPECIFICATION OF AMD RYZEN 7 2700X, I PURCHASED FOR MY PC BUILD,
DETAIL SOURCE: AMD MANUFACTURER WEBSITE**

SPECIFICATIONS

OF CPU CORES: 8
OF THREADS: 16
BASE CLOCK: 3.7GHZ
MAX BOOST CLOCK: UP TO 4.3GHZ
TOTAL L1 CACHE: 768KB
TOTAL L2 CACHE:4MB
TOTAL L3 CACHE: 16MB
UNLOCKED: YES
CMOS: 12NM FINFET
PACKAGE: AM4
PCI EXPRESS® VERSION: PCIE 3.0 X16
THERMAL SOLUTION (PIB): WRAITH PRISM WITH RGB LED
THERMAL SOLUTION (MPK): WRAITH PRISM
DEFAULT TDP / TDP: 105W
MAX TEMPS: 85°C

*OS SUPPORT:
WINDOWS 10 – 64-BIT EDITION
RHEL X86 64-BIT
UBUNTU X86 64-BIT
*OPERATING SYSTEM (OS) SUPPORT WILL VARY BY MANUFACTURER.

SYSTEM MEMORY

SYSTEM MEMORY SPECIFICATION: 2933MHZ
SYSTEM MEMORY TYPE: DDR4
MEMORY CHANNELS: 2

PC CASE
HOW TO CHOOSE THEM?

o To an inexperienced builder, the CASE may appear as simply a housing unit with the sole purpose of holding pieces of hardware without any other important aspect except perhaps that it can look attractive too.

o It can offer so much gaming experience than you might realize and more importantly, it can take away from the experience as well, so you need to pay attention to what each case has to offer.

o **SIZE AND FORM FACTOR** - All PC CASES are unique in one way or another, but they generally based on one of the following four modes: SMALL FORM FACTOR, MINI TOWER, MID TOWER & FULL TOWER. Naturally, the size of the case will decide which hardware pieces can and cannot fit into the set case but it is important to point out that these four form factors are all built around only a single piece of hardware, THE MOTHERBOARD.

o (i)SMALL FORM FACTOR CASES can only accommodate MINI ITX (INFORMATION TECHNOLOGY EXTENDED) MOTHERBOARDS.

o (ii)MINI TOWERS have enough room to fit a MICRO ATX (ADVANCE TECHNOLOGY EXTENDED) MOTHERBOARDS.

o (iii)MID TOWERS are made for ATX MOTHERBOARDS.

o (iv)FULL TOWERS are needed if you have got your eyes set on that EATX (EXTENDED-ATX) MOTHERBOARD.

o Each of these motherboards can be used to install a smaller motherboard meaning you can use a motherboard of any size in a full tower. Anything except an EATX motherboard in a mid-tower and so on.

o The compatibility can sometimes go in the opposite direction also, for example, some MID-TOWERS can even fit in the EATX motherboard. These are the exception and not any rules.

o The form factor of the PC CASE doesn't guarantee the compatibility of certain GRAPHICS Card or a COOLER. So always double the compatibility between the PC CASE you are purchasing and the graphics card or CPU cooler.

○ The most important thing to check for when it comes to the GRAPHICS CARD is the length, but the height is also becoming more crucial than ever due to the popularity of the bulky gaming cards with massive fans.

○ As for CPU COOLERS, the most important measurement to take is the height since LARGE TOWER COOLERS may not fit inside a compact case.

○ If you are planning to install a LIQUID COOLING SOLUTION, you need to make sure the case has adequate radiator support.

○ Components like RAM, SSDs, HDD and optical drives generally aren't affected by the size of the case except that smaller cases will be able to carry fewer of these storage devices.

○ Pay extra attention to the **specs sheet** if you are planning to buy a case that has support for an optical drive which requires 5.25" drive bay. Optical drive along with the optical drive bay is slowly but surely being phased out of modern gaming cases. If you've already bought a computer case only to discover it doesn't contain an optical drive bay, don't be disheartened as there are many great reliable and budget-friendly optical drives in the market which connect to your PC via USB.

○ **POWER SUPPLY** - Consider the power supply you will be using. Most PC cases use the standard ATX power supplies, but many small form factor cases can only fir the more compact SFX power supplies. Other PSU formats exist but as of now, these are the only 2 forms you need to know about in case you are building a DESKTOP PC.

○ I generally recommend MID-TOWERS to users who don't require a compact or a portable case, as the MID-TOWERS offer plenty of space which makes it easier to clean and better airflow.

○ FULL-TOWERS are generally more expensive so it's best to purchase them if you are planning on making good use of the extra space.

o While many MINI-TOWERS and SMALL FORM-FACTOR offer unparalleled degrees of portability, they come with some prominent disadvantages such as difficult to manage, not enough space inside the PC to fit all the components and generally running louder because of the stifling airflow.

o So, if you are planning not to carry around your case wherever you go, I suggest you go for a MID-TOWER CASE.

o **MODULARITY** - Now we have arrived at an aspect of modern gaming cases many of you are not aware of. Granted it's not for everyone but MODULAR CASES allow the users to add and remove parts such as trays, covers, mounts and so on. This adds a lot of flexibility and Customizability to an otherwise unchanging PC component. Excessive modularity is generally seen as overkill. But I recommend you Check out what the market has to offer before committing yourself to the constricting designs of NON-MODULAR CASES. Not all of them resemble the abstract pieces of modern art yet they offer tasteful designs that you wouldn't guess are modular.

o **FRONT PANEL CONTROLS** - Controls on the front panel of your case need not be limited to your standard USB ports, headphone and microphone jacks. Some cases feature an arsenal of amazing features in addition to these bare essentials like heat monitor, LCD panels, FAN controllers, volume controls, clocks, lighting controllers and so much more.

o **SOUNDPROOF CASE** - If you are building a high-end PC with loads of fans that all will be running at the same time, consider buying a soundproof case. The whirring of fans may be easy to ignore at first, but it can quickly turn into an unwanted distraction.

o None of these features modular or otherwise is necessary for the case to do its job well and the large majority of PC users will be more than content with their non-modular case that only has the standard few ports on the front. I made to make this section illustrate just a few ways in which cases can be made to accomplish so much more than simply hold the hardware like a piece of a cardboard box.

- **COOLING** – It is important that your PC cases must offer better airflow as there are a lot of cases in that market that are poorly built to accommodate this bare essential, as a result of which, poor airflow. Luckily, most of the modern cases adopt designs that facilitate proper airflow. The addition of case mounted fan adds to the better airflow design. Hence, I recommend installing at least two case mounted FANS, even in cases with excellent ventilation. This is the best way to increase overall airflow. A PC with more airflow will run more quietly, dissipate heat more efficiently and it may even draw a bit less power. The number of mounts that can be supported by the case depends on the size of these cases as well the size of the mounts too. SMALLER CASES stick to 120mm to 240mm mounts, but larger Cases not only support more mounts but sometimes support even bigger mounts. The same goes for the LIQUID COOLING SUPPORT, only instead of FANS, we have RADIATORS. Larger cases will have the room to support more and larger radiator mounts which will allow or a more expensive LIQUID COOLING SETUP.

- Manufacturers have become very good in designing cases with good airflow, but you can still find a lot of older models being sold, models that were made before such a large emphasis was made on the airflow design. While these models can generally be exceedingly affordable, they invariably end up doing more harm than good.

- So, make sure to do enough research before deciding the right PC case for you by letting the price dictate your decision.

- **AESTHETICS** – PC building has evolved from being just practical to the one that concerns itself with aesthetics now. Yes, beauty has entered into the world of PC building. The new trend in building PC is to have a case that is transparent that prominently features glass build. Taste differs, so there's still a fair bit of variety that exists. Don't fret if this isn't your cup of tea. Glass, of course, goes well with RGB lighting but there will always be cases with classic touch, clean and honest black exteriors for PC building enthusiasts who prefer a bit more inconspicuous approach as well as cases with aggressive angular designs that have become synonymous with the term gaming.

o You should also not be oblivious to the fact that the aesthetic of the exterior can affect the airflow. For example, you may think that all simple cases have excellent airflow, but some company sacrifices airflow benefits for their aesthetics in certain cases.

o Cases with the meshed front panel are way better for performance-oriented buyers. You can see even something as unassuming as the design of the front panel can affect the overall performance of the case. So, it is better to think about the aesthetics of the case even if you don't care about how it looks.

BUILD QUALITY & PRICE - All the features we talked about earlier will have a role to play when determining the overall price. This may lead you to believe that you can get a decent case no matter the price as long as it's non-modular and lacks any additional features like the ones we have mentioned both practical and aesthetic. The problem with many cheap cases is that they simply suffer from poor build quality more than anything else. This can manifest in the form of poorly designed infrastructure for **cable management,** insufficient rigidity in the **chassis (IMPORTANT** - Motherboard along with other heavy PC components are attached to the chassis of the case and need to be very rigid), sharp edges which can be harming to yourself, lack of thumbscrews and so much more and we must not forget about the airflow that's more likely than not going to be very poor, meaning below average airflow performance. So even if you dint care about the aesthetics or extra features, you will be doing your harm to the PC by picking up a very cheap $24 case. Performance-oriented gamers or video editors might have it harder since the cases that have amazing exterior and interior, which comes with great features more often than not tend to be more expensive especially the serviceable cases and excellent build quality. But distinguishing a good inconspicuous case among the sea of mediocre cases can be much more challenging. Luckily, **THE PRICE** is one aspect of the case that can be used as a good estimate of quality. My experience suggests a good buy will be centered around a $61 price range, which mostly has a good balance between affordability and quality. On the other hand, anything cheaper than $39 without discounts is most likely not going to do anything good for your PC. If you can't afford to fit into these price ranges, then it's time to go for discount hunting. There is no shortage of computer case manufacturers releasing new models to us year after year and with such a competitive market, the consumer is always treated to good models at decent discounts.

BEST GAMING CASE 2020

o It is a fact that even though computer cases don't increase the PC performance, but it surely can hamper them, hence selecting the ideal PC CASE is an important task.

HERE ARE THE 10 BEST GAMING PC CASES:

SMALL FORM FACTOR
MINI-ITX CASE

1) PC CASE: CORSAIR OBSIDIAN 250D
COST: $129/₹13,599
PURCHASE LINK: https://amzn.to/3acr8UY
FEATURES
Optimal Airflow.
2 built in fans, admirable job.
3 additional fan mounts
Can accommodate a full-sized GPU.
DOWNSIDE: larger & heavier than other MINI-ITX cases.

2) PC CASE: COOLER MASTER ELITE 110
COST: $57/₹4,499
PURCHASE LINK: https://amzn.to/2TpkuUv
FEATURES

Perfect for the mid-ranging game, considering the price point.
Compact and light along with quality and durable steel build
DRAWBACK: Not very spacious common among most of the mini-ITX cases.
Less hardware size compatibility
Poor heat management inside.
Even with all the provided fans, get a CPU liquid cooling unit, if selected CPU tends to run hot.

3) PC CASE: FRACTAL DESIGN NODE 202
COST: $129/₹16,119
PURCHASE LINK: https://amzn.to/2VxQM2A

FEATURES
Emulates PC console.
Comes with vertical stand.
Airflow design is well balanced.
Chambered, with GPU chamber having 2 fans.
CAN accommodate Full sized GPU.
A blower fan graphics card works well with this case.
Supports only SFX PSU.
No room or optical drives and 3.4" HDDs.

MINI-TOWER
MICRO-ATX CASES

1) PC CASE: COOLER MASTER N200
COST: $55/₹12,049
PURCHASE LINK: https://amzn.to/389W7zq
FEATURES

Better style, spacious and airflow.
Not for RGB enthusiasts.
Front mesh panel for better airflow, thereby performance.
Augmented by 3 mounted case fans
Sub optimal for liquid cooling builds
Noisy fans, ok for the price.

2) PC CASE: COOLER MASTER MASTERBOX LITE 3.1
COST: $50/₹11,039
PURCHASE LINK: https://amzn.to/2T97Av1
FEATURES

Tempered glass side panel & a black tined front panel.
Further complemented by the LED light built into the pre-installed FANS.
Decent airflow with aesthetics.
Supports only max 3 fans. But complemented by the additional radiator mount for liquid cooling.

MID-TOWER ATX CASES

1) PC CASE: CORSAIR CRYSTAL SERIES 570X
COST: $170/₹16,089
PURCHASE LINK: https://amzn.to/2TpdK9f

FEATURES

Features of MASTERBOX LITE 3.1 +
Uses fully transparent tempered glass (Front, top and both side panels)
Unlike MASTERBOX model, Design focuses on both airflow and aesthetics equally.
Design focused on LIQUID COOLING setups too.
6 Fan mounts & 3 Radiator mounts.
3 pre-installed RGB fans.
Drawbacks: Expensive

2) PC CASE: CORSAIR CARBIDE SERIES 100R
COST: $50/₹3,099
PURCHASE LINK: https://amzn.to/2PxjUms
FEATURES

Not aesthetic.
No radiator mounts.
Excellent & quality build.
Simplified cable management system.
Air cooling with a max of 5 fan mounts.
1 pre-installed fan.

3) PC CASE: NZXT 510

I purchased this for my PC build based on budget and decent build

COST: $70/₹6,445

PURCHASE LINK: https://amzn.to/2T8ItbF

FEATURES

Streamline cooling - well engineered airflow.
Glass side panel
2 pre-installed FANS
2 removable radiator mounting brackets.
USB 3.1 Gen 2 COMPATIBLE USB-C connector on the front panel.
Front panel & PSU intake has removable filters.
DRAWBACK: Non-glass side panel is flimsy, where dust can enter.

FULL-TOWER
E-ATX CASES

1) PC CASE: THERMALTAKE CORE V71
COST: $180/₹15,757 + Delivery + Import duty (If not US)
PURCHASE LINK: https://amzn.to/2IauBaP
Or
https://world.ubuy.com/?Goto=search/index/view/
product/B074ZLQZ8F?inf=37bc2f75bf1
BCFe8450a1a41c200364c&utm_source=uglow

FEATURES
Enlarged thick tempered side glass side panel, reduces
noise.
3 LED FANS + 1 REAR FAN = 4 pre-installed fans.
Front panel fan controller - Speed & LED.
Vertical GPU support.

FANS: HOW TO CHOOSE THE BEST FOR YOUR PC Build

The most important criteria in choosing a FAN are:

FAN SIZE (25-230mm)

o Measure the frames rather than the fans. The size goes from 25mm all the way to 230mm. The most commonly used fan size is 120mm and 140mm. The normal thickness for these is 25mm which is o for a majority of situations. There are also fans out there that are very thin for small form factor situations. Dimensions are present on the product boxing. So, make sure your selected fans are compatible with the CASE. Some cases allow you to mount either 2 x 140mm fans on the front or 3 x 120mm fans. I advise you to go for the bigger size fans because (i) Bigger fans enable better airflow without having to spin very fast, which automatically reduces noise level (ii) Even though the bigger fans are more expensive, a single big fan is still cheaper than 2 smaller fans.

FAN AIR LOW (CFM -> CUBIC FEET PER MINUTE)

o sometimes measured in m³/h. 1 CFM = 1.699011 m³/h. This number indicates the volume of air displaced by the fan. Higher the number, the more the fan can move. A higher number doesn't always mean the best fan as the fan can produce a considerable amount of sound at a higher speed. So, adjust accordingly in BIOS if you have to.

FAN RPM (REVOLUTIONS PER MINUTE)

o A bigger fan will remove more air at the same speed as compared to a smaller fan. Higher the RPM, the better the arrow will be and therefore performance. But this will increase the noise level. The opposite is true for low RPM, which has low noise levels.

FAN PWM (PULSE WIDTH MODULATION)

o This is indicated by a fan with a 4-pin connector rather than a 3-pin connector. With this special connector, connected on to the motherboard you can control the full precise control of the RPM range, you

can get the RPM to reflect temperature range Example:
Spike up fan RPM to 100% when CPU load is higher, etc,
the fan can also be adjusted to low RPM to make it
silent, based on your preference. Most of the 3-pin fan
doesn't have any of this function but certain
motherboard allows for the voltage of the fan to be
regulated, thereby regulating the RPM based on voltage
control.

FAN STATIC/AIR PRESSURE (mm H2O or Pa, Pascal/mm WG/mm WC)

o What happens when you have airflow Resistance within
   the CASE from CPU TOWERS, RADIATOR CASE ELEMENTS, etc.
   Higher the static pressure of the fan, better the fan
   can force the air through whatever resistance is there
   on either side of the FAN. The blade design is crucial
   for this, which is why they are much wider than your
   airflow fans. There are some industrial versions of
   fans that deliver an insane amount of static pressure
   but comes with a higher RPM along with loud noise. When
   it comes to water-cooling radiators, average case fans
   will do a passable job, but they aren't what you need.
   For pushing air through high-density heatsinks like
   radiators, you need a fan that can generate high-static
   pressure. That's where wide-bladed fans are effective.

o So, look for fans based on your case preference. There
   are a wide variety of fans that focus on speed and
   static pressure. Choose wisely if you are planning to
   buy extra. If you are a beginner stick with the design
   mentioned in number #35 of the chapter 'BEST TIPS -
   COMMON MISTAKES'.

o FAN NOISE (dB, Decibels) - Any fan noise below <20 dB
   is inaudible. Check out 'bequiet' banded fans. The
   noise levels indicate in the product manual or the
   manufacturer website are weighted decibels, meaning
   they are adjusted for the human ear. Indicated as
   'DBA'.

FAN BEARING TYPE

o This is important for noise, performance, and longevity
   of the fan. Some company fans with hydraulic bearing
   boast about 40,000 hours, some with rifle bearing boast

about 50,000-80,000 hours, about 300,000 with advanced fluid-dynamic bearings.

- **SLEEVE BEARING FANS** - They are the cheapest and most commonly used fans. They don't perform well in high temperatures or in a horizontal position which makes them perfect for computer cases. They have a shorter life span.

- **BALL BEARING FANS** - They are quieter and more durable. They are not affected when placed horizontally. They are very high-end in the world of fans. They cost a lot to the manufacturers too.

- **RIFLE BEARING FANS** - They come in between the sleeve and ball bearing. They are quiet, durable and can handle the horizontal alignment. They are also cheaper compared to the Baal bearing.

- **HYDRAULIC BEARING FANS** - They are sleeve bearing fans but better. They are quieter and last longer with the improved self-lubrication of the fan. They are the best all-around choice.

- **SSO BEARING** - They achieve higher precision and better longevity than the conventional ball, sleeve or hydrodynamic bearings. SSO bearing is a refined fluid-dynamic design.

HOW MANY FANS?

- If you are using more than 2 FANS in your case, it's better to create positive air pressure inside the case by having *more fans as intakes* and slightly fewer exhaust fans. This setup will reduce the dust build up inside of your case. This also allows you to run your fan at a lower speed resulting in a quieter environment.

POSITIVE VS NEGATIVE AIR PRESSURE

- Heart transfer relies on 2 main things for the best effectiveness: (i) A lower ambient temperature, how hot the air is around the HEATSINK (ii) Air movement. Living in a colder place and room air conditioner helps a lot. Since the components of the PC are enclosed in a CASE, the air used to cool these components can be considerably hotter than the rest of the room impeding cooling efficiency. The temperature inside the room itself can increase over time because of this. This is one of the methods, where a fan is useful to move the air inside faster. The drawbacks include - Noise, dust which can easily accumulate on the fans reducing their effectiveness, they also do plugs up the kinks of the HEATSINKS thus reducing their effectiveness. Adding more fans increases this unless done responsibly.

HOW TO PRACTICE SAFE COOLING? - The answer to this problem is a BALANCED AIRFLOW. A FAN can be configured in two ways:

○ **(i)** If all the fans act as an exhaust pulling the air out from inside, these fans act against each other reducing their efficiency. This movement of air only outside creates a negative air pressure inside. The result is air is pulled inside from all the nooks and corners of the case. This can result in dust build up in these areas and are pulled into the CASE.

○ **(ii)** If all the fans on the CASE are only pulling air inside, it has a similar issue as fans pulling air outside but dust doesn't accumulate in the nooks and corners of the CASE because of the POSITIVE PRESSURE inside because of which the air is pushed out through them. This doesn't help if you don't have filters in these nooks and corners of your CASE. So, the ideal way is to have filters on the fans for intake and extra filters in the nooks and corners of the CASE. If you don't have filters on your PC CASE, Cover the PC with a used pantyhose seems to do the trick. In the long run check for dust accumulation in the mesh panels and areas around the optical drive base. If present, time to make some adjustments in fan's intake/outtake ratios of your PC. There are options to adjust your FAN SPEED in your BIOS. Play around with it.

Check the next chapter to see the top best FANS you can buy from the market.

BEST PC FANS 2020

o Every PC requires at least one FAN. At least one exhaust fan to prevent the accumulation of hot air inside.

o Graphics cards are becoming bigger and bigger, producing more and more heat.

o With graphics card being the most integral part of a PC ecosystem, it's really surprising to see how fans are not considered an integral part of every gaming or video editing PC build.

o PC comes with prebuilt fans but not all of them.

o This list will help you decide the best fan most suited for your preferences:

1) PC FAN: COOLER MASTER SILENT FAN SI2
COST: $21/₹1,419
PURCHASE LINK: https://amzn.to/2I6BI3T
FEATURES

120mm size
1200 RPM
Performance oriented.
Ultra-silent operation at 19 dBA.
Economic solution for perfect performance.
RoHS compliance for protecting the environment.
Not the best in the market.
Least aesthetic.
Sleeve bearing model - not the best.
30,000 hours.

2) PC FAN: COOLER MASTER MEGAFLOW 200
COST: $17/₹4,246
PURCHASE LINK: https://amzn.to/3cmB1Bx
FEATURES

200mm size (only size available)
Efficient model: Quiet & powerful.
700 RPM. Large diameter makes up for it. Quiet operation
with low RPM.
Blue/Red LED versions/Black matte version.
Sleeve bearing model.
30,000 hours.

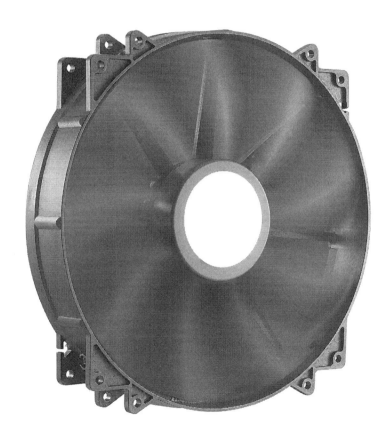

3) PC FAN: CORSAIR AIR SERIES AF120 QUIET EDITION
COST: $18/₹2,897
PURCHASE LINK: https://amzn.to/2VuXSVv
FEATURES

Features of SI2 + additional features.
120mm.
Operates at 21 dBA.
1100 RPM.
Hydraulic bearing
Replaceable color rings, multi-color option.
50,000 hours.

4) PC FAN: CORSAIR AIR SERIES AF120 PERFORMANCE EDITION
COST: $20/₹6,307
PURCHASE LINK: https://amzn.to/2PC5Ng1
FEATURES
120mm.
1650 RPM.
30 dBA (not good for gaming experience)
Similar to the quiet edition with some additional features.
Better performance.
50,000 hours.

5) PC FAN: CORSAIR LL SERIES LL120
COST: $40/₹2,558
PURCHASE LINK: https://amzn.to/2whzegx
FEATURES

120mm Size (only size available)
Hydraulic bearing type.
1500 RPM with only 24.8 dBA.
Fully customizable RGB LED lighting. You can buy this in dual and triple packs.
Best model with speed to noise ratio.
Expensive.
40,000 hours.

6) PC FAN: THERMALTAKE PURE 20
COST: $12/₹2,299
PURCHASE LINK: https://amzn.to/3ai58Il
FEATURES

200mm Size (only available size)
Elegant fan.
Outstanding performance.
This fan prioritizes on power and performance.
Cost effective
800 RPM
A little noisier than the competition with about 28.2 dBA
Sleeve bearing
Matte black/Transparent with blue LED light versions
available.
30,000 hours.

7) PC FAN: THERMALTAKE RIING 12
COST: $12.99/₹2,349
PURCHASE LINK: https://amzn.to/2uHS005
FEATURES
If you don't want the 200mm above version, this model will blow your mind.
One of the best models - Fast, quiet, stylish and affordable.
Incredible speed to noise ratio.
Many color choices.
120mm.
1400 RPM, 1000 RPM with low noise cable (LNC)
24.6 dBA.
Hydraulic bearing
40,000 hours.

8) PC FAN: NOCTUA NF-F12 PWM
COST: $20/₹2,810
PURCHASE LINK: https://amzn.to/2Tf8I0l
FEATURES
120mm Size.
SSO2 bearing.
1200-1500 RPM
22.4 dBA (18.6 dBA with LAN, low noise adapter)
Fan can generate high-static pressure, *perfect for water cooling radiators*.
6 years warranty
150,000 hours.

9) PC FAN: NOCTUA NF-S12B REDUX-1200
COST: $14/₹2,665
PURCHASE LINK: https://amzn.to/2TpGzCs
FEATURES

120mm.

SSO-Bearing (better than sleeve and hydraulic)

400 - 1200 RPM.

18.1 dBA.

Budget friendly

Best power to performance to noise ratio.

6 years warranty

>150,000 hours.

AIR COOLING VS LIQUID COOLING

- Water cooling is a superior method of cooling than air cooling, which is used for extreme gaming and overclocking (OC).

- AIO CPU COOLERS can be used for minimum overclocking and aesthetics.

HOW DO THEY WORK?

AIR COOLING:
- It relies on 2 key components

- **(i) THE HEATSINK** – HEATSINK is there to draw the heat away from the CPU and it is made of highly thermally conductive materials, usually aluminum or a combination of aluminum and copper. No matter how much thermal conductive they are, there is a limit to how much heat they can absorb, this is where the fans come into play.

- **(ii) FAN** – It spins to blow air through the HEATSINK and make sure it doesn't overheat.

LIQUID COOLING:

- The principle behind liquid cooling is a bit more complicated. It has 4 key components: (i) The Pump (ii) The Hose (iii) The Radiator (iv) Fan.

- The idea here is the same as air cooling. Instead of blowing air through the heatsink, it **pumps** water or any other liquid coolant through the **hoses** that connect to the CPU. But just circulating the water around isn't enough, it also needs something to absorb the heat. This is where the **radiator** comes in. The fan here keeps the radiator from overheating.

AIR COOLING VS LIQUID COOLING

- **(i) COOLING EFFICIENCY** – A much higher volume of water can be circulated more easily than air. Liquid cooling is more powerful and more efficient than air cooling will ever be. The big question here is, do you even need this type of cooling technique? If you are running your CPU at a factory setting, then there is no need to get liquid cooling. You won't get anything out of it. The same goes for some light overclocking. The liquid cooling will only ever become necessary if you are planning on pushing your CPU to the limit. Overclocking and liquid cooling go hand in hand.

- **(ii) PRICE** - you can always buy the liquid coolant just for your peace of mind and aesthetics. The manufacturing cost for it is way bigger than they are for air cooling. Liquid cooling units are very expensive. It is not a part of the budget PC.

- **(iii) CONVENIENCE** - Liquid cooling is very convenient. But installing and maintaining a liquid cooling setup can be an absolute nightmare unless you are experienced in dealing with computer hardware. Air cooling, on the other hand, is very easy to use and clean. The only thing you will have to do is take it out every once in a while, to clean the dust-out.

CONCLUSION: Now this comes to the final question, which cooling solution is the best? I will have to go with AIR COOLING because of its convenience, much cheaper and it really will be more than sufficient unless you are OVERCLOCKING (OC). Alternatively, if you are completely against the sound for the air-cooling fans makes, it is as good as a reason to go for the LIQUID COOLING. Also, you should consider investing in a liquid cooling unit if you are using a mini-ATX case or even a micro-ATX case with less air-cooling efficiency.

LIQUID COOLING
Everything basic you need to know

(Image Source: Thermaltake)

OVERVIEW

o The purpose of this section is to give beginner gamers the basic knowledge required to select, build and maintain components in a custom water loop. I'm not going to get technical about the hardware involved, but rather a simple overview to give the reader basic information on what custom loops are, how they are assembled and how to maintain them. This book is more for beginners to intermediate level gamers and video editors. I believe liquid cooling is more for extreme gamers who like to overclock their PC; hence I'll be covering the basics of water cooling. Unless aesthetics is your concern. As technology continues to advance, new solutions for old problems will arise, new problems with new solutions will need to be addressed. I'll try to cover the basics of everything.

o Before you go any farther, let me just say that water cooling a PC is not for everyone. It's for people who either need to use one of the advantages mentioned below or for people who have researched it and found their own reasons. I highly recommend that you, at the very least, read through this entire guide before starting this project. So, I suggest you do even more research past the information contained in this guide by reading and watching the video of the installation process to prevent any damage to your PC components.

CUSTOM LOOP PURPOSE:

○ A very important part of any process is figuring out why you're doing it in the first place. Lots of people are going to read this and ask, 'Why the hell do you need to go through all this trouble when a good air heatsink would be just as effective?' Liquid Cooling something is far more difficult, complicated and rewarding than just slapping a big heatsink on it and calling it a day, and it's therefore important to understand the process and theory behind it.

ADVANTAGES

○ **REDUCED OR RELOCATED NOISE AND HEAT** – The ability to move or relocate heat and noise to other locations is significant in some implementations. Most cars, for example, would look king OD weird if they all had air-cooled engines instead of a liquid solution. Some machines use radiators to move the noise of fans to a different location.

○ **HEAT CAPACITY** – Most Liquid simply has the ability to hold much more heat than metal or air, and therefore takes much more time and energy to heat up.

○ **EFFICIENCY** – Liquid radiators are more efficient at transferring heat to the air compared to conventional air heatsink fins.

○ **SIZE** – Water blocks are almost always significantly smaller in size compared to air heatsinks. This can allow for very minimal hardware space implementations while still being able to dissipate heat effectively.

- ○ **AESTHETICS** - This one is mostly for PC build enthusiasts, but I think we can all agree that a good water loop looks really looks amazing.

DISADVANTAGES

- ○ **COMPLICATED** - Compared to air cooling, Liquid Cooling is significantly more complicated and time-consuming. There are many more nuances that you have to look out for and workaround to get the full benefit.

- ○ **EXPENSIVE** - Liquid solution is going to be significantly more expensive as compared to air solution. This mainly because there are many more separate components in a Liquid loop compared to an air sink. There is always maintenance involved too.

- ○ **MAINTENANCE** - A water loop requires much more maintenance compared to an air sink. This requires time and patience.

- ○ **WATER LEAKS** - I saved this one for the end for a reason. If you can follow directions and not do anything reckless, water spills won't be an issue. The first thing people think of when they think about a water loop is, 'Will the water spill on to my expensive computer components?' I'll get more into this in later sections, but proper water loops will leave only an extremely small chance of damaging something, even if there are spills or leaks.

OVERVIEW OF WATER-COOLING COMPONENTS:

- ○ I'll give you a quick rundown of the various components involved in a PC water loop with measurements and statistics used to determine performance. I'll try to be as detailed as possible. Don't forget this is a basic guide.

WATER BLOCKS

o Water blocks are used to transfer heat from the PC
  components into the water. They are essentially heat
  exchangers that move heat energy to the water from the
  heat generating-component. Water blocks rely on surface
  area and flow rate to transfer heat quickly and
  effectively. Just like air heatsinks, the more surface
  area there is, the more heat can be transferred. To add
  surface area, water block manufacturers rely on fins,
  pins and channels. Depending on the design, a water
  block will make use of any one of those 3 parts. There
  is no single best solution for a good water block. The
  restriction of the block is often used to compare
  blocks. This is a measurement of how much water can be
  pumped through the block in a given amount of time.
  High restriction blocks often perform better with a
  more powerful pump and a loop of its own. Low
  restriction blocks may sacrifice performance, but they
  also allow you to chain more blocks together. Since
  performance is your goal, the former option is
  effective.

CPU BLOCKS

o CPU water blocks are the most common type of block. Often made of copper and coated with nickel for a shiny silver finish. CPU blocks make use of pins and fins mostly. Some CPU blocks are designed with channels, but there aren't many out there. They attach to your motherboard just like any other aftermarket heatsink, with a backplate and other mounting hardware.

GPU BLOCKS

GPU blocks are designed to fit on your graphics card. There are 2 main types of GPU blocks (i) FULL COVER GPU BLOCKS - They are designed as the name suggests to fully cover the GPU PCB (GPU Circuit board). Blocks of this type often support a single card and PCB design. They cool the GPU core, memory and power delivery (VRMs) with a single block. Universal GPU blocks are often designed to fit on any GPU. They may include brackets for many different types of mounting scenarios, just like CPU blocks. Even though most GPUs today use standard mounting holes and specifications, universal GPU blocks, despite the name, are not always universal. Because universal blocks only cool the GPU itself, you will often need separate cooling on the power delivery (VRMs) and memory. This often comes in the form of stick-on heatsinks. The picture below shows the GPU blocks.

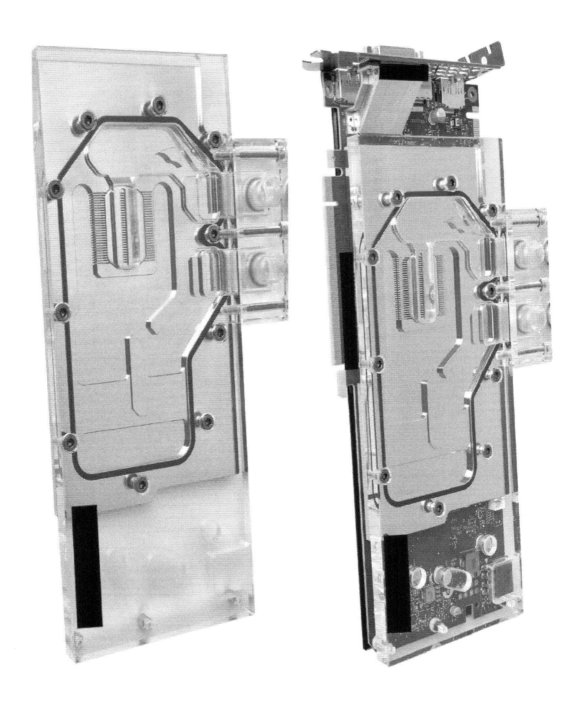

CHIPSET/OTHER BLOCKS

o   In addition to cooling your GPU and CPU, some people
     like to attach water blocks to additional heat-
     generating components in their PC. Chipset blocks are
     similar to GPU blocks. They come in universal and
     board-specific versions. Board-specific blocks are
     almost always limited to a single motherboard version.
     Board-specific blocks are very rare, even for expensive
     and popular motherboards. Other places people have put
     water blocks are RAM. Most RAM blocks are custom
     designed and rather expensive. Nowadays, RAM doesn't
     really generate enough heat to warrant a fully custom
     solution. Hard Drives. Yes, there have been water
     blocks designed to fit around hard drives. No, they
     aren't really necessary. There have been a few PSUs
     that have connections for water loops. Again, this
     isn't really necessary and it's very expensive.

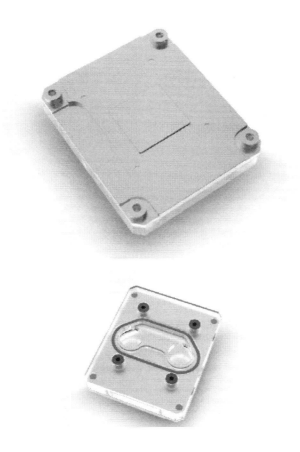

PUMPS

- Pumps are responsible for circulating water around your loop. They often vary in physical design, size, power consumption and noise generation.

PUMP MEASUREMENT

- Pumps are categorized and measured with head pressure and flow rate, in addition to dB for noise and watts for power consumption. Flow rate is the measurement of how much liquid a pump can move with no restriction. Usually measured in gallons/liters per hour, the flow rate doesn't tell you much unless you also know the head pressure, because no water loop is going to have 0 restrictions. Head pressure is how high a pump can push liquid at full load (with 0 for unrestricted flow or 100% restriction). It's measured by seeing how high a pump can push water through a thin tube and is usually measured in feet or meters. A pump with lots of flow is useless if it can't push that water through minor restrictions. Similarly, a pump with lots of head pressure and not a lot of flow isn't very useful either.

COMMON PUMP DESIGNS AND IMPLEMENTATIONS

- The most common pump today is a variation on a single design, the *Laing DDC pump*. The pump only has a single moving part and is very reliable. It's essentially a large magnet with an impeller attached to it in the middle that gets moved by electromagnets around the perimeter of the pump. Because of its reliability and effectiveness, lots of companies have taken the design and changed minor details, like the top housing geometry for more flow or head pressure. Unless you are looking for an extremely powerful pump, your best and cheapest bet is a DDC pump from any one of the known component manufacturers. Other pumps have more powerful motors or other features that can't fit inside the DDC form factor but often require more maintenance and care.

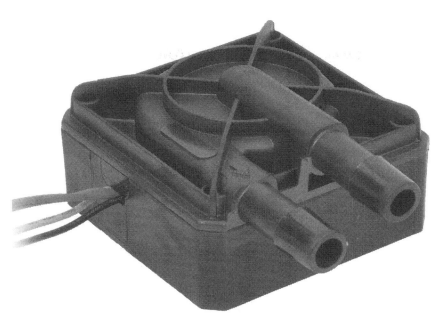

RADIATORS

o They are designed to transfer heat from one substance to another efficiently. However, the term 'radiator' usually refers to a liquid-air heat exchanger. Simply put, the point of a radiator in a custom loop is to get heat out of the liquid and into the air so it can go pick up more heat from the components.

SIZING YOUR RADIATOR

o This is one of the most important parts of your liquid cooling unit loop. This is the only part in the loop that takes the heat out of the unit. So, when choosing a radiator, it is always safe to go for the best. Avoid bad quality and undersized radiators.

o Your blocks take the heat from your PC components. Your radiator takes the heat out of the loop.

o A 240mm length, 120mm breadth and 30mm thickness (240 x 120 x 30 mm) worth of radiator per component is the recommended standard size.

o Take 1 x 120mm fan worth of the radiator per component. 120mm is the most widely used fan on CPU, all in one water cooling loop, powered GPUs.

o A single 120mm fan covering the radiator with 30 mm radius is usually more than enough to handle a standard component and even a little bit of overclocking.

o Under extreme overclocking – 2 x 120 mm (240mm) fans covering a 30mm thick radiator per component.

o When you start stacking components in your loop and adding more GPUs or CPUs (dual-processor system) and in case of extreme overclocking, it is ideal to add a 240mm radiator along with 2x 120 mm fans per component is recommended.

o Additionally, some radiators are thicker than others. This, combined with fin density, determines what the ideal type of fan you want to use on the radiator is. Thickness is measured in mm and comes in all sorts of measurements, the thickest I've seen being 80mm and about 20mm for the thinnest. Fin density is measured in FPI or Fins Per Inch. 30 FPI is on the high side while 5-10 is low. Thicker and denser radiators ideally need fans with high static pressure to push air through the fins. Thinner radiators with less fin density perform better with fans that have lots of airflows.

o The different components in the PC that need to be cooled using a liquid cooling system are: (i) CPU (ii) VRM (iii) GPU. VRM for the chip that is drawing a lot of power. But if you are using a lot of components like two GPUs etc, the rule dictates, cooling unit per component, this adds a lot of clutter of things. This is where the thickness of the radiator matters. Adding thickness to the radiator increases the surface area or the number of fins. Fin density of the radiator is increased resulting in more dissipation of heat. Thereby increasing the cooling capacity. This is where the debate comes, THICKNESS VS LENGTH, trying to look for that sweet spot. But if you go beyond 60 or 80mm thick radiator, you are going to have a huge pressure drop across the radiator because of the air that is being pushed by the fan through the radiator is immensely slowing down.

o CPU MONOBLOCKS – A Monoblock is a compromise in cooling for easier application of water cooling. It is easier in that you can cool the VRM and CPU in one block and avoid clearance issues. Monoblocks don't help cool the CPU any more than a regular block. They just add VRM cooling to the mix. Which unless you have a chip that is drawing lots of power and extreme overclocking there isn't much need. That being said a big beefy Monoblock does look cooler.

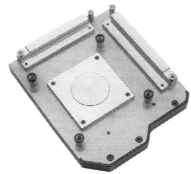

FANS

- The 2 main important specifications to meet the need to be used for liquid cooling are:

- (i)STATIC PRESSURE (ii) AIRFLOW OPTIMIZED.

- The benefit of having these features in the fan makes it strong to react against the resistance of the airflow. This is important because the fins of the radiator are aligned straight but the air coming out from the fans are being blown in the shape of a cone and not in the straight line complimenting the radiator. This causes resistance in the airflow. The thickness of the radiator determines the amount of pressure drop that is going to be there. There is a significant difference between the airflow fans and the static pressure fans, with the airflow fans having more number of fins, the fins being slightly angled with more gaps in between them as compared to the static pressure fans. The difference is still minimum unless you are trying to get the maximum out of your loop.

- PUSH VS PULL - PUSH is when the fan sits behind the radiator, pushing the air through it. PULL is when the air sits on the opposite side of the radiator and pulls the air from inside the fins of the radiator and expel them out. There is a constant debate to which method is more beneficial, with the reality being the same amount of pressure drop.

- Cleaning the radiator is an important process requiring time and dedication. You need to learn the press of cleaning. It's a part and parcel of the liquid cooling system.

TUBING AND FITTINGS

- Tubing and fittings are often where lots of people mess up and end up having to wait a week for a tiny fitting arrive to set up their loop. It's also the place where a lot of money ends up, especially if you buy premium fittings.

MEASUREMENTS AND TYPES:

TUBING IS MEASURED WITH 3 SEPARATE IMPORTANT MEASUREMENTS:

- **INNER DIAMETER (ID)** - This is the diameter of the inner wall of the tubing. Common sizes are 1/2', 3/8' and 7/16'.

- **OUTER DIAMETER (OD)** - This is the diameter of the outer wall of the tubing. Common sizes are 1/2', 5/8' and 3/4'.

- **WALL THICKNESS** - This is the difference between OD and ID and is extremely important. Tubing with an ID of 1/2' typically has an OD of 3/4', but it is in no way standardized. When ordering your tubing and fittings, make absolutely sure your tubing will work with your fittings.

TUBING SUITABLE FOR WATER LOOPS COMES IN DIFFERENT MATERIALS:

- **TYGON** - Flexible and good for tight loops. Not exactly cheap but will make life a lot easier. This is recommended.

- **CLEARFLEX** - Not as flexible as Tygon, but about half the price. A good middle ground.

o **VINYL** - Extremely cheap, but also prone to some nasty kinks. I would avoid vinyl if you can.

o Some transparent tubing also has a nasty habit of clouding up when used for about a while. Whether this has to do with a coating on the inside or some other problem remains to be seen, but it would be worthwhile to do a research on whatever tubing you're thinking about getting to see what other people are saying about it.

SPRINGS AND COILS

o Some people like to prevent kinks and achieve tighter bends with cheaper tubing is by add springs or coils to it to keep it around. Coils go on the outside of the tubing and are sometimes added for aesthetic reasons and are typically made of plastic. Springs go inside the tubing, are meant to stay hidden and are usually made of metal. Springs will impede flow by a relatively negligible amount. For springs, make sure they will fit the ID of whatever tubing you're using, and for coils make sure they fit the OD.

FITTING - MEASUREMENTS AND TYPES:

o There are only two types of fittings, compression fittings and barbs. Barbs are fittings that grab onto the inside of the tubing and keep it secure. Compression fittings are almost exactly like barbs, but they have a compression ring on the outside for extra security. Most people who use barbs use zip ties for security. Compression fittings cost anywhere from $4 to $14 apiece and barbs are usually under $4 depending on what you get. For barbs, all you have to check is if the ID of your tubing matches the fitting size. For compression fittings, you have to look at all 3 measurements because they all matter. Failure to check this often results in compression rings that are too small or large. The other thing you need to check is if your fitting will fit onto the component it was selected for. The most common thread size, by far, is G1/4. Even though almost every component you buy will have G1/4 threads, it's always good to double-check.

RESERVOIRS AND T-LINES:

o The purpose of reservoirs and T-lines is the same: to remove air from the loop, and the way they go about it is similar.

o **RESERVOIRS** - A reservoir is meant to hold extra water in a loop to allow for air bubbles to slowly be replaced by water as it circulates. It holds a relatively large amount of water in a tank that is essentially stored until it gets replaced by air. The only downside of a reservoir is that it costs money and takes up space. Some reservoirs have pump mounts and other goodies that might be useful for your loop.

T-LINES - These days T-lines aren't really worth the trouble because a good reservoir isn't hard to find. I'm only mentioning it because you may hear it talked about from time to time. A T-line is just a part of your loop (near the top of the loop) that has been T-ed off and had a section of tubing added. This effectively functions as a tiny reservoir but holds a very small amount of water. Some people use little T-lines for fill ports.

Image courtesy: Cooler Master

Image courtesy: BI-PARTS

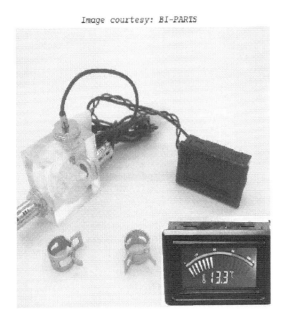

Image courtesy: Thermaltake

OTHER COMPONENTS

- People like to put other little things in their loops like *flow meters, temperature probes and special coolant additives*. These are some of the useful ones that you might want to know about.

- **FLOW METERS** – Simply used for seeing if your pump is pushing water around the loop, flow meters don't really measure flow all that well, despite the name. Passive meters are usually a paddlewheel that the coolant spins to indicate flow. Active meters have a wire for feedback to your motherboard like a fan RPM sensor.

- **TEMPERATURE PROBES** – They are used for measuring the temperature of the water. They usually look similar to a T where the base of the T is the actual sensor and the water flows from one branch to the other. Keep in mind, the temperature of the water is not equal to the temperature of the components being cooled. Water cooling water rarely gets above 40C.

- **COOLANT AND ADDITIVES** – Everybody has their own opinions on what the best liquid to run in your loop is. Yes, there are some additives that might improve this or that or make this look cool or some other special thing. However, the easiest and cheapest liquid to use in your loop is, by far, distilled water and something to stop stuff from growing. There are also no coating or fogginess of the tubes. You have two easy options for that: Biocide and a Silver Kill Coil. Biocide is exactly what it sounds like: liquid that kills living things. You simply add a couple of drops for every X amount of water and it prevents algae from growing. Silver Kill Coils are actually even easier. You simply put them somewhere in your loop, preferably where water flows and it prevents growth.

- **SETTING UP YOUR FIRST LOOP** – So you just read the descriptions and now you want to build a loop for yourself, awesome and Goodluck you decided to take on this project. Now you need to start picking your components. Please take these next sections as *recommendation only*. This should not be the only guide you read before taking this project on. Do as much research and read as many guides as possible to get more understanding of how this stuff works before you spend your money.

o **SELECTING COMPONENTS** - The component selection is a very important part of the process. You need to make sure everything fits beforehand and if you haven't had any experience with it just yet, it's pretty intimidating to spend so much money on something you're unsure about. Therefore, you need to be absolutely sure you're getting the right stuff for your hardware and do a lot of research. I will not be recommending specific components for your circumstances. It is your job to research and finds the best solutions for your system.

o **WATER BLOCKS** - Water blocks are the base of your water loop. If you can't find any blocks that fit your hardware, there isn't much point to pursuing the venture. For CPU blocks, the process is relatively easy. Pick a block based on your research and make sure it's going to fit on your socket. Just like aftermarket CPU coolers, make absolutely sure you have all the materials required to mount your block. Lots of blocks today come in AMD or Intel specific versions, and not all of them support every socket. For GPU blocks, it's a little more complicated. If you're looking for a full cover block, then you need to figure out two things - Is your card a reference PCB design? If it is, look for a waterblock and double-check on the manufacturer's compatibility list to see if it's supported. If it's not a reference design, look and see if a waterblock was still made for it, as is the case with some of the higher-end cards with a non-standard PCB layout. If a full cover block is unavailable, you might have to look for a universal block. Mounts for universal blocks are very similar to CPU blocks for your GPU and its mounting holes. Each GPU has its own mounting system. Find yours and check with the manufacturer's compatibility list to see if it will work. Generally, to reduce corrosion, people like to select blocks made of the same metal. For example, if you have a copper block on your CPU, try and get a copper block for your GPU as well. For nickel plated blocks, try and get blocks that are both nickel-plated. This isn't a huge concern, but it's worth mentioning. Keep in mind that this is only a problem with metals. Delran or Acetal tops aren't going to have an effect on your loop metals.

o **PUMP** - Pump selection is another important part of the process. Like I said in the previous sections, you will most likely be picking up a pump based on the Laing DDC pumps. Do some research and find out, based on your water block selection, what pump would be good for you.

o **RADIATORS** - Your radiator selection will be heavily based around your case selection. While I can't give specific details for every situation, I can give you a few hints on radiator selection: Pick a fin density and thickness that works for your fans. At the end of the day, any fans, even ones with low static pressure, will push air through any radiator. Don't worry too much if you don't know the ratings of your fans. Radiators are actually bigger than the fan slots that the mount on. Make sure you have enough room to actually fit the radiator on the fan mount you select. As a general rule of thumb, try to have at least a 120mm radiator for every GPU and CPU water block in your system. If it looks like a crossflow radiator would work better in your system than a regular one, go for it. ***Never ever buy or use an aluminum radiator*** in a computer water loop. You will regret it later when your blocks are corroded down to nothing. If you want to do push-pull with your radiator, chances are you are going to need extra mounting hardware (like longer screws and more washers). Don't forget that!

o **TUBING AND FITTINGS** - When you pick out your fittings, double-check that your fittings work with your tubing and components. Make sure to get enough tubing for your loop. I usually get about 10 feet even though I could probably get by with 5. It's always good to have a little bit of headroom. I also like to buy 1 or 2 more fittings just to have a couple of extras. There isn't much to say here other than to get what you like best.

o **OTHERS** - When you pick out the remaining components for your loop, it's very important to ask yourself 'is this going to physically fit in my computer?' It helps to get product measurements and a ruler and check out your case. Other things you should be wary of are: - Make sure you buy whatever solution you picked for stopping algae growth (Silver Kill Coil or Biocide). - Pick up any springs or coils if you think you need to make any tight bends - If using barbs, get some hose clamps or zip-ties to keep them secure - Make sure you have a plan for mounting the reservoir. Bay reservoirs are significantly easier to mount and are very handy. - Don't forget your flow meters or temperature probes!

o **PUTTING THINGS TOGETHER** - Throughout this portion of the guide, I will assume you already have a computer set up and ready with the PSU, motherboard, GPU and all your other components ready to go. Some people like to build their loop outside of the PC and test it that way, but I was never a fan of the practice and therefore won't be covering it. Ok, so you got all your components selected and ready to roll. Your parts just arrived and you're bouncing off the walls with excitement just thinking about putting your loop together. First things first: tools. In addition to your water-cooling components, you also need a couple of other tools that will help a lot when putting things together: A friend or another semi-educated person willing to help you out. Having another pair of hands is extremely helpful when putting everything together. Even if they don't have technical skills, somebody standing by with a paper towel or a person to hold the flashlight is always good. LOTS of paper towel. I'm talking an entire roll at the very least. Water WILL spill and you will need to clean it up. Experience with hardware in general A flashlight. Very helpful if you lose a screw or something. Sometimes the mounting for certain components can get tricky. Screwdrivers and hex keys. You should have a good assortment of Phillips and flat screwdrivers. Additionally, some components (like some water blocks) use hex screws instead of regular screws. A 12 V power supply with enough current to run your pump. Because you are going to need to turn in on and off many times, using a PC power supply can get tedious. Dykes (wire cutters) for cutting stuff and pliers (both needle nose and blunt) for bending, pulling, gripping and breaking stuff. A funnel that can fit inside your tubing. Very useful for filling and flushing. Makes the whole process about 30x less frustrating. Ruler or other measurement tools for the planning stage. 6-8 hours of time. I completed my first CPU only loop in about 4 hours and boy was it a long, stressful process. I highly recommend that you complete the entire thing in one sitting, if possible. Once you get that stuff together, get your parts out for cleaning.

○ **CLEANING** - The first thing you want to do when you have all your components together is clean the hell out of everything. Contrary to popular belief, water cooling components will not come ready to run. You need to do some preliminary cleaning. If you have relatively clean water where you live, then flush out the radiator, blocks, tubing and reservoir with tap water. If you don't have access to clean water, then buy a couple of extra jugs of distilled water to flush everything. For the radiator and reservoir, I like to get a good amount of water inside and shake it back and forth to get all the crap out. For the blocks, I like to take each one apart. Make sure there aren't any metal shavings or chips that might be stuck. Be careful not to stretch or break the rubber seals in the water blocks! If you stretch them, you just threw out $100. I also like to run some water through the tubing to make sure there isn't any leftover coating inside (a funnel is very helpful for this purpose) The pump is a special case. Some pumps are designed so that water can flow even when it's off, but some aren't. For the DDC style pumps, I simply take them apart (watch the rubber O ring!!) and wash the impeller and top. I would advise strongly against getting water on your pump electronics. Once you flush everything out, use a paper towel or other absorptive material to dry the water blocks and pump components completely. If you are going to leave them overnight, make sure you get every drop-off.

○ **PLANNING** - Simple Loop Plan Now you're ready for the planning stage. This is a very, very important part of the process and will determine how difficult it's going to be to put your loop together. This part consists of determining your loop order, where you plan to mount each radiator, reservoir and pump, which way you want to mount fans and determining how long each tubing section needs to be. Don't actually mount anything just yet. (and as tempting as it is, DO NOT run your new water-cooling pump dry) Get your measurement device out and start figuring. It is VERY helpful to take a picture of how you plan to set up your loop and how each tubing section will fit into the PC. Measure the approximate distance for each tubing run. Loop order isn't a concern if you're reading this guide. Aim for no crosses and make each tubing run as short as possible. However, make sure you account for bends. Once you have the length, add 2-3 inches and cut it long. It's much better to have too much tubing than too little. Cut the tubing carefully and as straight as possible with dyes, tubing cutters, a razor blade or sharp scissors. If you have a cut down the length of the tubing, cut that section completely off. Any sort of cut will eventually manifest into a leak. Because priming your pump is such a PITA, try and keep it as low in the loop as possible to make it easier to get water inside. At the very least, make sure your reservoir is above the pump. Double-check and triple-check that you have the optimal layout for your hardware and tastes. It would really suck to cut your tubing and realize that it's not long enough halfway through. Once done, you're ready for the next part.

MOUNTING AND INSTALLING

o The next part is - you guessed it! - mounting everything. This part is, of course, going to be different for everyone. Here are some guidelines to help make sure you don't break anything:

o **DON'T OVER TIGHTEN FITTINGS** - Usually, a hand-tight with a little help from a wrench/pliers is all it takes to get a good seal. The fittings have O-rings that will break with too much pressure. If a length of tubing is too long when you install it, cut it by about half as much as you think you need to. I can't count the number of times when I swore it needed an inch off when it was really half that.

o **DON'T OVER TIGHTEN RADIATOR SCREWS** - The screws can, and will, go right through the fins on the radiator and create a nice leak for you to clean up once you start filling. Not only that, but damage from over-tightening is not covered under any warranty for radiators.

o **MAKE SURE YOU CAN FILL YOUR LOOP EASILY** - If your designated fill hole isn't able to be easily reached by a funnel or other filling device, make sure you add a tube that you can remove later and make filling much easier.

- **DON'T OVER TIGHTEN THE MOUNTING SCREWS ON THE WATERBLOCKS** - I've had waterblocks that could be tightened to produce almost 200 lbs. of pressure on the CPU because it was designed for multiple heights. This isn't at all necessary and can break components if you aren't careful.

- **FOR BARB FITTINGS, USE ZIP TIES AS RUDIMENTARY COMPRESSION RINGS** - Tubing can, and sometimes will slowly slip off barbs over time. This method minimizes the effect

- **DON'T FORGET YOUR KILL COIL** - If you're using a silver kill coil, be sure to actually include it in your loop and don't forget about it!

FILLING AND PRIMING

- Once you've got everything hooked up, do yourself a favor and double-check EVERYTHING. Make absolutely sure that all your connections are solid and ready for the water. Once you're ready, start slowly filling up your loop with water or coolant until you can't fit anymore. A very important part of the process that people often miss is pump priming. Priming a pump simply means to make sure your pump has water in it before it starts pumping water. Failure to do so could cause your pump to run dry (which will ruin it very quickly). There really isn't an easy way to tell if you have water inside the pump other than by turning it on for a second to see if it starts moving water. If it doesn't sound like water is moving (it should be quite loud and very obvious) then shut off the pump immediately. Throughout this process, you WILL spill water on something. Once you do, very carefully absorb it with the paper towel and continue filling. If you spring a leak, get a wad of paper towel, absorb the leak and slowly start to drain your loop. If water gets on the computer components, that's fine, just carefully pat it dry and keep going. Keep filling and running the pump until it gets back around to the fill area and can keep going around with no extra water. Then run the pump and keep filling as the air bubbles start to get pushed out. Carefully tip your case back, forth, left and right (I've even turned cases upside down, although this might actually give you more bubbles depending on how your loop is set up). As more bubbles come out, your pump should start to quiet itself down.

TESTING & HOPING

- It is at this point that I like to set my power supply up and let the pump run overnight for some extended leak testing. People like to put a paper towel near all of the fittings and potential leak points to identify little drops. If anything feels damp at all, you have a problem. Check fittings first, then look for cuts in the tubing, bad seals and other things. If there were no problems, congratulations, you completed your first custom loop! Hook everything up to you PC power supply and enjoy the temperatures and quiet. For the first few weeks, I would double-check the fittings and make sure no sneaky leaks have popped up, but that's about it. Check your water level in the reservoir occasionally. Water does evaporate, but large amounts of missing water are a telltale sign of a leak. If you did find a sneaky leak, it's time to drain your loop. Carefully disconnect a tube near the bottom of your loop and allow all the water to drain out. Paper towels really come in handy for this part. Once drained, check all the things that could have gone wrong. Chances are, it's a fitting that was over tightened or not tightened enough. Check for good seals in compression fittings and barbs. Finally, make sure there isn't a tiny cut in the tubing or other leak points. If you found something obvious, remedy the situation and refill her. If not, keep looking! Little air bubbles could come loose as the water settles and get into your pump which may make a grinding noise if it makes it that far.

MAINTENANCE FOR YOUR LOOP

- Every 6 months or so, you are going to want to perform some routine maintenance on your loop. This maintenance is pretty straightforward and generally easy to perform: Drain the loop and fill it again Water circulating around a cooling system eventually gets pretty dirty and refilling it with clean water will help keep your blocks clean and your temperatures down Clean all the water blocks, radiators and the reservoirs Use the same methods as you did when you first got them Replace the tubing Depending on how stained it's gotten, replacing your tubing may be worthwhile Once you finish, fill up your system just like you did when you first set it up and check for leaks.

CONCLUSION

o Water cooling systems, while relatively complex, are actually easier to set up than most people think. I wrote this guide in the hopes that it would convince or at least help convince more people with the time and knowledge to go out and set up your own loop. This is not the best water-cooling guide out there, nor the most complete. As always, this will be a work in progress forever. Whether or not you learned something from this guide, I hope you enjoyed reading it as much as I enjoyed writing it. Once again, thanks for reading and good luck with whatever project you plan to pursue.

o Here I have covered the basics of liquid cooling. Now you know the basic components required to create one. I recommend you watch a lot of videos to get ideas and different techniques required to be an expert in this. This is a vast subject and I believe require multiple sources, as many advanced PC builders have adopted their own techniques, like you will in time.

BEST AIO WATER COOLING UNIT 2020

HERE ARE THE 10 BEST GAMING PC CASES:
Always check for compatibility with your CPU,
CASE AND MOTHERBOARD.

1) PC FAN:
CORSAIR HYDRO SERIES H100I RGB PLATINUM
COST: $159/₹11,819
PURCHASE LINK: https://amzn.to/2I8cFNZ
FEATURES
Radiator Dimensions: 277mm x *120mm* x 27mm
Compatible with CORSAIR iCUE.
Fan Dimensions: *120mm* x 25mm
Two 120mm CORSAIR ML PRO Series RGB magnetic levitation PWM
fans.
Fan Speed: 2400 RPM
Dynamic multi-zone RGB pump.
240mm dual radiator.
Powerful software.
Fan Static Pressure: 4.2 mm-H2O
Noise Level: 37 dBA
Fan Airflow: 75 CFM
AM4 Support.

2) PC FAN: THERMALTAKE FLOE DUAL RING RGB 240 TT EDITION
COST: $$146/₹14,999
PURCHASE LINK: https://amzn.to/2wlhHUy
FEATURES
Tt LCS Certified
Advanced addressable LED lighting with Thermaltake's patented TT RGB PLUS Software.
Patented Riing Plus RGB TT Premium Edition Radiator Fan.
Digital Lighting Controller.
High Efficiency Radiator
High Performance Waterblock and Durable Sleeved Cable
High Reliability Pump
FAN Dimension:120 x 120 x 25 mm
FAN Speed:500~1400RPM
Noise Level:19.8 ~ 24.7 dB-A
RADIATOR Dimension:393 x *120* x 27 mm
AM4 Support.
FAN Max. Pressure:0.17~1.54 mm-H2O

3) PC FAN: NZXT KRAKEN X52
COST: $120/₹10,850
PURCHASE LINK: https://amzn.to/3coNXqs
FEATURES

Includes Aer P radiator-optimized fan.
CAM Powered for complete software control.
Individually addressable RGB and infinity mirror design.
Advanced lighting modes for a fully dynamic lighting experience.
Industry-leading 6-year warranty.
Radiator: 275 x 123 x 30mm.
Radiator Size: 240
AM4 Support.
RAM Height Clearance 35mm.
Fan Speed 500~2,000 +/- 300RPM.
Fan Noise Level 21-36dBA.
Dimensions Aer P120: 120 x 120 x 26mm.

4) PC FAN: DEEPCOOL CAPTAIN 240 RGB LIQUID

COST: $90/₹14,749
PURCHASE LINK: https://amzn.to/3aK0frO

FEATURES

AM4 & TR4 Support
Radiator Dim. 290.00 x **120.00** x 27.00 mm.
Fan Dim. **120.00** x 120.00 x 25.00 mm.
Fan RPM 500 - 1800 RPM +/- 10%.
Fan Noise 30 dBA (Max).
Equipped with Automatic Pressure Relieving Radiator, It
Never Leaks.
Fully Addressable RGB Effects and Optimized Pump LED.
Fan Air Pressure 2.42 mama

5) PC FAN:

COOLER MASTER MASTERLIQUID ML240R RGB

COST: $110/₹9,150

PURCHASE LINK: https://amzn.to/2wUxU3h

FEATURES

Dual Dissipation.
Addressable RGB LED.
Push-Pull Fans.
Sleeved FE.
Exclusive Wired ARGB Controller.
AM4 support.
Radiator Size: 240
Radiator Dimension: 275 x 118.5 x 27 mm.
FAN dimension: *120* x 120 x 25 mm.
FAN Speed: 650-2000 RPM (PWM) ± 10%.
FAN Air Pressure: 2.34 mmH2O (Max).

6) PC FAN: ASUS ROG RYUO 240 RGB
COST: $187/₹18,790
PURCHASE LINK: https://amzn.to/3aqB9hD
FEATURES

ROG-designed radiator fans for optimized airflow and static pressure.

LiveDash one-stop control center for lighting and OLED display.

Individually addressable RGB and NCVM coating pump cover accentuates the sleek, modern aesthetics.

Reinforced, sleeved tubing for increased durability.

AM4 & TR4 Compatibility.

Radiator Dimension: 272 x 121 x 27 mm.

Radiator Size: 240

Fan: 2 x ROG Designed radiator FAN

Fan size: 2 Fan Slots (120mm).

Fan Dimension: *120* x 120 x 25 mm.

Fan Speed: 800 ~ 2500 RPM +/- 10 %.

Fan Static Pressure: 5.0 mmH2O.

Fan Air Flow: 80.95 CFM / 137.5 m3h.

Fan Noise: 37.6 dB(A).

FAN Control Mode: PWM.

(CORSAIR HYDRO SERIES H100I RGB PLATINUM)

THERMALTAKE FLOE DUAL RING RGB 240 TT
EDITION

NZXT KRAKEN X52

DEEPCOOL CAPTAIN 240 RGB LIQUID

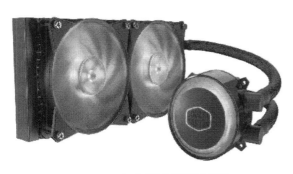

COOLER MASTER MASTERLIQUID
ML240R RGB

ASUS ROG RYUO 240 RGB

WHAT IS PCIe?

o Peripheral Component Interconnect Express (PCIe or PCI-E) is a serial expansion bus standard for connecting a computer to one or more peripheral devices. PCIe provides lower latency and higher data transfer rates than parallel buses such as PCI and PCI-X. Every device that's connected to a motherboard with a PCIe link has its dedicated point-to-point connection. This means that devices are not competing for bandwidth (this was the case for PCI connections) because they are not sharing the same bus.

o Peripheral devices that use PCIe for data transfer include graphics adapter cards, network interface cards (NICs), storage accelerator devices and other high-performance peripherals.

o With PCIe, data is transferred over two signal pairs: two wires for transmitting and two wires for receiving. Each set of signal pairs is called a "lane," and each lane is capable of sending and receiving eight-bit data packets simultaneously between two points.

o PCIe can scale from one to 32 separate lanes; it is usually deployed with 1, 4, 8, 12, 16 or 32 lanes. The lane count of a PCIe card is a determining factor in its performance and therefore in its price. For example, an inexpensive PCIe device like a NICs might only use four lanes (PCIe x4). By comparison, a high-performance graphics adapter that uses 32 lanes (PCIe x32) for top-speed transmission would be more expensive.

o PCIe bus slots are typically backward compatible with other PCIe bus slots, allowing PCIe links that use fewer lanes to use the same interface as PCIe links that use more lanes. For example, a PCIe x8 card could plug into a PCIe x16 slot. PCIe bus slots are not backward compatible, however, with connection interfaces for older bus standards.

o For laptops and mobile devices, mini PCI-e cards can be used to connect wireless adapters, solid-state device storage, and other performance boosters. External PCI

Express (ePCIe) is used to connect the motherboard to an external PCIe interface. In most cases, designers use ePCIe when the computer requires an unusually high number of PCIe ports.

o PCI Express (PCIe) is a new protocol that eliminates a lot of these shortcomings of PCI, provides more bandwidth and is compatible with existing operating systems.

o PCI Express is a serial connection that operates more like a network than a bus. Instead of one bus that handles data from multiple sources, PCIe has a switch that controls several point-to-point serial connections. These connections fan out from the switch, leading directly to the devices where the data needs to go. Every device has its dedicated connection, so devices no longer share bandwidth as they do on a normal bus.

o The components of your PC will all connect to your motherboard in one way or another, most often through the PCIe slots.

o Every PC motherboard has several PCIe slots you can use to connect GPUs, RAID cards, Wi-Fi cards or SSD add-on cards.

o The PCIe connection is how you will connect many of your most important components like your graphics card to the motherboard.

o Most GPUs require a PCIe x16 slot to operate at their full potential.

o PCIe slots come in a variety of sizes, x1, x4, x8, x16, x32, with X4 and X16 being the most common.

o The number after the x tells you how many lanes (how data travels to and from the PCIe card) that PCIe slot has. A PCIe x1 slot has one lane and can move data at one bit per cycle. A PCIe x2 slot has two lanes and can move data at two bits per cycle, so on.

o HDDs are still used to a high extent in data centers as they are seen as reliable to some extent, cheap to replace and they don't wear down. This technology is 40 years old. Hence their performance is limited.

o HDDs and SSDs have only one command queue and can send 32 commands per queue. NVMe has 64,000 command queues and can send 64,000 commands per queue. So, it is clear utilizing NVMe and PCIe together would make perfect sense for a data center where so much information is being processed every second.

o PCIe communicates directly with the system CPU as opposed to a SATA controller, so in essence, it's cutting out the middleman to access information quicker.

o Combining NVMe and PCIe is now on the rise.

o PCIe 3.0 is the most common version of the connection on the market right now. But some of AMD'S most recent motherboards support PCIe 4.0.

o A single PCI Express lane, however, can handle 200 MB of traffic in each direction per second. An x16 PCIe connector can move an amazing 6.4 GB of data per second in each direction. At these speeds, an x1 connection can easily handle a gigabit Ethernet connection as well as audio and storage applications. An x16 connection can easily handle powerful graphics adapters.

o When the computer starts up, PCIe determines which devices are plugged into the motherboard. It then identifies the links between the devices, creating a map of where traffic will go and negotiate the width of each link. This identification of devices and connections is the same protocol PCI uses, so PCIe does not require any changes to the software or operating systems.

o Each lane of a PCI Express connection contains two pairs of wires —> one to send and one to receive. Packets of data move across the lane at a rate of one bit per cycle. An x1 connection, the smallest PCIe connection, has one lane made up of four wires. It carries one bit per cycle in each direction. An x2 link contains eight wires and transmits two bits at once, an x4 link transmits four bits, and so on. Other configurations are x12, x16 and x32.

○ **PCI EXPRESS 3.0** – PCI Express 3.0 specification was made available in November 2010. New features for the PCI Express 3.0 specification include several optimizations for enhanced signaling and data integrity, including transmitter and receiver equalization, PLL improvements, clock data recovery, and channel enhancements for currently supported topologies. PCI Express 3.0's 8 GT/s bit rate effectively delivers 985 MB/s per lane, nearly doubling the lane bandwidth relative to PCI Express 2.0.

○ **PCI EXPRESS 4.0** - PCI Express 4.0 was officially announced in 2017, providing a 16 GT/s bit rate that doubles the bandwidth provided by PCI Express 3.0, while maintaining backward and forward compatibility in both software support and used mechanical interface. PCI Express 4.0 specs will also bring OCuLink-2, an alternative to Thunderbolt connector. OCuLink version 2 will have up to 16 GT/s (8 GB/s total for ×4 lanes), while the maximum bandwidth of a Thunderbolt 3 connector is 5 GB/s.

○ With the right hardware, a motherboard with two x16 PCIe connections can support two graphics adapters at the same time. Several manufacturers are developing and releasing systems to take advantage of this feature: NVIDIA Scalable Link Interface (SLI): With an SLI-certified motherboard, two SLI graphics cards and an SLI connector, a user can put two video cards into the same system. The cards work together by splitting the screen in half. Each card controls half of the screen, and the connector makes sure that everything stays synchronized.

PCIe GENERATIONS COMPARISON

	TOTAL BANDWIDTH X16	RAW BIT RATE (G/s)	FREQUENCY	INTRODUCED
1. PCIe 1.0	8 GB/s	2.5 GT/s	2.5 GHz	2003
2. PCIe 2.0	16 GB/s	5 GT/s	5 GHz	2007
3. PCIe 3.0	32 GB/s	8 GT/s	8 GHz	2010
4. PCIe 4.0	64 GB/s	16 GT/s	16 GHz	2017
5. PCIe 5.0	128 GB/s	32 GT/s	32 GHz	2019
6. PCIe 6.0	256 GB/s	64 GT/s	32 GHz	Coming Soon

PCIe 5.0 and PCIe 6.0 are the future generation PCIe.

o This is the MSI B450 Gaming PRO Carbon AC motherboard (https://amzn.to/38wOl38)
(Image Source: MSI Manufacturer Website)

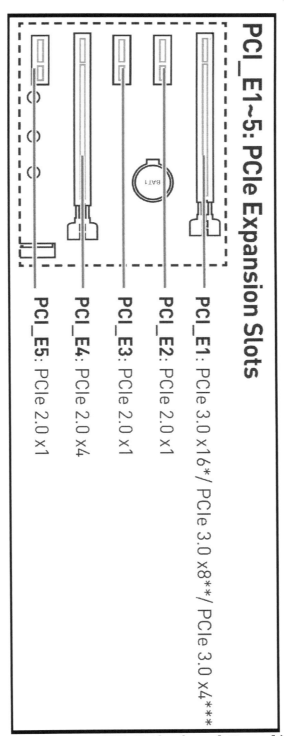

(Image Source: MSI Motherboard Manual)

GRAPHICS CARD: HOW TO CHOOSE THE RIGHT ONE?

o Though some CPUs are capable of outputting basic graphics on their own, if you want to something fancy like VIDEO EDITING or GAMING, then you would want a dedicated GRAPHICS CARD, which connects to the motherboards PCIe slot.

o This is one of the most exciting PC components when choosing to build your own PC.

o GPU (Graphics Processing Unit) is the chip that the graphics card carries on the PCB (Printed Circuit Board). Sometimes it can also be mentioned to describe the graphics card itself.

o The term Graphics card, Video card, and GPU are all loosely and interchangeably used to mention the same PC component.

o Most modern motherboards and graphics cards will work together as long as you have an available PCIe slot.

o If you are buying an especially heavy and powerful GPU in which case you want to look for motherboards with reinforced PCIe slot to handle the weight and don't forget to tighten that screw which attaches the GPU to the back of the CASE.

o If you are planning to run multiple graphics cards together, you will need to select a motherboard that supports multiple GPUs.

o The different graphics cards can be based on the same GPU (the chip and not the graphics card). Example: The two largest PC Graphics card makers, AMD and NVIDIA will release a reference version of a new graphics card like the RADEON RX 580 by AMD or the GeForce GTX 1080 by NVIDIA. Then vendors like MSI, Asus, Gigabyte, etc will use this reference design that is customized along with unique coolers, I/O ports, and sometimes higher clock speed. This means all these models have the same GPU chip but are customized to include other features.

o It is also possible for a single graphics card to have 2 GPUs like AMD's R9 295X2, RADEON PRO DUO or NVIDIA's TITAN Z. All these guarantees tremendous graphics horsepower but depends on how one much the games involved support Multi-GPU graphics card performance.

o Multi-GPU connections in NVIDIA are called SLI (Scalable Link Interface) and AMD it's called CROSSFIRE.

o **GPU ARCHITECTURE** - It is the platform or technology a GPU is built on. Example: NVIDIA's GTX 970, 980, 1070, 1080, these graphics can be used at different tiers to form a Multi-GPU setup. GTX 970 and GTX 980 are based on the Maxwell GM204 GPU architecture whereas GTX 1070 and GTX 1080 are based on the Pascal GP104 GPU architecture.

o New architectures are developed by AMD and NVIDIA almost every 2 to 3 years. They often shrink the size of the physical components of the processor which allows them to fit more features and transistors on to the GPU.

o Architecture changes allow reducing the amount of power required to run the graphics card.

o So, it is very important to compare the generations of graphics cards too and not just the features alone.

<u>KEY SPECIFICATIONS TO LOOK</u>

o **VIDEO MEMORY/VIDEO RAM/VRAM** -It has the same function as that of the system RAM, it holds whatever data currently being accessed by the GPU. These data are the textures and images makeup what is displayed to you on your screen. This is extremely important when running high-resolution Games/videos. Having more VRAM necessarily doesn't guarantee more FPS (Frame Per Second). But will affect the resolution if lesser than recommended. 4GB of VRAM is currently the sweet spot to go for when selecting the high performing budget graphics card. 4GB of VRAM is great for running 1080p games, 2GB for lower-end cards with some settings turn down. 6-8GB allows enough headroom needed to run the 1440p and 4K, assuming that the card has the RAW power necessary to run those resolutions in the first place. One of the indicators of such RAW power is called Core Clock. Don't forget to look for the number of stream processors including the speed they run at.

○ **CORE CLOCK** - It is the frequency at which the GPU is running. It is measured in Hertz (Hz). This can be used as a measurement to compare the powers of different GPUs in different generations. This indicates performance. The higher the core clock, the better is the performance. A clock speed of 3.5 GHz to 4.0 GHz is generally considered a good clock speed for gaming but it's more important to have good single-thread performance. This means that your CPU does a good job of understanding and completing single tasks. This is not to be confused with having a single-core processor. While a CPU tries to maximize the use of the processor by using two threads per core, a GPU tries to hide memory latency by using more threads per core. The number of active threads per core on AMD hardware is 4 to up to 10, depending on the kernel code

○ **BOOST CLOCK** - This is the speed a card can boost itself to withstand a heavy processing load like in Gaming or Video editing. when your GPU is working hard it may boost itself up an extra 100MHz or 200MHz to provide a bit of a performance increase for the heavy load. When not overclocking, your boost clock will be extremely important for your graphics card since it will be the highest possible clock your card can reach.

○ **THERMAL THROTTLING** - The speed of the graphics card can drop down significantly if it's too hot. This is called thermal throttling. This is where the importance of the right cooling unit comes in so that you get the maximum performance out of your Graphics card.

○ **MEMORY CLOCK** - Video memory runs at a certain speed called the Memory Clock. This is one of the few specifications that help us determine the memory bandwidth. Others include Memory Bus Width (How many bits of data that can travel to and from the VRAM in each clock cycle) and the type of memory (GDDR5, GDDR5X or HBM). HBM (High Bandwidth Memory) - This is a vertically stacked RAM that is seen in certain AMD graphics cards. If you increase the Memory Clock but don't see performance gains, then chances are your GPU memory bandwidth wasn't particularly limited in the first place, so there's no need to increase the memory clock speed.

○ **MEMORY BANDWIDTH** - This is measured in gigabytes per second (GB/s). This is like a tube connecting the GPU (chip) to its VRAM. Bigger the memory bandwidth, the more effectively your GPU can use its VRAM. Having a very high memory won't be effective if its memory bandwidth is too low to use all of it at once.

○ **CUDA CORES** - CUDA (Computer Unified Device Architecture) is NVIDIA's custom programming language. They are the physical cores in an NVIDIA GPU. In AMD GPU they are called the STREAM PROCESSOR and they use the OpenCL programming language.

○ **TRANSISTOR CLOCKS** - They are the number of transistors in the GPU. It is not important to know the number here.

○ **WATTAGE** - Wattage required for the GPU to choose the PSU can be a bit confusing. The power consumption of GPU is mentioned in the range. There is two value to keep a note of, the maximum power consumption and recommended power supply. The first value is the maximum power consumed by the GPU and the second value is important in choosing the right PSU (power supply unit). This is the minimum wattage required when purchasing a PSU, including the wattage of the GPU.

The following specification is not important enough to know unless you are going to do an in-depth technical analysis:

○ **TEXTURE UNITS** - They assist in applying textures to 3D models.

○ **ROPs (RASTER OUTPUT PIPELINES)/ RENDER OPERATIONS UNIT** - They are involved in the final process of outputting pixels to the display or rendering. They also deal heavily with Anti-aliasing.

- **THERMAL DESIGN POWER (TDP)** – It is the maximum amount of heat the GPU is specified to produce when running normal applications. It is measured in Watts. It doesn't correlate to the maximum amount of power consumed by the graphics card.

- **THE MANUFACTURING PROCESS** – The manufacturing process of a GPU refers to the 'half-pitch' of a memory cell in a processor or half the distance between identical features. It's measured in nanometer. A new process is developed every 2-3 years. AMD's RX480 is made on a 14nm process and NVIDIA's 10 series GPUs are made on a 16nm process. This is why this generation of GPUs has a significant big performance leap then the previous generations. The last generation had 22 nm processors.

BENCHMARKS

- The only real way to know how the card is going to run is to see its performance in real situations. Specifications can give a general idea of how a card might perform relative to another but there is no way to know for sure until you put it to the test.
- So, before you purchase a graphics card, do enough research, read and watch reviews and comparisons about the card.

HOW TO CHOOSE THE BEST BUDGET GRAPHICS CARD

- Don't buy a Graphics card below $80.
- Make sure you have a reliable PSU.
- Check the power cable supplying the graphics card.
- Don't go for more than 600W PSU for any budget Graphics card.
- Don't use a budget graphics card with low-end CPU.
- Always see the compatibility between GPU and your CASE.

o Don't waste a lot of money on the extreme OC (overclocking) EDITION.
o Don't go for SLI or CROSSFIRE version of a budget graphics card.
o 4GB edition is better than 2GB editions.
o The budget graphics card is not good for 4K videos. If you have to buy, stick with 1080p.

√ More details in the next chapter, don't miss out.

Below is the datasheet of the graphics Card I purchased to build my PC:

(Image Source: MSI)

SPECIFICATION

Model Name	Radeon™ RX 580 ARMOR 8G OC
Graphics Processing Unit	Radeon™ RX 580
Interface	PCI Express x16
Cores	2304 Units
Core Clocks	up to 1366 MHz
Memory Speed	8000 MHz
Memory	8GB GDDR5
Memory Bus	256-bit
Output	DisplayPort x 2 / HDMI x 2 / DL-DVI-D
HDCP Support	Y
Power consumption	185 W
Power connectors	8-pin x 1
Recommended PSU	500 W
Card Dimension(mm)	269 x 125 x 38 mm
Weight (Card / Package)	653 g / 1152 g
DirectX Version Support	12
OpenGL Version Support	4.5
Multi-GPU Technology	Crossfire™, 2-Way (Bridgeless)
Maximum Displays	5
VR Ready	Y

FEATURE

BLACK & WHITE DESIGN

Inspired by advanced armor shielding with a classy black & white finish, ARMOR cards fit any build.

TORX FAN

This Award-winning Fan design combines two different fin designs for cool & quiet gaming.

ZERO FROZR

Eliminates fan noise by stopping the fans in low-load situations so you can focus on your game.

ADVANCED AIRFLOW CONTROL

Indentations in the aluminum fins direct more airflow onto the heatpipes for enhanced cooling performance.

OC PERFORMANCE

MSI OC graphics cards are equipped with higher clock speeds out of the box for increased performance.

CUSTOM PCB

An optimized PCB design with enhanced power delivery provides a solid base for high performance gaming.

Military Class 4 Components

Using only the highest quality components means you get reliable and stable in-game performance.

VR Ready

Certified to provide the performance required for a smooth experience in your VR adventures.

CONNECTIONS

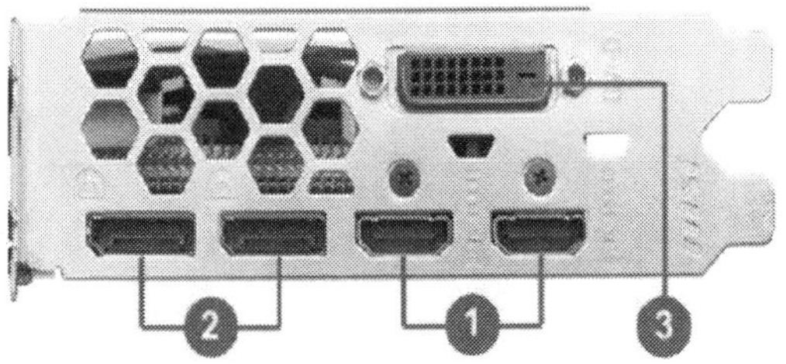

1. HDMI
2. DisplayPort
3. DVI-D

Image source: MSI

AMD VS NVIDIA - WHICH VIDEO CARD IS BETTER?

o The technologies are constantly changing day-to-day, so it is important to constantly research the ideal GPU for your system.

o Do check out for Gaming PC (https://www.pcworld.com/article/3106426/the-best-graphics-cards-for-pc-gaming.html) - It is updated here every 3 months for the best GPU out there in the market for VIDEO EDITING & GAMING. The buy is based on budget etc.

o For video editing, check out (https://graphicscardhub.com/best-graphics-card-for-video-editing-rendering/)

o AMD and NVIDIA have much fewer differences than they used to.

o AMD used to have a bad reputation because of half-baked software and awful drivers. But they don't anymore.

o Their software is good now. A few years earlier they made 'RADEON' settings which is great. It lets you record all your gameplay.

o They have been updating and releasing their drivers faster. NVIDIA does the same thing.

o NVIDIA supports VARIABLE REFRESH RATE MONITORS. Variable refresh rate (VRR), sometimes also called dynamic refresh rate (DRR), refers to technologies that enable dynamic refresh rates for monitors, where the refresh rate of the monitor is continuously synced to the output rate of the content being displayed. NVIDIA supports and syncs VRR of GPU with that of the monitor.

o NVIDIA has their proprietary G-SYNC monitors but can be expensive.

o RADEON GPUs can only be connected to free-sync monitors.

o Only AMD supports Free-Sync over HDMI cable.

- AMD's RADEON RX 570 (**https://amzn.to/2T2oKdG**) & RX 580 (**https://amzn.to/2wSgFjf**) is dominating the low-end market. They are a few years old, but they give a killer price to performance ratio.

- AMD tends to give more bang for the buck. They give you more raw frame rates than NVIDIA.

- If you look for the high-end super 4K fast video card for gaming especially, only NVIDIA card is the choice.

- AMD doesn't have a high-end offering.

- Adobe premiere pro works amazingly with NVIDIA GPU.

- Nvidia or AMD GPU for Video Editing? Most of the popular video editing software like Adobe Premiere Pro support CUDA or OpenCL frameworks (or both) for GPU acceleration. CUDA is Nvidia's proprietary parallel computing platform and programming model for Nvidia graphics cards. On the other hand, AMD uses OpenCL (Open Computing Language) which is an open-source parallel programming framework. Nvidia also supports OpenCL but it is not as good and efficient when it comes to OpenCL computations compared to AMD GPUs. So, if you are getting a graphics card for video editing purposes especially for software like Adobe Premiere Pro, After Effects then Nvidia Graphics Cards will perform a bit better than the AMD ones. However, for applications using only the OpenCL framework, AMD graphics cards may perform better than Nvidia ones.

- Using two or more video cards in tandem is known as "SLI" for NVIDIA cards and "Crossfire" for AMD cards. This can get you better performance, sometimes even for less money than you'd spend on a comparable single card solution. However, whether it's worth it is a whole different story.

- How to create SLI and Crossfire Work: First you Will need a compatible motherboard, 2 compatible GPU and a bridge that connects both the GPUs together, which either acmes with the motherboard or the GPU.

- **SLI** - Here you need the same GTX model. The manufacturer can be different.

- **CROSSFIRE** – This allows for 2 different GPUs to be bought together. Do check the NVIDIA's SLI page and AMD's CROSSFIRE page.

- After the installation of both the cards and the necessary bridge, you can open up your driver's control panel and enable SLI or Crossfire. Make sure your drivers are up to date. Now play a game, if your drivers support SLI or Crossfire for that game, you'll notice a significant performance boost.

- **IMPORTANCE OF MULTI-GPU** – Main reason being, price to performance ratio. In some cases, running 2 mid-range GPUs together delivers better performance and price compared to a single GPU. Most of the single high-end GPUs are very expensive. This is ideal for *multi-monitor and high-resolution gaming*.

- **MULTI-GPU DRAWBACK** – (i) Running 2 GPUs together can result in more power requirement, more heat, and noise. Heat should be managed well in such cases. Even the noise can be distracting at times. If you don't want to handle these issues, then the single GPU is for you. But they can be very expensive (ii) SLI and CROSSFIRE are not always supported by all the games. It can also be caused by the driver incompatibility. AMD and NVIDIA are always updating their drivers. In case if the game is not working, you will have to stick with a single GPU or will have to deal with the GPU driver itself.

- (iii) MICRO SHUTTERING – SLI OR CROSSFIRE can make the video choppy.

- In my experience, it is better to stick with a single GPU without having to tweak the setting and deal with all the extra issues that come with the setup. The extra money you have to pay for the single GPU setup is worth it.

- Some dual-GPU configurations may not require any work, but it's hard to know. You always run the risk of having more work when you get multiple cards. But in some cases, it may be worth the trouble.

Some BEST GPU for VIDEO EDITING include:

1) GPU: EVGA GeForce GTX 1060 6GB SC Gaming, only 6.8 in, Perfect for mITX Build Graphics Card 06G-P4-6163-KR

WATTAGE: 120W

COST: $420/₹49,077

PURCHASE LINK: https://amzn.to/2Pu8Fv3

2) GPU: ZOTAC Gaming GeForce GTX 1660 Ti 6GB GDDR6 192-bit Gaming Graphics Card Super Compact - ZT-T16610F-10L

WATTAGE: 120W

COST: $280/₹24,550

PURCHASE LINK: https://amzn.to/2wVeITj

3) GPU: XFX Radeon RX 580 GTS XXX Edition 1386MHz OC+, 8GB GDDR5, VR Ready, Dual BIOS, 3xDP HDMI DVI, AMD Graphics Card (RX-580P8DFD6)

WATTAGE: 185W

COST: $169/₹29,207

PURCHASE LINK: https://amzn.to/2I6vMaV

4) GPU: ZOTAC GeForce GTX 1050 Ti Mini, 4GB GDDR5 DisplayPort 128-bit Gaming Graphic Card (ZT-P10510A-10L)

WATTAGE: 75W

COST: $256/₹16,285

PURCHASE LINK: https://amzn.to/3c9MV1z

Some BEST GPU for GAMING include:

1) <u>BEST BUDGET GPU</u>

ZOTAC GeForce *GTX 1650 Super Twin Fan* 4GB GDDR6
128-bit Super Compact Gaming Graphics Card (ZT-T16510F-10L)

WATTAGE: 100W

COST: $160/₹15,599

PURCHASE LINK: https://amzn.to/2Vr97OB

2) BEST 1080P GPU

ASUS GeForce *GTX 1660 Super* Overclocked
6GB Dual-fan EVO Edition VR Ready
HDMI DisplayPort DVI Graphics Card (DUAL-GTX1660S-O6G-EVO)

WATTAGE: 125W

COST: $240

(If you live outside US, you need to import this & can be expensive)

PURCHASE LINK:

https://world.ubuy.com/?goto=search/index/view/product/B07ZHWQ81N?Inf=37bc2f75bf1bcfe8450a1a41c200364c&utm_source=aglow

3) BEST 1440P GPU

Sapphire *Radeon RX 5700* 8GB GDDR6
HDMI/Triple DP (UEFI) PCI-E Graphics Card
WATTAGE: 225W
COST: $350/₹32,388
PURCHASE LINK: https://amzn.to/2I1bCPM

4) <u>BEST 4K/60HZ GPU</u>
NVIDIA – NVIDIA GeForce *RTX 2080 Super* 8GB GDDR6
PCI Express 3.0 Graphics Card – Black/Silver
WATTAGE: 250W
COST: $700/₹49,077
(If you live outside US, you need to import this & can be
expensive)
PURCHASE LINK:
https://world.ubuy.com/?goto=search/index/view/product/B07W3P4PC2?Inf=
37bc2f75bf1bcfe8450a1a41c200364c&utm_source=aglow

BEST GAMING GRAPHICS CARD 2020

$100-150
APPROPRIATE FOR A ~$500 BUILD

1) GPU

ZOTAC GeForce GTX **1650 Super** Twin Fan 4GB GDDR6
128-bit Super Compact Gaming Graphics Card (ZT-T16510F-10L)

WATTAGE:

FEATURES:

It has Turing NVENC engine, which is a killer app for NVidia right now.

MEMORY TYPE:

GDDR6

(This GPU has speed of 192 GB/s)

Vs

GDDR5

(Which has speed of about 128 GB/s)

COST: $160/₹15,599

PURCHASE LINK: https://amzn.to/2Vr97OB

$200-250
APPROPRIATE FOR A ~$750 BUILD

1) GPU: MSI Gaming GeForce GTX **1660 Super** 192-bit HDMI/DP 6GB GDRR6 HDCP Support DirectX 12 Dual Fan VR Ready OC Graphics Card (GTX 1660 Super Ventus XS OC)

COST: $230/₹22,888

PURCHASE LINK: https://amzn.to/389ImAO

FEATURES

GDDR6-This faster speed (336 GB/s) push it closer to its Ti counterpart.

It also has Turing NVENC for recording GAME PLAY & STREAMING.

$300-350
APPROPRIATE FOR A ~$1,000 BUILD

1) GPU: Sapphire 11294-01-20G Radeon Pulse **RX 5700**
8GB GDDR6 HDMI/ Triple DP OC w/ Backplate (UEFI)
PCIe 4.0 Graphics Card
COST: $573/₹37,066
(If you live outside US, you need to import this & can be expensive)
PURCHASE LINK: https://amzn.to/2vpZHrV
FEATURES
Is a better performer for this price,
with extra performance that can be unlocked with BIOS update
or
with soft power play tables mod.
Want the best performance and not afraid to tinker grab this one.

2) GPU: ZOTAC Gaming GeForce **RTX 2060** Twin Fan 6GB GDDR6 192-bit Gaming Graphics Card, Super Compact, IceStorm 2.0, ZT-T20600F-10M
COST: $320/₹30,399
PURCHASE LINK: https://amzn.to/32G58iL
FEATURES
Provide full RTX & LSS support, Turing NVENC encoding. Want good performance and a more robust feature set go for this one.

$400-450
APPROPRIATE FOR A ~$1,250 BUILD

1) GPU: PowerColor RED Devil Radeon **RX 5700 XT**
DirectX 12 AXRX 5700 XT 8GBD6-3DHE/OC 8GB
256-Bit GDDR6 PCI Express 4.0
CrossFireX Support ATX Video Card
COST: $470/₹46,900
PURCHASE LINK: https://amzn.to/2wh3mbz

$500-550
APPROPRIATE FOR A ~$1,500 BUILD

1) GPU: Gigabyte GeForce **RTX 2070 Super** Windforce
8G Graphics Card, 3X WINDFORCE Fans,
8GB 256-Bit GDDR6, GV-N207SWF3OC-8GC Video Card

COST: $499/₹46,200

PURCHASE LINK: https://amzn.to/32Ar8eK

FEATURES

Better than Radeon 5700 XT,
while maintaining the NVIDIA exclusive features.
NVENC encoding engine, Ansel, Ge Force Experience,
Custom resolutions, CUDA, Studio drivers.

$600-650
APPROPRIATE FOR AN EXPENSIVE BUILD

1) GPU: ASUS Dual GeForce **RTX 2080** DirectX 12
DUAL-RTX2080-O8G-EVO 8GB 256-Bit GDDR6
PCI Express 3.0 HDCP Ready SLI Support Video Card

COST: $650/₹66,269

(If you live outside US, import duty applies)

PURCHASE LINK:

https://world.ubuy.com/?Goto=search/index/view/product/B07GK4X6C2?inf=37bc2f75bf1bcfe8450a1a41c200364c&utm_source=uglow

FEATURES

Even with all the RTX goodness,
it doesn't deliver for the more money
you are paying as compared to the 2070 SUPER.
I suggest you save the money for a better one.
Same goes for the RTX 2080 SUPER.

BEST OF THE BEST

1) GPU: MSI GeForce RTX 2080 Ti Gaming X Trio
11GB GDDR6 Gaming Graphic Card
COST: $1,199/₹1,15,650
PURCHASE LINK: https://amzn.to/398L9M7

2) GPU: NVIDIA TITAN RTX
COST: $2,349/₹3,29,999
PURCHASE LINK: https://amzn.to/2VxpSro

WHAT IS RAM & HOW TO CHOOSE THEM?

o Primary memory or temporary storage, this is called RAM. RAM stands for RANDOM ACCESS MEMORY.

o RAMs are stored on the motherboard in modules that are called DIMMs (DUAL IN-LINE MEMORY MODULE). The DIMM is a dual in-line module because it has two independent rows of pins on either side of the notch at its lower end.

o It can have 168, 184, 240 or 288 pins.

o DIMM is installed on the motherboard memory slots or DIMM slots.

o A motherboard can have a various number of memory slots. An average motherboard will have between 2 and 4 of the memory slots.

o For the data or program to run on the computer. It needs to be loaded into the RAM first.

o The data or program is first stored in the Hard drive and it is then loaded on to the RAM.

o Once it's loaded onto the RAM, the CPU can now access the data or run the program.

o A lot of time if the RAM is too low. The RAM won't have all the memory that the CPU needs. When this happens, some of the data has been kept in the slower hard drive to compensate for the low memory. So instead of the data going from the RAM to the CPU, it has to do extra work by going back to the hard drive. This process slows down the PC.

o To solve this issue – You need to increase the amount of RAM on your computer. By increasing the memory, more amount of data can be stored in the RAM for the CPU to access. And there is no need to constantly access the slower hard drive.

o This is the reason why a computer with higher RAM performs better than one with lower RAM.

o RAM requires constant electrical power to store data and when the power is switched off, the nth data is erased.

o Different types of RAM:

(i) DRAM (DYNAMIC RAM)

o This type of RAM contains capacitors. Capacitors are like small buckets that store electricity. It is in these capacitors, data is stored in the form of 1 or 0. That is how computers read data, in the form of 1 or 0. Since Drams have capacitors, they need to be refreshed constantly with electricity because capacitors are incapable of holding electricity for a long time as they instantly leak. Hence the name Dynamic. It means capacitors have to be dynamically refreshed otherwise they lose information that they are holding

(ii) SDRAM (SYNCHRONOUS DYNAMIC RAM)

o This is the type of memory used in RAM DIMMs today. SDRAM also uses capacitors like DRAM but the main difference being speed. Older DRAM's technology operates asynchronously with the system clock, which means that it runs slower than the system clock because its signals are not coordinated with the system clock. But the SDRAM runs or operates synchronously with the system clock. Which is why it is faster than the DRAM. Here all the signals are tied to the system clock for better-controlled timing.

o So as tasted before RAM is stored on the motherboard in modules that are called DIMMs. And these DIMMs come in different memory sizes. Today they range anywhere from 128MB to 32GB per DIMM.

o Before going deep into the speed of RAM, it is important to know certain information,

o The term 32 or 64-bit data path refers to the number of bits of data that are transferred in 1 clock cycle.

o The more bits that are transferred in one clock cycle then the faster the computer will be.

o DIMMs with a 64-bit data path means that they can transfer 64 bits of data at a time.

o Prior to DIMM, existed **SIMM** (old & discontinued) has a 32-bit data path. They transferred 32 bits of data at a time. That is why DIMMs are faster than SIMMs.

o A single bit or 1 bit of data is the smallest form of data that the computer can read. 8bits = 1 Byte.

o So, if a memory DIMM is rated 64-bit data path, that means it has an 8-byte wide data path/bus. (64 bit/8= 8 Bytes).

o SDRAM'S are rated at different speeds FOR example: Old SDRAM, way back in the late 1990s was labeled PC-100. 100 STANDS FOR 100MHz, the maximum speed at which it operates. Since the SDRAM only comes in 64-bit modules, it has an 8-byte wide bus as discussed earlier. To figure out the tidal bandwidth of PC-100, 100MHz x 8bytes = 800 MB/s. In short PC-100 SDRAM can transfer data at maximum speed of 800 MB/s. Another example: An SDRAM labeled PC-133, here 133 is the clock speed, can transfer at a maximum speed (bandwidth) of 1066 MB/s. This correct and not 1064 because the actual clock speed is (133.3333 x 8 = 1066).

o Another type of memory was called RDRAM WHICH WAS DEVELOPED BY RAMBUS Inc. And they developed the RIMM (RAMBUS IN-LINE MEMORY MODULE). These Rims have 128 pins. It looks similar to DIMMs with the exception that the bottom notches were located near the center of the module. Debuted in 1999 which revolutionized the speed of the memory. This was a breakthrough. But they failed to keep up with the technology. DIMMs have progressed much faster. RDRAM speed was at 800 MHz, which was considered to be extremely faster as compared to the then SDRAM. RDRAM had only a 2-byte wide bus whereas SDRAM had an 8-byte wide bus. So, when you calculate the bandwidth, RDRAM has maximum speed of, 800MHz x 2 bytes = 1600 MB/s.

o To keep up with the faster speed of computers, new technology was developed called the DDR.

(iii) DDR (DOUBLE DATA RATE)

- In this, it sends double the amount of data at each clock cycle, compared to non-DDR. A non-DDR (single data rate) uses only the raisin edge of the clock signal to transfer data. But DDR uses both the rising and falling edge of the clock signal to send data, which gives DDR the ability to send twice the amount of data. DDR is also labeled, different from non-DDR. DDR label may include both the clock speed and the total bandwidth in its name. Example: DDR-333 PC-2700, here 333 is the clock speed and 2700 is the actual total bandwidth. In calculations: 333 MHz x 8 bytes = 2700 MB/s.

(iv) DDR2

- This is the new technology that succeeded DDR. It is faster than DDR because it allows for higher bus speeds. It has 240 pins compared to DDR (184 pins). DDR2 is labeled just like DDR but with a slight difference for example: A DDR2 DIMM could be labeled DDR2-800MHz PC2-6400. The difference is the '2' in their label.

(v) DDR3

- DDR3 is twice as fast as DDR2. It also used less power than DDR2. It also has 240 pins. But the notches in the DIMM are in different places, slightly away from the center. Hence DDR3 DIMMs can't be used in the motherboards of DDR, DDR2 or DDR4. It is labeled as DDR3-1600 MHz PC3-12800.

(vi) DDR4

- This is the 4th generation of DDR SDRAM. They have 288 pins. It uses less power than its previous generation of DDR. They offer a higher range of speed than DDR3. Such as DDR4-4266MHz PC4-34100. They have a maximum bandwidth of 34100.

- **ECC** - There are times and circumstances where memory corruption can't be tolerated example in servers. Servers are always up and running and some servers can't be offline for any reason like servers that control financial data, emergency medical data or government data. These servers can't go down for any reason. That is why some RAM modules have EC (ERROR CORRECTING CODE). It detects if the data was correctly processed by the memory module and make corrections if it needs to. You can tell if the RAM module has ECC by counting the number of memory chips on the module. A standard NON-ECC DIMM will have 8 memory chips whereas the ECC DIMM will have up to 9 memory chips. Most RAM modules today are non-ECC because of the advance in technology that has minimized memory errors and made non-ECC more stable. ECC DIMMs are still used in servers.

HOW TO CHOOSE THEM?

- Today PCs are commonly equipped with a minimum of 4GB RAM.

- How much RAM do you require for your PC depends on how you are planning to use them?

- 8GB of RAM IS typical a safe recommendation for light users. With 16GB or more RAM is a good bet for heavy users.

- RAM plugs into a motherboard via rectangular slots and is termed as DIMM slots.

- **DIMM (DUAL IN-LINE MEMORY MODULE) SLOTS** - The number of DIMM slots on a motherboard determines how much RAM you can add. It most commonly varies from 2-8 slots.

- You can add one RAM module at a time, but you will get the best performance when you install RAM in matched pairs.

- RAM is usually purchased in kits of 2 or 4 DIMMs. For Example: If you are planning to equip your PC with 16GB of RAM, then you will typically buy 2 x 8GB of RAM modules.

- When choosing RAM, you will see designations like DDR4, DDR3, DDR2, DDR, etc, that indicate the generations and speed numbers. If it shows DDR4 3000. DDR4 2600, DDR4 1600, etc, the right-side number indicates the speed of the RAM.

○ Your motherboard will support a wide range of RAM types but make sure you compare your motherboard with your RAM for compatibility in the PCPARTPICKER.COM site.

○ Make sure to purchase the RAM that is in the AMD SUPPORTED MEMORY WEBSITE:https://www.amd.com/system/files/2017-06/am4-motherboard-memory-support-list-en_0.pdf

○ The memory in other lists may or may not work but why do you want to take a risk.

○ **SANCTIONED OVERCLOCKING:** It is clear that RAM stores data or programs from the HDD or SSD for the CPU to access them. Now the amount of data stored and speed at which it is transferred to CPU solely depends on the RAM. I the data is transferred at a slower rate than the CPU's demand, PC becomes slower. But if the RAM data is sent to the CPU at a rate higher than it can digest, the CPU won't be able to read them. This shows that **faster the RAM doesn't always mean faster the PC performance.** So, it is important to find that sweet spot perfect enough for the CPU to read all the data send from RAM. JEDEC (Joint Electron Device Engineering Council) established a baseline for this. They specify, 2133 MHz for DDR4. AMD for their part has specified a range of speeds with the most frequently used configuration. Now, wait a minute, so how come major brands like Corsair, G.skill advertising speeds that are up to almost double the standard put forward by JEDEC? This is where the sanctioned overclocking Comes in to play. XMP (EXTREME MEMORY PROFILE) – Extreme Memory Profile lets you overclock RAM and compatible DDR3/DDR4 memory to enhance the VIDEO EDITING/GAMING features built into PCs with Intel/AMD processor. Get that extra edge you need to dominate. You can activate the XMP feature in the BIOS. This is mentioned later in the BIOS SETUP chapter. Every RAM module even the higher end XMP ones have the JEDEC standard speeds fed in. Along with that a faster XMP profile is stored on a special chip called SPD (Serial Presence Detect) that identifies each module. These details allow the speed to move back and forth between the JEDEC standards and XMP. For compatibility, JEDEC comes first and it's only when you specifically enable XMP in BIOS that it will run at those higher speeds.

o In almost every case largest improvement in performance (PERFORMANCE VS DDR4-2133) over 2133 is achieved by 2666 MHz, then there is another modest improvement when you jump into 3200 MHz, and from there is no significant improvement, things go downhill contrary to marketing and purely synthetic benchmarks.

o Is buying 3000 MHz good, it sounds like a sweet spot? It also depends on what budget are you building your PC. If you are on a budget, a slight increase in DDR4 speed from 2133 to 3600 will cost you close to $64, which you can use it to buy a better CPU. But if you are willing to shed a considerable amount, this slight change in speed can give you a Small edge in the world of GAMING. Again, it depends, if you are a VIDEO EDITOR, you could invest in a better CPU, trying to get more cores. The more the CPU cores, the better the performance when it comes to video editing. As mentioned earlier core limitations are there when it comes to performance.

BEST MEMORY RAM 2020

HERE ARE THE 10 BEST RAM:
MAKE SURE YOUR RAM IS COMPATIBLE WITH YOUR MOTHERBOARD

BEST HIGH-END RAM

1) RAM: CORSAIR DOMINATOR PLATINUM RGB
32GB (2X16GB) DDR4 3200 (PC4-25600) C16
COST: $200/₹32,164
PURCHASE LINK: https://amzn.to/2vn5PS3
FEATURES
Advanced DDR4 memory modules.
XMP 2.0 support for trouble-free, automatic overclocking.
Memory Configuration Dual / Quad Channel.
Memory Type DDR4.
LED Lighting WHITE.
Tested Speed 3200MHz.

BEST HIGH-END RAM

1) RAM: ADATA XPG SPECTRIX
16GB 3000MHZ D41 DDR4 RGB
COST: $210/₹15,000
PURCHASE LINK: https://amzn.to/2PDp5kQ

FEATURES
DDR4 RGB RAM memory with a hybrid liquid-air cooling system.
Programmable RGB lighting
Overclocking unleashed.
Hybrid cooling.
Hermetically sealed.
Two Colors to Choose from.

BEST RAM

1) RAM: CORSAIR VENGEANCE LED
32GB (2x16GB) DDR4 3200MHz C16
COST: $300/₹42,999
PURCHASE LINK: https://amzn.to/2Tghgny
FEATURES
Compatible with CORSAIR ICU.
Stunning led lighting.
Designed for high-performance overclocking
Built-in heat spreaders.
Limited lifetime warranty.
Custom performance PCB and carefully screened RAM.
Maximum bandwidth and tight response time.

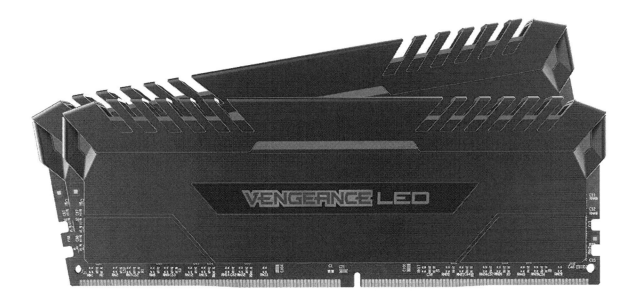

BEST DDR4 RAM

1) RAM: G.SKILL TRIDENT Z RGB
COST: $167/₹19,973
PURCHASE LINK: https://amzn.to/2x3CigB
FEATURES
Tested Speed 3200MHz.
Warranty Limited Lifetime.
exposed light bar with vibrant RGB LEDs.
award-winning Trident Z heat spreader.
vivid RGB lighting.
Trident Z Means Overclocking

BEST BUDGET RAM

1) RAM: KINGSTON HYPERX FURY
COST: $80/₹7,600
PURCHASE LINK: https://amzn.to/32KRF9f
FEATURES
Updated low-profile heat spreader design.
Cost-efficient, high-performance DDR4 upgrade.
Ready for AMD Ryzen.
Speeds up to 3733MHz.

BEST HIGH FREQUENCY RAM

1) RAM: HYPERX FURY RGB 3733MHZ
COST: $106/₹9,999
PURCHASE LINK: https://amzn.to/2Tf35yW
FEATURES
Stunning RGB lighting with aggressive style.
XMP-ready.
Ready for AMD Ryzen.
Speeds up to 3733MHz.

BEST DOUBLE CAPACITY MEMORY

1) RAM: G.SKILL TRIDENT Z RGB DC
COST: $863/₹79,999
PURCHASE LINK: https://amzn.to/3coVbL7
FEATURES
Designed for performance.
high-capacity DDR4 memory,
Extended Heat spreader.
Design Your Own RGB Style.
Asus Aura Sync Ready.
XMP Ready.
Limited Lifetime Warranty.

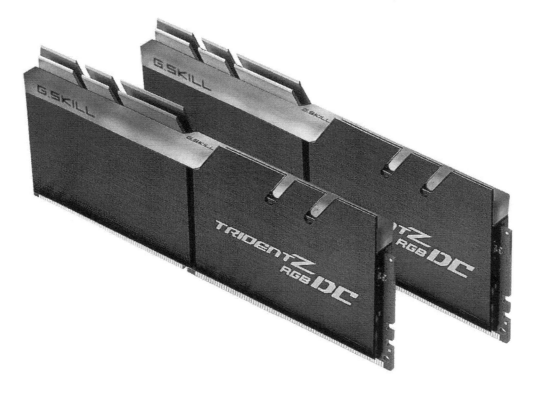

BEST RGB RAM

1) RAM: G.SKILL TRIDENT Z ROYAL
COST: $185/₹33,500
PURCHASE LINK: https://amzn.to/39hMNuW

FEATURES

Radiant Crystalline Light Bar.
Luxurious Aluminum Heat spreaders.
Software Lighting Control.
Extreme Overclocking Performance.
Platform Compatibility.
XMP 2.0 Support.
Limited Lifetime Warranty.

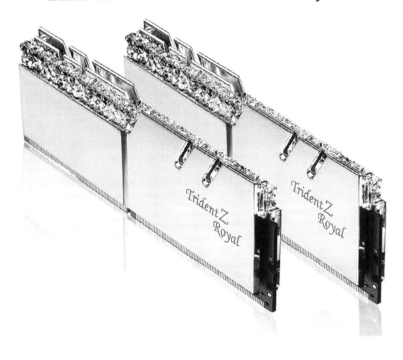

BEST LOW-PROFILE RAM

1) RAM: CORSAIR VENGEANCE LPX
COST: $149/₹14,000
PURCHASE LINK: https://amzn.to/2wkSxW7
FEATURES
DESIGNED FOR HIGH-PERFORMANCE OVERCLOCKING
COMPATIBILITY TESTED.
XMP 2.0 SUPPORT.
ALUMINUM HEAT SPREADER.
LOW-PROFILE DESIGN.

STORAGE DEVICES AND HOW TO CHOOSE THEM?

o Every PC needs somewhere to store its data and that is going to come in the form of a traditional hard drive (HDD) or solid state drive (SSD).

o The common way to connect your storage drive to the motherboard is through the SATA 3.0 connections. That is supported by any motherboard that you can buy from the market.

o Your HDD is in turn powered by SATA power supply cable from PSU.

o NVMe SSD is the newer protocol that offers increased bandwidth, lower power consumption, lower latency, and other advantages.

o NVMe SSDs come in 2 form factors: (i) Cards that plug into PCIe slots (ii) Compact versions that plug into M.2 slots.

o If you are planning to buy the NVMe SSD, make sure your motherboards support them.

o SSD - A good SSD (M.2 NVMe SSD - Fastest) is always required for fast reading. It's even more powerful when the **entire drive** is selected for this purpose. To run your operating system along with the ADOBE PREMIERE PRO or GAMING. It is better to leave more than 50% of the assigned SSD empty for the best performance. Any extra data storage should be made in a separate HDD or SSD.

o SSDs include power failure protection enabling the device to shut down safely in the event of a power outage with no loss of data and a reduced risk of data corruption.

o The future certainly looks bright for NVMe PCIe tech especially when 3D-NAND is making its way into commercial and industrial storage.

o **3D NAND** - 3D NAND is the stacking of memory (or silicon) chips on top of each other. Some manufacturers call this V (for vertical) NAND. The aim is to make your device faster, hold more information, run more efficiently and use less energy. The concept has been around for several years but only until recently have developments taken a significant step forward.

o 3D NAND will be faster, more powerful, use less energy and have more storage capacity than current 2D NAND.

o From the above information, it is clear to go for a storage device that is SSD, M.2, PCIe all with V-NAND technology to keep up with the current technology and get the best out of it.

Always use **PCPARTPICKER.COM** to compare the compatibility between different components of the PC you are planning to build.

HARD DRIVES, SSD, M.2, NVME, SATA, AHCI HOW ARE THEY ALL RELATED?

o This is the most confusing part, but I have broken it down to the simplest terms.

o The knowledge you gain from here will enable you to purchase better drives for your compatible PC.

o SSD has no moving parts, unlike HDDs. They use flash memory for data storage as compared to mechanical HDDs that use rotating magnetic disks to store data.

o In recent years SSD has gotten faster and more capable of moving data at a faster rate.

o To unlock the full capacity of the SSD, Engineers developed a new technology to unlock the faster speed of SSD - M.2 & NVMe was developed.

o Before M.2 & NVMe, the interface standard that was used for HDD and SSD was SATA 3.0 and the standard that was used for the software to communicate with SATA was AHCI (Advanced Host Controller Interface). This software was primarily developed for mechanical HDD. It was never optimized for SSD and this technology dates back to 2004. Thus, AHCI became a bottleneck for SSD.

o SATA 3.0 BUS with AHCI - allows data transfer speed of about 600 MB/s (theoretical rate).

o ***M.2 SSD with an optimized protocol like NVMe*** doesn't use the SATA BUS, instead, it uses the PCIe BUS which is much faster than the SATA. This allows the SSD with a data transfer rate of 3GB/s (theoretical rate), which is extremely fast. This means it is 5 times faster than SATA with AHCI.

o Speed factor can also highly depend on the SSD and motherboard used when it comes to M.2 NVMe SSD.

o NVMe - also known as NON-VOLATILE MEMORY EXPRESS is a communications protocol specifically developed for SSD. It reduces the CPU OVERHEAD, STREAMLINES OPERATIONS which LOWERS LATENCY, resulting in increased input/output operations per second - Which translates to increased speed. This was developed to fully take advantage of the capability of PCIe storage devices and to perform many of the input/output operations in parallel. The parallel operations mean many calculations are done at the same time. Major operations are broken down into multiple minor operations which are processed independently and take place at the same time.

○ NVMe (Non-Volatile Memory Express) is an interface protocol built especially for Solid State Drives (SSDs). NVMe works with PCI Express (PCIe) to transfer data to and from SSDs. NVMe enables rapid storage in computer SSDs and is an improvement over older Hard Disk Drive (HDD) related interfaces such as SATA and SAS. The only reason SATA and SAS are used with SSDs in computers is that until recently, only slower HDDs have been used as the large-capacity storage in computers. Flash memory has been used in mobile devices such as smartphones, tablets, USB drives, and SD cards. SSDs are flash memory.

○ This process of NVMe communication protocol is very similar to how the multi-core CPU with multiple threads works.

○ Another advantage NVMe has over AHCI is called a COMMAND QUEUE.

○ COMMAND QUEUE – Consider COMMAND as operations and QUEUE as the line formed by the COMMAND to be executed in the storage drive. When one command is executed in the storage drive, it goes to the next command in the queue. AHCI allows only 1 queue with 32 Commons per queue. Whereas NVMe allows 64K queues with each queue capable of 64 commands. In theory, if you were to max out NVMe express, it would have completed 4,096,000,000 commands.

○ Not all M.2 SSD have NVMe technology or use PCIe BUS like M.2 NVME SSD. Some M.2 SSD uses the SATA bus like the M.2 SATA SSD. The latter is much slower.

○ There is no speed advantage between the M.2 SATA SSD and a standard 2.5-inch SSD.

o M.2 was formerly known as the 'NEXT GENERATION FORM FACTOR - NGFF'. Standard used for mounting expansion cards only.

o M.2 and NVMe is a type of interface (FORM FACTOR). Here it connects the storage device to the motherboard or the hard drive controller.

o M.2 uses the same technology as SATA (600 Mbps Speed) hence speed is bound by the same rules. Hence as good as SATA.

o M.2 was a way to make SATA compatible.

o SATA I (150 Mbps Speed) —> SATA II (300 Mbps Speed) —> SATA III (Current Generation - 600 Mbps Speed).

o The M.2 SSD connects directly to the motherboard in the M.2 slot. Which means there are no data or power connection cables needed.

o NVMe (Non-Volatile Memory Express) - Uses PCIe X4. Times 4 means, it has 4 serial connections. A single serial connection is 600 Mbps in Speed. **4 serial connection means 2400 Mbps Speed Connection.**

o NVMe connection, allows a solid state drive to have its data read straight from a PCIe slot on the motherboard. The drive draws power directly through the motherboard. Also, the NVMe drive will draw data through the motherboard at a faster rate than SATA 3.

o NVME & PCIe - PCIe lanes are essentially data lanes on a motherboard. There's a limited amount, and the different ports and slots on a motherboard are given certain lanes. On a typical newer motherboard, you'll see slots of various sizes corresponding to the number of PCI-E lanes available (x1, x2, x4, x16, etc). NVMe can queue more data at once due to having access to more PCIe lanes.

o M.2 has 2 slots, one slot is 6 pins from the left and the other slot is 5 pins from the right. It has a total of 30 pins. Whereas NVMe has only one slot, 5 pins from the right and has a total of 34 pins.

o M.2 can perform at maximum SATA speed which in practical means 560 MB/s in the best-case scenario. Whereas PCIe X4/NVMe has a practical speed of about 2100+ MB/s.

o Intel has a new technology called 'OPTANE'. This technology will double or triple the NVMe technology speed.

o In some cases, you need to tell the motherboard the type SSD you have plugged on to the motherboard. Do this by logging on to the BIOS > ADVANCED MODE (F7) > ADVANCED (TOP) > ON BOARD DEVICE CONFIGURATION > M.2_1 CONFIGURATION (scroll down) > if AUTO (Sometimes AUTO MODE doesn't properly detect the drive) > AUTO —> PCIe MODE.

o If you got a motherboard that supports NVMe and SATA on the M.2 slot means you can use a regular SATA M.2

o If you are using an old PC, there is a high chance your PC is not equipped with this M.2 or NVMe slots. If so, You can always purchase a **M.2 NVMe + M.2 SATA SSD PCIe x4 Adapter – Vantec M.2 NVMe + M.2 SATA SSD PCIe x4 Adapter (UGT-M2PC200) [** https://amzn.to/2HTXeZB **]**. You can click/copy the link given to buy the product. This is an adapter that goes into the PCIex4 slot. Make sure this slot is present on your motherboard. You will have to insert the M.2 NVMe SSD card at an angle of 30°. The adapter usually comes with a screw and a washer (This needs to be inserted from the bottom of the card and screwed from top) to tighten the card. Gently screw them in and not too tight as it can break the card. The adapter also comes with a regular-sized backplate which goes to the back of the regular-sized PC like Mid-Tower PC. By default, the adapter comes with a low profile backplate. There should be a slot for a regular M.2 SSD drives too which is rather connected through SATA data cable. Make sure to connect your Samsung 970 EVO Plus 500GB PCIe NVMe M.2 (2280) Internal Solid State Drive (SSD) (MZ-V7S500) [https://amzn.to/2vezxZd] to the first slot on the adapter. Now insert the adapter gently like the graphics card. See if the drive appears under DRIVES AND DEVICES. It usually will appear only if the drive is formatted. Now go the THIS PC > Right Click > DEVICE MANAGER > Storage Controller > Standard Express NVM Controller (If there) > This PC > Right

Click Manage > Storage > Disk management > system detects a new drive and ask what type of partition you need > MBR (Master Boot Record) or GPT (GUID partition table). Select GPT > click OK > Now it will show the unallocated disk that requires partition > Right-click on the unallocated space given > NEW SIMPLE VOLUME WIZARD > Follow through all default > Format. Now the drive appears under drives and devices.

o For gaming, both NVMe and SATA 3 will offer very similar boot speeds. They are both so fast that other hardware, such as RAM and CPU performance, ends up being the bottleneck.

o NVMes are only useful for transferring those larger files, so unless you regularly move around large photo and video editing files or find a great deal on an NVMe drive, you may as well stick to a standard SATA 3 SSD because you can get a much bigger size for the same price.

In short: 7200 RPM Hard Drive - average read/write speed of 80-160MB/second. SATA 3 SSD - read/write speed up to 550MB/second. NVME SSD - read/write speed up to 3500MB/second.

BEST STORAGE DEVICES 2020

HERE ARE THE 10 BEST SSD FOR GAMING:
TIP: NVMe TECHNOLOGY IS MUCH FASTER THAN SATA.

BEST PREMIUM SSD

1) STORAGE DEVICE: SAMSUNG 970 EVO PLUS
COST: $109/₹9,999
PURCHASE LINK:
https://amzn.to/3cAfipQ
(500GB)
https://amzn.to/2Ie9qoa
(1TB)
https://amzn.to/2IbfjST
(250GB)
FEATURES
powered by the latest V-NAND technology
Read/write speeds up to 3,500/3,300 MB/s, up to 53% faster than the 970 EVO.
Optimized firmware.
Get up to 1,200 TBW with a 5-year limited warranty for lasting performance
Exceptional Endurance.
Form Factor M.2

2) STORAGE DEVICE: CRUCIAL P1 1TB NVME
COST: $105/₹10,699
PURCHASE LINK:

https://amzn.to/39gDb3u
(1TB)

https://amzn.to/3cpJK5U
(500GB)

FEATURES
Can be faster than SATA.
Respectable brand.
Solid power efficiency.
Reduced performance when full.
QLC results in weaker random IO.
NVMe™ PCIe® technology delivers
sequential read/write speeds up to 2,000/1,700 MB/s.
Lasting Value.
5-year Limited Warranty.

BEST VALUE SSD

1) STORAGE DEVICE: INTEL SSD 660P SERIES
COST: $92/₹11,900
PURCHASE LINK:
https://amzn.to/2VQ1lyb
(1TB)
https://amzn.to/2VGA9Sq
(512GB)
FEATURES
PCIe and Intel QLC 3D NAND in one SSD.
SSD 660p fits low-cost and high-capacity—up to 2TB—into one drive.
More value for better price.
sequential Read: Up to 1,800MB/s, Sequential Write: Up to 1800MB/s Random 4KB Reads: Up to 220,000 IOPS, Random 4KB Writes: Up to 220,000 IOPS
5-year limited warranty.

2) STORAGE DEVICE: CRUCIAL MX500 1TB
COST: $115/₹10,120
PURCHASE LINK:

https://amzn.to/32HwhC2
(1TB)
https://amzn.to/2VDUuYk
(500GB)
https://amzn.to/2vzBHmf
(2TB)
https://amzn.to/39oKkiw
(250GB)

FEATURES

Capacities up to 2TB.
efficiency of next-gen micron® 3d band.
A higher level of reliability.
Manufacturer's 5 Year Limited.
Company's 45-day money-back period
One of the fastest SATA drives and a great value.
Competitive price per GB.
Nowhere close to NVMe performance.

BEST BUDGET SSD

1) STORAGE DEVICE: Western Digital Blue
COST: $120/₹11,156
PURCHASE LINK:
https://amzn.to/3ayfWCv
(1TB)
https://amzn.to/2IjNojH
(2TB)
https://amzn.to/39kNnbh
(250GB)

FEATURES

High capacity with enhanced reliability.
3D NAND technology enables Sequential Read Speeds up to 560MB/s and Sequential Write Speeds up to 530MB/s.
every WD Blue 3D NAND SATA SSD is verified for compatibility.
Downloadable WD SSD Dashboard and Acronis Software.
5-Year Limited Warranty.

2) STORAGE DEVICE: SAMSUNG 860 EVO
COST: $120/₹11,156
PURCHASE LINK:

https://amzn.to/2TDHvn4
(1TB)
https://amzn.to/3cs5A8U
(500GB)
https://amzn.to/2TvTEdz
(250GB)

FEATURES

As fast as SATA gets.
balanced blend of price, performance, and reliability.
Innovative V-NAND Technology with Enhanced Read/Write
Performance.
Up to 550 MB/s Sequential Read.
Up to 520 MB/s Sequential Write.
SATA bottlenecks.
Sometimes higher prices.

POWER SUPPLY UNIT (PSU) & HOW TO CHOOSE THEM?

- Buy a well efficient PSU (Power supply unit). Shed a few extra bucks if you have to. But not for cheap components. It's nothing but overkill.
- This is one of the last pieces of a puzzle when building a PC. This is because it is important to know the total wattage required to power all the components in the PC before purchasing the PSU.
- Buying a power supply sounds pretty straight forward right? Calculating the power (wattage) needed for your components, matching the power requirement with that of the PSU. It all sounds pretty straight forward to me. It's far from straight forward. It seems there is a lot more to consider when purchasing a PSU or your next rig.
- The wattage listed on the box is only a part of the story.
- Other important factors like reliability, efficiency, build quality can widely vary among different models.

- **WATTAGE** – Your power supply needs to meet the wattage requirement of all your PC components. CPU & GPU are the most power-hungry components in any PC. An underpowered PC might not work at all. Hardware manufacturers always provide rough estimates of how much power their product consumes indicated as **THERMAL DESIGN POWER (TDP)** or maximum power consumption. Ideally, your PSU not only needs but exceeds the power requirements of your PC because PSU works best when they are left with a bit of room for breathing, this allows for future up-gradation, adding more components if necessary. Also, if you want maximum efficiency out of the PSU, it should run between 50%-80% of its total output. In short, the wattage should be 50%-80% more than the calculated total wattage required for the PC components. This prevents the heating up of your PSU. So ideally it would be wise to choose a PSU with a wattage double the requirement form its PC components. This will ensure quieter, durable and extra wiggle room for future up expansion and overclocking.

- After figuring out the wattage required by your PC components (You can use **PCPARTPICKER.COM** to check the total wattage of your components), it is important to realize that some unscrupulous brands can label their power supplies with **PEAK WATTAGE** instead of what they can deliver continuously. So, when your PC demands for that power, it can short the power supply, causing serious damage to other components as well, this is more so in a hotter climate.

o Always rely on reputed brands like CORSAIR, EVGA, SeaSonic, Thermaltake, etc.

o **EFFICIENCY** - It is another important fact not to overlook. This is important in terms of energy cost and **heat output**. One way to go for a much efficient PSU is by going for PSU labeled with **80 plus rating.** 80 plus comes in BRONZE, SILVER, GOLD (This is an ideal middle ground for most users), PLATINUM & TITANIUM in the order of their efficiency. For gaming, there is no need to even consider platinum or titanium PSUs. These are ideal for systems that are under heavy load most of the time like the servers and workstations. I have purchased (Refer pictures below). This rating indicates how well a PSU COVERTS power from your wall socket to the lower voltage required by your PC components. These PSUs are so efficient, they promise not to waste power more than 20%. The EVGA SUPERNOVA 650 G+, 80 PLUS GOLD 650W, FULLY MODULAR, FDB FAN, 10 YEAR WARRANTY, INCLUDES POWER ON SELF TESTER, POWER SUPPLY 120-GP-0650-X1.

o This PSU comes with **(i)** 80 PLUS Gold certified, with 90% (115VAC) / 92% (220VAC~240VAC) efficiency or higher under typical loads **(ii)** Heavy-duty protections, including OVP (Over Voltage Protection), UVP (Under Voltage Protection), OCP (Over Current Protection), OPP (Over Power Protection), SCP (Short Circuit Protection), and OTP (Over Temperature Protection) **(iii)** Whisper Silent with 135mm Fluid Dynamic Bearing Fan **(iv)** Fully Modular to reduce clutter and improve airflow **(v)** 100% Japanese Capacitors ensure long-term reliability.

o You can always go for SEMI/MODULAR PSU.

RAILS - This spec in the specs list sounds more confusing like **+12V RAILS,** they determine how many rails feed power to all the different components of your PC. Still, what is a RAIL? Rails is a printed circuit pathway through which the unit draws power. **MULTI-RAIL POWER SUPPLIES** distribute power among multiple rails, but **SINGLE RAIL PSU** only has a single pathway. SINGLE RAIL PSU feeds the full power of the unit from one rail to all parts connected to it which ensures that every component has ample power to work with. Theoretically, it also carries the drawback of putting your hardware at huge risk from power surges. MULTI-RAIL PSUs, on the other hand, can handle power surges because of its in-built over-current and short-current prevention system in each rail. This MULTI-RAIL PSU comes with the indicated power supply for each component. It is also mentioned both on the PSU and in the product manual. (Refer to the picture below)

(Image Source: EVGA)

EVGA 650 / 750 / 850 / 1000G+ Specifications

ЄVGA 650W GOLD

	+5V	+3.3V	+12V	-12V	+5Vsb
AC Input	100-240 VAC, 10-5A, 50-60 Hz				
	+50°C ambient @ full load				
DC Output	+5V	+3.3V	+12V	-12V	+5Vsb
MAX output, A	24A	24A	54A	0.3A	3A
Combined, W	120W		648W	3.6W	15W
Output power, Pcont	650W @ +50°C				

80 PLUS GOLD

EVGA 650G+ / 750G+ Cable Configuration

Modular Connector				Cables	Cable Color
MB				1 x ATX 20+4-Pin	
CPU1	CPU2			2 x EPS/ATX12V 8(4+4)-Pin	
VGA1	VGA2	VGA3	VGA4	4 x PCI-E 8(6+2)-Pin	
SATA1	SATA2	SATA3		3 x SATA 5-Pin x 3	Black
PERIF1	PERIF2			2 x Molex 4-Pin x 3	
FDD				1 x Molex to FDD Adapter	

○ **PIN CONNECTORS** - Always make sure all the pins required to power all the components in your PC came with the PSU. You can check the product manual on the manufacturer's website for this. There will be pin connectors for the motherboard (MB), CPU, GPU (Graphics Processing Unit), HDD, SSD, Optical drive, Front panel, etc.

○ **MODULAR POWER SUPPLY (MODULARITY)** - Some PSUs are modular. This means they allow you to plug in only the cables that you need for your build to avoid having a messy bundle of extra wires cluttering up your case. This helps in CABLE MANAGEMENT a lot. This is important because it helps to keep the inside of the case clean and free from dust. This is, in turn, important to maintain the heat inside the case for maximum PC performance. Dust build-up can seriously impede PC performance. This is also important for the aesthetics of the PC. This feature is always reflected in the price. Modular PSU is more expensive than the semi/non-modular. You can still buy semi-modular if you are good at cable management and is the cheaper option to modular PSU. The CASE available in the market does a good job of hiding these cables well.

○ A good PSU also needs to run quietly. When purchasing always make sure you have a **QUIET FAN**, mentioned in the features of the PSU. Different branded companies come up with different technologies and name for it. The PSU I purchased (refer to the picture below) comes with a FLUID DYNAMIC BEARING FAN.

PSU FANS - look for any one of these (i) ZERO RPM FAN MODE, here the fan spins only when required (ii) RIFLE/FLUID DYNAMIC BEARING FANS, you will get quiet performance even when your power supply is working at its maximum.

○ You can always select the NON/SEMI modular PSU to save money and if you don't mind the extra wires that can be unappealing. This also limits the external devices you need to plug on to the PC at the time of building or later for upgrading.

○ **MULTI RAIL VS. SINGLE RAIL POWER SUPPLIES** - Effectively they are the same in the way they deliver power to your components. However, there is a benefit that one of them offers over the other, safety. For low wattage units, this doesn't matter, as the max Amperage will be triggered on either single-rail or multi-rail PSUs in the event of an overload. However, as you reach higher wattage units, you'll find that it's very difficult to hit the max Amperage of the PSU on a single-rail unit. Chances are in the event of an overload on the +12V power source, it's going to potentially burn your components or itself before OCP kicks in. In this scenario, multi-rail PSUs are better simply because each rail has a lower Amperage rating that is a portion of the power supply's maximum. It'll make the OCP easier to trigger, and therefore, more likely to save your components from harm. But when considering a power supply to purchase with efficiency, clean power delivery, ripple, noise, etc. the answer is, pick either, because the results will be the same.

- Always select higher wattage than the calculated power consumption value as this will give room for upgrading later.
- Corsair also produces amazing PSUs. Along with the above-mentioned features. Corsair's AXi models feature less than 1% voltage regulation for incredible stability if you are an extreme overclocker, perfect for high-end gaming PC. They have 80+ titanium efficiency and they are available in capacities to around 1600watts of continuous power to make sure even the most demanding system keeps running without a hitch. The top-end 1600i comes with gallium transformers for superior efficiency in a smaller form factor. Their 100% 105° Japanese Capacitors deliver 94% efficiency. All the models that end with an 'i' are compatible with Corsair's IQ software interface which will allow you to control and monitor all compatible corsair products right from your desktop including your power supply unit's noise and performance level.

Both the EVGA & CORSAIR comes with a 10 years warranty.

Below image shows the components I selected for my PC build and their wattage requirement:
Use the PCPARTPICKER to select and add the components to see the required wattage.

⚡ Wattage Breakdown   ✕

Note: Wattages are estimates only. Actual power draw may differ from listed values.

Component	Estimated Wattage
AMD Ryzen 7 2700X 3.7 GHz 8-Core Processor	13W - 105W
MSI B450 GAMING PRO CARBON AC ATX AM4 Motherboard	17W - 70W
Corsair Vengeance LPX 32 GB (2 x 16 GB) DDR4-3200 Memory	29W
Western Digital Blue 1 TB 3.5" 5400RPM Internal Hard Drive	3W - 15W
Samsung 970 Evo 500 GB M.2-2280 NVME Solid State Drive	2W - 10W
MSI Radeon RX 580 8 GB ARMOR OC Video Card	46W - 185W
Total:	414W

THE EVGA SUPERNOVA 650 G+, 80 PLUS GOLD 650W, FULLY MODULAR, FDB FAN, 10 YEAR WARRANTY, INCLUDES POWER ON SELF TESTER, POWER SUPPLY 120-GP-0650-X1
PURCHASE LINK:
https://world.ubuy.com/?goto=search/index/view/product/B00K8 5X2A2?inf=37bc2f75bf1bcfe8450a1a41c200364c&utm_source=uglow)
(If you live outside the US, Import Duty)
You can go for the compatible corsair substitute
AMAZON PURCHASE LINK
(**https://amzn.to/398IYbt**)

(Image Source: EVGA)

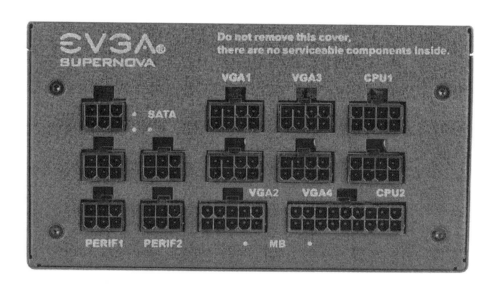

BEST POWER SUPPLY UNIT 2020

BEST PSU FOR PC GAMING

1) PSU: CORSAIR RM850X
COST: $140/₹14,499
PURCHASE LINK: https://amzn.to/3cwUqPZ

FEATURES

80 PLUS GOLD CERTIFIED - High efficiency operation for lower power consumption, less noise and cooler temperatures.
ZERO RPM FAN MODE.
100% ALL JAPANESE 105°C CAPACITORS - unwavering power delivery and long-term reliability.
FULLY MODULAR CABLES.
FULLY MODULAR CABLES.
PSU Form Factor - ATX.
Fan bearing technology - Rifle Bearing.
Multi-GPU ready.

(CORSAIR RM850X)

BEST HIGH-END POWER SUPPLY

1) PSU: SEASONIC PRIME 1000 TITANIUM
COST: $280/₹33,189
PURCHASE LINK: https://amzn.to/39nZowK

FEATURES
ATX 12 V
Fully Modular.
80 PLUS Titanium Certified.
12 Years Warranty.
MICRO TOLERANCE LOAD REGULATION.
PREMIUM HYBRID FAN CONTROL.
FLUID DYNAMIC FAN BEARING.
Multi-GPU setup.
Gold plated connectors.

(SEASONIC PRIME 1000 TITANIUM)

BEST BUDGET POWER SUPPLY

1) PSU: COOLER MASTER MASTERWATT 750W
COST: $95/₹8,500
PURCHASE LINK: https://amzn.to/3cqQznT
FEATURES

The 80 plus Bronze certification guarantees that MasterWatt delivers an average efficiency of 85 percent.
Cooler Master 120mm Silencio FP fan combines sealed LDB bearings with quiet fan blades offering a long lifetime of quiet cooling.
SEMI-FANLESS UP TO 15% LOAD.
DUAL FORWARD AND DC-TO-DC CIRCUIT DESIGN.
The MasterWatt uses 16AWG cables for PCI-e cables. Less resistance and better efficiency, providing you a safer user environment.

(COOLER MASTER MASTERWATT 750W)

BEST COMPACT POWER SUPPLY FOR MINI-ITX BUILDS

1) PSU: FSP DAGGER 500W
COST: $124/₹11,650
PURCHASE LINK:
https://world.ubuy.com/?goto=search/index/view/product/B07SYSLZDR?inf=37bc2F75bf1bcfe8450a1a41c200364c&utm_source=uglow

FEATURES
Micro ATX Compatible.
80 PLUS Gold certified.
Efficiency >= 90% at typical load.
100% Japanese made electrolytic capacitors.
Fanless under 50% load.
Fully modular for easy installation.
Expensive.

(FSP DAGGER 500W)

(FSP DAGGER 500W)

BEST DIGITAL POWER SUPPLY

1) PSU: NZXT E850
COST: $140/₹13,450
PURCHASE LINK: https://www.kccomputers.in/store/power-supply/80-gold/nzxT-e850-power-supply-np-1pm-e850a-uk/
FEATURES

Digital power monitoring.
NZXT CAM software integration - Power indicators monitored and tracked through CAM software.
Delivers precise & stable voltage while ensuring optimal efficiency under load.
Silent operation with 0 RPM fan when operating under 100 watts.
fully modular design.
80 Plus Gold certified.
FAN: Bearing: FDB (Fluid Dynamic Bearing)
Sleek design.
Expensive.

(NZXT E850)

BEST RGB POWER SUPPLY

1) PSU: GAMDIAS ASTRAPE P1-750G
COST: $95/₹25,525
PURCHASE LINK: https://amzn.to/2PJX8YK

FEATURES

80 PLUS Gold up to 90% Efficiency.
10 Years Warranty.
100% Japanese Capacitors.
Fully Modular & Flat Cables.
One Touch to Easily Switch 26 Lighting Effects Including White Light, Neon-Flex RGB, Multi-color, and LED off.
135mm FDB silent fan.
DC to DC design for steady voltage output and powerful single +12V rail
Support ATX12V v2.4, ERP 2013 Lot6.
Complete protections: OVP, UVP, OPP, OCP, SCP, SP, ICP Silent mode.

(GAMDIAS ASTRAPE P1-750G)

HOW TO CHOOSE THE BEST MONITOR FOR
VIDEO EDITING
&
GRAPHIC DESIGN

o You can get an excellent monitor for editing your photos. At the same time have great screen quality in Video Editing or when hopping into your 3D modeling software of choice.

o Monitors have lots of features that sound confusing and at times it is difficult to tell what features are important and what is just marketing speak.

o The first question to ask yourself before purchasing a monitor will be, **what medium are we planning to present our work in?**

o When working in motion Design, Video Editing or 3D animation, our work stays mostly digital and will be shown on screens.

o Types of screens: is it going to be shown on the Movie screen, or uploaded on to your mobile devices for Instagram, etc. This is important. How your target audience will experience your work is very important.

o Proofing Devices – The devices should be able to make use of the maximum quality your work comes with.

o You can always spend too much time on details, color accuracy or frames per second and overproduce your work, which the target audience might not even be able to appreciate because of the sub-par quality of their devices.

o Some examples of Monitor features that might not be entirely necessary, depending on your work and target group: (i) getting a 4K Monitor when you usually output smaller-resolution 1080p or 720p resolution videos (ii) Buying a highly color accurate Monitor when your target group only uses low-quality Mobile screens (iii) Going for a 144Hz Display (144Hz means the display refreshes 144 times per second to show a new image) when your animations run at 25FPS. For a 144Hz monitor to work at 144Hz, the game or your video MUST run at 144FPS or higher. If the frame rate falls below 144FPS, it is very noticeable and the game appears "choppy" or has extremely heavy "motion blur" (iv) You can easily save some money here, so it is good to know how accurate and high quality your work has to be, to find the minimum feature requirements in a Monitor. Of course, you might need the features elsewhere, 144Hz when you are gaming, for example, or the 4K display for having multiple applications open at once.

PANEL TYPES

o **THE TN PANEL (TWISTED NEMATIC):** This type of panels has the fastest performance. This means they have low response times, highest refresh rates, minimal motion blur; Low input lag. Even with all this, its display has the worst viewing angle and the worst color. It's cheap to buy these monitors. Best used for GAMING.

o **THE VA PANEL (VERTICAL PANEL):** This type of panels has the longest response times typically with higher refresh rates possible. The viewing angles here are typically better than TN, worse than IPS but with good color, best contrast, and best image depth. High-end models can be compared to the TN panel monitors for their performance. Best for general use.

o **THE IPS PANEL (IN-PLANE SWITCHING):** Performance wise it has slower response times than TN, faster response times than VA. Gaming quality refresh rates are rare. These types of monitors have the best viewing angle and color. It is one of the most expensive monitors and good for professional use.

o **THE IPS PANEL** is the best panel type for our kind of work, Video Editing. We need the best color display possible to be able to accurately edit our project contents.

o Having a high viewing angle lets us view the Monitor from different angles, so even a colleague or client standing or sitting next to you can take a look at what you are seeing, without obscuring the contrast and colors too much. Top of the line Monitors with IPS Panels usually have at least a 178° Viewing angle vertically and horizontally, which is very helpful.

o The downsides to an IPS Panel Monitor are the *Price* and *the latency*. The Latency doesn't concern us that much, as we are buying the Monitor for professional use and not high-end gaming.

- The IPS Panel monitors are not good for GAMING. Go for the TN Panel monitors for that.

- Since monitors are an integral part of video editing, it should be worth spending a premium for the highest possible quality display that will serve us well for a long time.

- These monitors can last for a long time as compared to the PC components because of their slower technical progression. A single best monitor can easily go through 2 to 3 generations of PC upgrades.

MONITORS WITH MATTE OR GLOSSY REFLECTIONS

- There are different display devices available in the market with a reflective screen and it looks expensive. But in the world of video editing, we should stay clear of these types of reflective monitors as they can easily reflect light off from any other light source or reflective surfaces. It can even reflect our face. All these can be very distracting from our work along with less color and contrast appreciation due to the distraction.

- Professional Monitors have Matte surfaces. The reflections that bounce off the surface of these displays are being scattered and dimmed at the same time, to make the picture quality as clear as possible. Always go for a matte finish over a glossy finish for professional work.

GAMUT & COLOR ACCURACY

- The color gamut depicts a range of colors within the spectrum of colors that are identifiable by the human eye (visible color spectrum). Within this visible Color spectrum, there are areas that a monitor can be rated for. 'SRGB' and 'Adobe RGB' being the most popular.

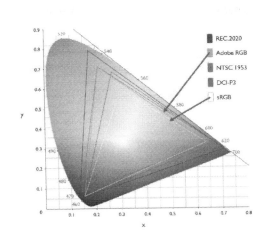

o Based on the GAMUT depiction above, you can notice that Adobe RGB covers a larger color spectrum than sRGB.

o **THE ADOBE RGB COLOR SPACE** is a color space developed by Adobe Systems, Inc. in 1998. It was designed to encompass most of the colors achievable on CMYK color printers, but by using RGB primary colors on a device such as a computer display.

o **SRGB** is an RGB color space that HP and Microsoft created cooperatively in 1996 to use on monitors, printers, and the Internet.

o **SRGB** gives better (more consistent) results and the same, or brighter, colors. Using Adobe RGB is one of the leading causes of colors not matching between monitor and print. sRGB is the world's default color space. Use it and everything looks great everywhere all the time.

o You will find many monitors supporting a higher percentage of the sRGB spectrum more easily than the Adobe RGB spectrum.

o **NOTE:** Our best goal when buying a good monitor is to maximize the percentage of both sRGB and Adobe RGB. As discussed above, to get the best possible color ranges we will have to look at monitors with *IPS panels*, as TN panels lack accuracy in this area. But even within Monitors that have IPS panels, there are still great differences.

○ Most Monitors have at least 90% sRGB Spectrum coverage and above 70% Adobe RGB spectrum coverage. The higher the coverage percentage, the more expensive are the Monitors. Monitors with 99% or even 100% of Adobe RGB coverage can cost a good premium.

○ You have to think about how important color accuracy is in your work. If it matters a lot, better to invest in a monitor with the most color accuracy. But these monitors can be very expensive.

COLOR BIT DEPTH

○ Bit depth refers to the color information stored in an image. The higher the bit depth of an image, the more colors it can store. That is because the 1 bit can only store one of two values, 0 (white) and 1 (black). An 8-bit image can store 256 possible colors, while a 24-bit image can display over 16.7 million colors.

○ The 2 different types of color bit depths monitors come with are 8-bit and 10-BIT.

Bits Per Pixel	Number of Colors Available	Common Name(s)
1	2	Monochrome
2	4	CGA
4	16	EGA
8	256	VGA
16	65536	XGA, High Color
24	16777216	SVGA, True Color
32	16777216 + Transparency	
48	281 Trillion	

○ Bit depth is a technical measurement that describes the number of color values per channel – Red, Green, and Blue. When a camera shoots 8-bit, it is recording 2^8 unique colors per channel, which adds up to 256 total. 256 shades of green, blue and red each, all mixed up together to form an image. It's important to note that each pixel is a mixture of all three colors. The sensor is still receiving the full visible spectrum, but the processor is trying to efficiently compress that glut of information into a usable image format that still preserves image detail – not an easy task. A 10-bit image comes out to 1024 unique colors per channel, and 12-bit brings us to 4096. You can have a lot more subtlety and nuance when working in 10 or 12 bit, but

the difficulty of encoding it climbs exponentially.
There's a reason that smaller, more consumer-oriented
cameras only shoot 8-bit.

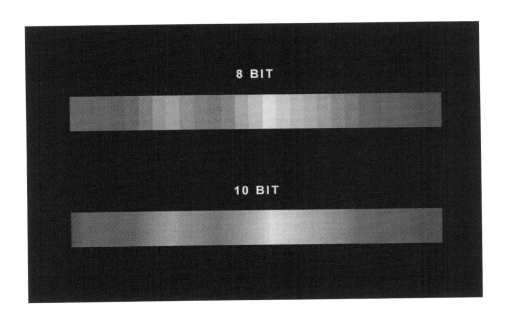

8-BIT COLORS

o 8-bit video is the lowest bit depth that can reasonably be
    expected to look "realistic" and not noticeably disrupt
    colors in strange ways.

o 8-bit will not survive a strong color grading process,
    leaves less room for correction, and does not capture
    the richness of the full-color spectrum as well as 10-
    bit or 12-bit. Because of this, it is a less than ideal
    candidate for shooting log footage.

o This is the most basic stripped-down video signal that can
    be called viable. Unless you have high expectations
    from grading your footage in post-production, an 8-bit
    video can be a viable option.

o 8-bit is like having more than enough colors, but every so
    often you find a need that you just can't fill with
    these types of monitors.

o 8-Bit Codecs Include: (i) h.264 (ii) AVCHD

10-BIT COLORS

○ A 10-bit recording is the broadcast standard in many ecosystems and is a mandatory minimum in many production companies like Netflix.

○ This meets the demands of HDR displays and future-proof the images captured.

○ 10-bit color is the ideal set of colors. At this point, you're pretty well set for all of your day-to-day needs.

○ 10-Bit Codecs Include: (i) ProRes 422 HQ (ii) DNxHD

○ More colors are always better, but the question is whether your PC hardware and software apart from your Monitor can support this.

○ Like mentioned before, you will need a Graphics Card that supports 10-BIT. Quadro or Radeon Pro Workstation GPUs are the choices for this. Also, your work will have to be in at least 10 bits too. If you are working on a JPG Image, MP4 Movie or Render your Animation to a png-sequence, these formats store color in 8-bits per channel This meaning that your 10-BITs per channel monitor will not show any additional Bit depth in your work. Unless you work on Canon RAW, RED 10-BIT or EXR Sequences, you will be able to see the higher color range, that a 10-BIT Monitor will grant you. Especially in Gradients, or Vignetted uniform Backgrounds, you can quickly spot if a Monitor is making good use of its 10-BIT capability.

FRAME RATE CONTROL (FRC)

○ This is a way for the monitors to achieve a higher bit rate. Another way as you know is through 10-bit and higher color bit depths.

○ 8-Bit Monitors can increase their Bit depth by rapidly flashing pixels close to each other, which gives the impression of higher Bit Depth, as multiple pixels and colors are blended this way. FRC can produce flickering and will never be as accurate as true 10-BIT support.

o Choose a 10-bit monitor as long as it hasn't achieved the 10-bit through FRC.

MONITOR SIZE AND RESOLUTION

o The size of the monitors is usually mentioned in inches (") diagonally across the screen. This makes it difficult to know the exact height and width of the monitor. Hence you will have to look up the aspect ratio to know how tall and wide the screen of the monitor is.

o **ASPECT RATIO** - You have to understand what aspect ratios are to easily move designs, images and compress digital video files/content from one medium to another without making an error in your calculations. For the record, the proportional relationship between the height and width of a rectangle is what is aptly referred to as an aspect ratio.

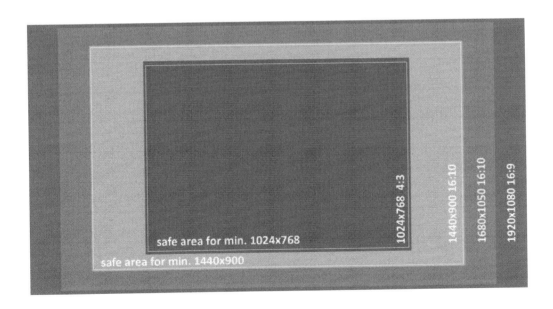

o Now check out these monitors, both are 25". Can you notice the difference? (Image Source: DELL & L.G)

○ The only difference here is the aspect ratio. The left monitor has the aspect ratio of 4:3 and the right one with 16:9.

○ The most popular professional monitors for video editing are sized 24" or 27" inches and up, with an aspect ratio of 16:9.

○ Many reasons why people choose wide Screen monitors are (i) Cinematic appearance (ii) Better fits our eye's Field of Vision (iii) Most of the work being created is in a wide-screen format (vi) GAMING - Objects of interest are usually placed on a landscape that extends horizontally.

o The size and resolution of the monitor's panel have a greater influence on the pixel distance. Hence it is important to understand the increase in monitor size should go hand in hand with the resolution. Larger the monitor, higher the resolution.

o Imagine yourself sitting at a fixed distance from the monitor. Now the monitor gets larger and larger. You are now able to appreciate the individual pixel size on the monitor screen. The only way to prevent this is by either (i) Increasing the resolution of the monitor or (ii) By moving away from the monitor as the monitor gets bigger and bigger. The second option is unreasonable. Hence the only viable option is to increase the resolution of the monitor.

o Examples of monitors with higher resolution without appreciating the individual pixels on them are (i) For 24″ monitor sizes go for Full HD (1920px x 1080px) (ii) For 27″ go with at least WQHD: 2560px x 1440px (iii) And for 32″ and up you will need 4K displays (3840px x 2160px). Here the viewing distance should remain constant.

4K AND HIGH DPI DISPLAYS

o Don't go for small monitors with high resolution. Example: Less than 23″ monitor with high resolution, where the information is shown on the screen like the text, icons menus, etc can shrink significantly. This can be very straining for the eyes.

o The display scaling in windows can be used to increase the size of these smaller, texts, menus, etc but some of the third-party software might not support that and can make these blurry.

o In short, Bigger monitor deserves better resolution. It is a good investment.

CONTRAST RATIO

o Manufacturers often claim to have an extremely high dynamic contrast ratio. This is a pure marketing gimmick and doesn't help up selecting the ideal monitor for us.

○ Two most common thing manufacturer mention in their specs sheet include: (i) Dynamic Contrast Ratio (ii) Static Contrast Ratio

○ **DYNAMIC CONTRAST RATIO** – This value is obtained by measuring the widest distance between dark and light a monitor can project at different brightness settings. "Different" is the important word here, as you certainly won't switch around your brightness or turn on and off the backlighting all the time to get that great contrast the manufacturer is speaking of.

○ **STATIC CONTRAST RATIO –** What we want is the widest distance between dark and light a monitor can project at the same brightness setting and not the other way around unlike dynamic contrast ratio. This is what we should be looking out for when buying the best monitor for Graphic Design, Video Editing, 3D Animation or many other visually demanding use cases out there.

○ Always go for IPS Panel Monitor that has at least 500:1 static contrast ratio which is better than 1000:1.

BRIGHTNESS

○ Candela is the SI unit of light intensity measured in CD/m^2. Higher the CD/m^2, the greater is the brightness of the monitor.

○ The environment in which your work is equally important. If you are working in a darker environment like during night in a slightly dark room. Contrary to the belief, having a bright monitor is counterproductive as your eyes will adjust to accommodate more light. Hence excess light will cause eye strain. A monitor with high CD/m^2 works wonders in a bright, highly lit environment like outdoors, etc.

○ Monitor with 300 CD/m^2 – 350 CD/m^2 brightness is a good value for most environment settings.

○ You can always increase the brightness but never above the limit of the monitor.

MONITOR REFRESH RATE (60Hz, 120Hz, 144Hz)

○ The higher the refresh rate of a Monitor the more individual Images per second it can display.

○ The 'HZ' used in a monitor's description is used to describe its refresh rate. The higher the Hz, the more often the screen will refresh. For example, a 60Hz monitor will refresh its image 60 times per second, while a 144Hz monitor will refresh its image 144 times per second. (Image courtesy: Samsung, 32" CHG70 Gaming Monitor with Quantum Dot)

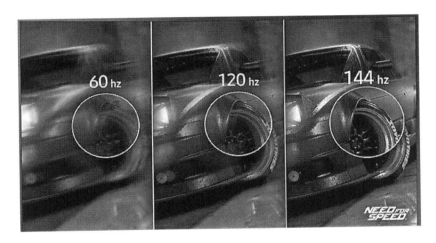

○ When you are playing games that run at over 60fps or watching movies that have higher frame rates than 60fps or playing back anything on the Monitor such as a Video Editing timeline. Your screen will also output more than 60 Images per second.

○ The human eye can differentiate between a game playing at 60fps and 144fps.

○ The question remains, is it important for your professional work? Are you animating at 25fps? Are you editing videos with 60 fps or higher? Or if you are a game developer, who optimizes VR with games that have high movement in them?

○ If you are such a gamer or game developer who uses 60fps or higher most of the time, then you should look for a monitor that delivers the same. 91% of the time, video editors, graphics designers, etc don't require 60fps or higher.

CURVED, FLAT OR ULTRA WIDE

○ Sometimes it just drops down to your personal experience, the type of monitors you are comfortable working with.

○ Even though ultra-wide monitors have some software that simulates multiple displays, it just doesn't feel like the real thing.

○ Curved and ultra-wide monitors give much space to work with, within the constraints of a single monitor. This also depends on how comfortable you are in working in such an environment.

○ Having multiple monitors give you the flexibility to have different types of work running, for example, different types of videos with different resolutions and color.

○ Gaming is undoubtedly benefited from the curved and ultra-wide monitors. The difference is well appreciated. But I wouldn't recommend these for the most line of works.

○ Aesthetically they are much better looking than the flat monitors.

HOW MANY MONITORS TO BUY?

○ Most of the video editors, graphics designers, and 3D animators work with at least 2 monitors.

○ You can have one monitor for your Software palettes, Main GUI as well as your Timeline and have a second Monitor for your Footage and Previews or Images you are working on. This is a perfect setup or video editors.

○ A 24-inch lower quality Monitor for your Software Interface and a 27-inch Monitor with great color and contrast is a very popular setup among video editors.

- ○ Most of the monitors have VESA mounts that let you attach them to the monitor arms. This will free up a lot of space on your work desk and a nice angle to work with.

- ○ Still, you prefer to go with a single monitor, I would recommend a larger monitor with high resolution.

- ○ Go or 27″ and higher monitor with a WQHD resolution. (Photo above, Image source: Samsung, 86.4cm (34") Ultra WQHD Curved Monitor) - (https://amzn.to/2IpZ9Fs)

ADDITIONAL FEATURES

- ○ **PIVOT** - Some monitors can pivot 90°. This helps in switching between 16:9 ratio to 9:16 ratio. This is highly beneficial in helping to read those long websites and documents that fit this ratio. This feature combined with a monitor arm gives plenty of flexibility.

- ○ **MONITOR HOOD** - This is very helpful when you find yourself working outdoors in a very bright environment or places that reflect a lot of light which can be very distracting for your work.

- ○ **CONNECTORS** - These days monitors come with USB and headphone jack without having to reach for your PC. This comes in handy or devices that have short cables. Monitors thus can act as a hub for USB.

- ○ **MULTIPLE DISPLAY CONNECTORS** - Monitors come with multiple Display Input Connectors, such as HDMI, Display Port, DVI, and VGA. This help in attaching multiple PCs to your monitor and switch between them using the display source switcher without having to change the cable every time you need to change the PC.

- ○ **WARRANTY** - Make sure the warranty provided by the manufacturer is good as this is the place where the manufacturer tries to save money.

- ○ **SPEAKERS/AUDIO** - In-Built speakers come in handy when you want to change between headphones.

CALIBRATING THE MONITOR

o To bring out the true potential of a monitor it is important to calibrate them. The color and brightness of the monitor should be calibrated to the set values. This will make sure the project you are working on will look the same on different devices you will be playing the video.

o These projects should look similar on the monitor as they should look on the TV, Mobile phones, etc.

MONITOR CALIBRATION TOOL – As the name suggests this is a great tool to calibrate your monitor. The only thing you will have to do is to connect it to the PC and attach it to your monitor. It hardly takes any time. Since different monitors come with different preset calibration values, this device helps in creating an equal set value, especially if you are working with multiple monitors. The best one in the market right now is Datacolor SpyderX Pro (https://amzn.to/2wFgYh0).

BEST MONITOR FOR VIDEO EDITING SHOULD HAVE OF THE FOLLOWING FEATURES:

FEATURES	CHOICE
1. PANEL TYPE	IPS PANEL
2. SURFACE FINISH	MATTE FINISH
3. COLOR ACCURACY	ADOBE RGB & sRGB SHOULD BE AS HIGH AS POSSIBLE IN PERCENTAGE.
4. COLOR DEPTH	8-BIT FOR MOST. 10-BIT & HIGHER, IF YOU CAN MAKE USE OF IT.
5. SIZE	24" FOR FULL HD RESOLUTION. BIGGER THE MONITOR, HIGHER THE RESOLUTION
6. CONTRAST RATIO	STATIC CONTRAST RATIO OF AT LEAST 500:1. 1000:1 IS BETTER. AVOID NON-DYNAMIC CONTRAST.
7. BRIGHTNESS	BEST BETWEEN 300 - 350 CD/m^2 ALSO DEPENDS ON THE WORK ENVIRONMENT.
8. REFRESH RATE	FOR MOST IT'S 60Hz. FOR HIGH-SPEED FOOTAGE LIKE GAME DESIGN, GO FOR 100Hz, 120Hz, 144Hz.
9. MULTIPLE MONITOR	I PREFER 2 FLAT STANDARD SIZED MONITORS FOR PROFESSIONAL WORK. ULTRA-WIDE & CURVED FOR AESTHETICS.
10. ADDITIONAL FEATURES	GO FOR PIVOT, USB / AUDIO CONNECTORS, MULTIPLE DISPLAY CONNECTORS SUCH AS HDMI, DVI, VGA, DISPLAY PORT, VESA MONITOR ARM MOUNT CAPABILITY, IN-BUILT SPEAKERS.

BEST MONITORS

BEST ALL-AROUND VIDEO EDITING MONITOR

1) MONITOR: DELL ULTRA SHARP UP2716D
COST: $312/₹45,000
PURCHASE LINK: https://amzn.to/2Iqbdqe

FEATURES

SIZE - 27" / 16:9
PANEL - IPS
Color Accuracy - 100% Adobe RGB Bit
Depth - 10bit
Resolution - WQHD 2560×1440
Brightness - 300 CD/m²
Contrast - 1000:1

BEST FOR SERIOUS PRINT WORK AND GRAPHIC DESIGN

1) MONITOR: EIZO COLOREDGE CG2420
COST: $1479/₹1,57,900
PURCHASE LINK: https://amzn.to/2xflymw

FEATURES

SIZE – 24" / 16:10
PANEL – IPS
Color Accuracy – 99% Adobe RGB
Bit Depth – 10-BIT
Resolution – Full HD 1920×1200
Brightness – 400CD/m²
Contrast – 1500:1

4K EXTREME BUDGET MONITOR

1) MONITOR: PHILIPS 276E8VJSB
COST: $230/₹19,695
PURCHASE LINK:

https://world.ubuy.com/?Goto=search/index/view/product/B07JXCR263?inf=37bc2f75bf1bcfe8450a1a41c200364c&utm_source=uglow

FEATURES

SIZE – 27″ / 16:9
PANEL – IPS
Color Accuracy – 70% Adobe RGB
Bit Depth – 10-BIT
Resolution – 4K 3840×2160
Brightness – 350 CD/m²
Contrast – 1000:1

2) MONITOR: ASUS PROART PA329Q
COST: $878/₹1,37,500
PURCHASE LINK: https://amzn.to/38wO0gN
FEATURES

4K monitor with great color accuracy
SIZE -32" / 16:9
PANEL - IPS
Color Accuracy - 99.5% Adobe RGB
Bit Depth - 10-BIT
Resolution - 4K 3840×2160
Brightness - 350 CD/m²
Contrast - 1000:1

HOW TO CHOOSE THE BEST GAMING MONITOR?

o The monitor is one of the most important parts of the gaming world.

o The performance of the PC is expressed through the monitor. Whatever the PC can do is measured through the monitor, so it is important to choose the right monitor.

o There are a lot of factors that determine the right kind of monitor for your gaming alone.

o The first question you should ask yourself is, what is the intended purpose? Is it Gaming, Video editing or professional use?

o The higher the resolution, the better is the quality.

FEATURES TO LOOK FOR IN A GAMING MONITOR

PANEL TYPE

o IPS PANEL is the ideal choice.

SURFACE FINISH

o MATTE FINISH (Non-Reflective), to prevent glare.

COLOR ACCURACY

o ADOBE RGB & sRGB should be as high as possible in percentage.

COLOR DEPTH

o 8-BIT for most. 10-BIT & HIGHER, if you can make use of it.

SIZE

o 24" for FULL HD RESOLUTION. Bigger the monitor, the higher the resolution.

o 32" is plenty big for a typical desktop view distance.

- 32″ monitor with QHD (2560 x 1440) resolution is the sweet spot now.

- FHD (1920 x 1080) for the highest frame rates.

CURVED OR FLAT

- Curved monitors give you a larger field of view (FOV).

- It is less eye-straining.

- It can cause a lot of glare and can be distracting in a well-lit environment. hence perfect for a controlled environment.

- Ultra-wide monitors are effective.

- Buy an ultra-wide with a minimum size of 32″.

- A 1800r means 1800mm curve radius with a max viewing angle of 1.8m.

- Lower the curvature, the more curved the display is.

RESOLUTION

- More pixels for more picture quality.

- Minimum needed for gaming: 1920 x 1080 -- also known as 1080p / full HD (FHD) / HD.

- Better sharper images on a QHD < 4K monitor.

- A high-resolution QHD or more is preferred for a monitor above 27″.

OPERATING SYSTEM

- The operating system should be able to support the high resolution.

- Windows can operate best at 90-110ppi pixel density. if you have the pixel density more than that, everything on the monitor will be shrunk. objects and texts will appear much smaller.

PIXEL DENSITY

- 109ppi (PIXEL PER DENSITY) is ideal.

- Larger monitor with less resolution has poor pixel density.

CONTRAST RATIO

- Static contrast ratio of at least 500:1. 1000:1 is better.

- Avoid non-dynamic contrast.

BRIGHTNESS

- Best between 300 - 350 CD/m^2

- It also depends on the work environment.

REFRESH RATE

- For most it's 60Hz. for high-speed footage like game design, go for 100Hz, 120Hz, 144Hz.

RESPONSE TIME

- Shorter is better.

- It tells you the time required for an individual pixel to change form black to white or one shade of Grey to another.

- Larger response time will result in blurry pictures esp. in gaming.

- Choose response time from 5ms (most common) to 0.5ms (fastest).

AMD FREE-SYNC VS NVIDIA G-SYNC

- This helps gaming monitors, laptops and Television to help fight screen tearing, stuttering and input latency (the time between when you move your mouse and when the cursor moves) during fast-paced games and video.

- As the name says, free-sync requires AMD GPU and g-sync requires NVIDIA GPU.

- G-sync monitors usually cost more than free-sync ones.

- G-sync and free-sync offer comparable performance GPU for the typical user.

- G-sync monitors operate from a 30Hz refresh rate up to the monitor's maximum.

- Free-sync displays are not as consistent. monitor with free sync supports adaptive refresh up to monitor's maximum refresh rate. the minimum refresh rate should not go below 40Hz.

- Low frame rate compensation - this is viable if the minimum refresh rate is 2.5 times that of the maximum refresh rate. And it should not go below 40Hz.

- If you plan on doing a lot of competitive gaming with HDR content, consider getting a g-sync ultimate or free-sync premium pro display.

MULTIPLE MONITOR

- I prefer 2 flat standard-sized monitors for professional work. ultra-wide & curved for aesthetics.

GPU (GRAPHICS PROCESSING UNIT)

- Higher pixel needs higher processing power GPU. if not, the high resolution will be a hindrance rather than a quality.

- Most GPU doesn't support refresh rate more than 60Hz for a 4k UHD or 5k monitors.

- GPU required for 4k gaming to push past 60fps can be very expensive. example: NVIDIA GeForce GTX titan x

o Multi-GPU is ideal for multi-monitor and high-resolution gaming, based on the requirement.

o The minimum GPU requirement depends on the type of game.

o For gaming at QHD resolution go for at least a GTX 1060 or RX 580. here you don't have to have to turn the in-game settings down to low. for 4k gamers go for at least a 1070 TI or RX VEGA 64.

ADDITIONAL FEATURES

Go for a pivot, USB / audio connectors, multiple display connectors such as HDMI, DVI, VGA, display port, VESA monitor arm mount capability, in-built speakers.

BEST GAMING MONITOR 2020

BEST 4K GAMING MONITOR

1) MONITOR: ACER NITRO XV273K
COST: $650/₹58,000
PURCHASE LINK: https://amzn.to/2xzxe3O

POSITIVE FEATURES

PANEL TYPE: IPS
COLOR ACCURACY: Accurate DCI-P3 color gamut
SCREEN SIZE & ASPECT RATIO: 27", 16:9
CONTRAST RATIO: 1,000:1
BRIGHTNESS: 350 CD/m² – Native, 400 CD/m² – Peak (HDR Mode)
RESOLUTION: 4K @ 144 Hz
REFRESH RATE: 144 Hz
RESPONSE TIME (GTG): 1 MS VRB
PIXEL DENSITY: 163 pixels per inch (PPI)
G-SYNC/FREE-SYNC: Free Sync compatible and G-Sync Compatible (without HDR)
MULTIPLE MONITOR:
VESA: Yes
ADDITIONAL FEATURES: HDMI®, 2x HDMI®-in, 2x Display Port, 1x USB 3.0 Upstream, 4x USB 3.0 Downstream

NEGATIVE FEATURES

o HDR only looks slightly better than SDR because of no dynamic contrast.
o sRGB mode has inaccurate white point.
It's Expensive.

BEST BUDGET 4K GAMING MONITOR

2) MONITOR: BENQ EL2870U
COST: $293/₹24,500
PURCHASE LINK: https://amzn.to/2vTSelv

POSITIVE FEATURES

PANEL TYPE: TN
COLOR ACCURACY: 72% NTSC
COLOR DEPTH: 10 bits
SCREEN SIZE & ASPECT RATIO: 28", 16:9
CONTRAST RATIO: 1,000:1
BRIGHTNESS: 300
RESOLUTION: 4K @ 60 Hz – 4K resolution and HDR tech, 3840x2160p
REFRESH RATE: 60 Hz
RESPONSE TIME (GTG): 1ms (GTG)
PIXEL DENSITY: 158 pixels per inch (PPI)
G-SYNC/FREE-SYNC: Free Sync. No G-Sync.
MULTIPLE MONITOR:
ADDITIONAL FEATURES: 2 x HDMI 2.0; 1 x DP 1.4
VESA: Yes
WARRANTY: 3 Years

NEGATIVE FEATURES

o No G-SYNC
o Refresh rate only 60Hz
Plain design

RAID SETUP - HOW TO SAVE YOUR DATA?

o Storage is a very important part of fault tolerance. If something were to happen to a company's data, such as a disk failure that results in data loss that could have a serious impact on how the company performs. The same could happen to you, loss of data due to disk failure is a serious issue.

o **DATA LOSS PREVENTION** - So it is important to make sure if there is a disk failure, data is not lost. One of the best ways to prevent data loss is through RAID (REDUNDANT ARRAY OF INDEPENDENT DISKS)

o **RAID (REDUNDANT ARRAY OF INDEPENDENT DISKS)** - In a RAID setup, data is stored in multiple disks so that in the event of a disk failure no data will be lost.

o There are 4 common types of RAID: (i) RAID 0 (ii) RAID 1 (iii) RAID 5 (iv) RAID 10.

o **RAID 0 STRIPING** - It is not fault-tolerant. It shouldn't even be called RAID because not only does it provide fault tolerance, it increases the data loss because in a RAID 0, the data is not duplicated but the data is 'striped' across multiple disks. The incoming data is spread over 2 disks. So, if one of these disks fails or damage to one of the disks, all the data will be lost. The only advantage in setting up RAID 0 is speed. If your 2 disks are working instead of one, then accessing data is much faster.

o **RAID 1 MIRRORING & DUPLEXING** - This setup is fault-tolerant. In a RAID 1 setup, the data is copied to more than 1 disks so that each disk has same data. So, in the event of a single disk failure due to internal or external factors, no data will be lost because there is a copy of the same data in the other disk.

o **RAID 5 STRIPING WITH PARITY** - In this type of setup, a minimum of 3 or more disk is required. This is the most common setup that is used because it is fast, and it can store a large amount of data. Here the data is not copied but striped across the different available disks. In addition to the data, there is another very important piece of information that is being evenly spread across all the disks. And this information is called **PARITY**. Parity will be used to rebuild the data in the event of a disk failure. The downside of this type of setup is that parity storage takes up space equivalent to that of an entire disk. This reduces the collective amount of data that can be stored in this array. Example: If all 4 disk array totals to about 4TB, only 3TB will be available or data storage. The entire disk of 1TB will be used to store PARITY. If there is a failure of one disk in this setup, you will not lose any data. RAID 5 setup is designed to handle a single disk failure. All you have to do here is replace the failed disk and the RAID 5 setup will use the parity information from the other disks to rebuild the data on to the new drive. However, if 2 disks were to fail at the same time in a RAID 5 setup, all the data Would be lost because RAID 5 is not designed to handle 2 disk failures at the same time. *It can only handle one disk failure in this type of setup*.

o **RAID 6 STRIPPING WITH DOUBLE PARITY** – In this type of setup, you need to have a minimum of 4 or more disks. This setup is just like RAID 5 setup where the data is striped across all the disks and parity is also spread on all the disks. But the difference is, in RAID 6 parity is spread twice on all the disks and the reason for this *double parity* is for this type of setup to handle 2 disk failure at the same time. So, in a RAID 6 setup, if two disks were to fail at the same time, which is pretty rare, no data will be lost. And all you would have to do is replace the failed disks and then RAID 6 setup would use the double parity from the other disks to rebuild the data on the new drives. So in this setup, for example: If you are using 4 disks of 1TB each for this setup, totaling storage space of about 4TB, only 2TB can be used to store data and the other 2 disks will be used to store the double parity. Read performance from both the RAID 5 & 6 is about the same but the write performance by the RAID 6 setup suffers greatly because RAID 6 has to write 2 independent parity blocks instead of one parity as compared to the RAID 5 setup.

o **RAID 10** – RAID 10 = RAID 1 + RAID 0. A combination of RAID 1 setup and RAID 0 setup is used to create the RAID 10 setup. You need to use a minimum of 4 disks. In this type of setup, a set of 2 disks are mirrored using RAID 1 setup. Then both sets of 2 disks are striped using a RAID 0 setup. This will give it the benefits of fault tolerance from RAID 1 and the speed of RAID 0. The downside in a RAID 10 is that you can only use 50% of the total storage capacity for data storage. If you are using 4 disks for data storage in RAID 10 setup, only 2 disks can be used to store the data.

RAID 5 SETUP IN WINDOWS 10

HOW TO SETUP RAID 5 USING STORAGE SPACES

o RAID 5 SETUP requires a minimum of 3 separate Hard drives (HDD).

o Make sure your computer is connected to 3 or more hard drives.

o Open 'settings' on windows 10 > Click on 'system' > Select 'storage' > Under 'More storage setting', select 'Manage storage spaces'.

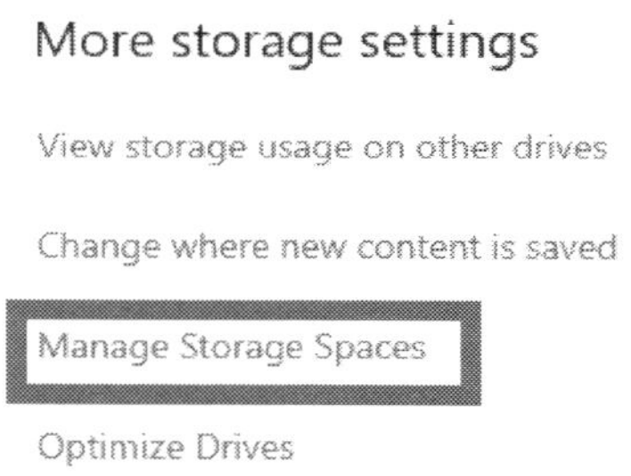

More storage settings

View storage usage on other drives

Change where new content is saved

Manage Storage Spaces

Optimize Drives

o Under manage storage spaces > Select 'Create a new pool and storage space' > Here you can select drives (at least 3 drives) to create storage pool – preferably these drives have to be the same size. You can run the RAID-5 setup son after installing the windows for your new PC. If there are any unformatted drives among the selected three, it's more likely going to be deleted by the windows. You can partly recover this later from the recycle bin. Now click 'Create Pool'.

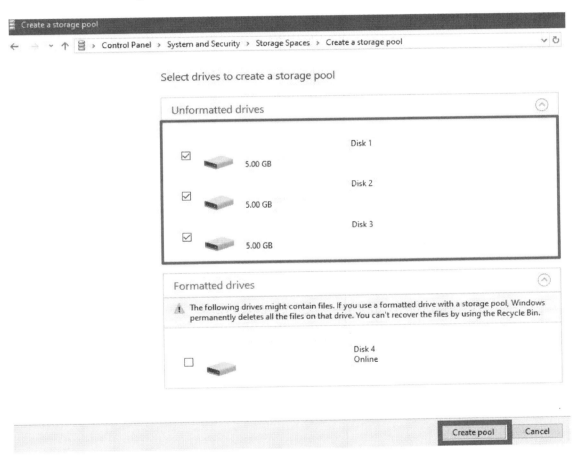

o Here you have to enter the name, resiliency type, and size for the storage space. Under Name: Storage Space > Drive letter: D,E,F etc > File system: NTFS > Resiliency: Select **'parity'**- This is equal to RAID-5 setup.

o Size section – This is important because a pool can be larger than the actual physical capacity, and if you run out of space, you'll need to add more drives, so beware when you change the size option. The formula to calculate the parity of storage space is, maximum=(n-1)/n*maximum. You can't always rely on the formula. Do refer to the sheet below. You can always get the NAS system and select the RAID 5 option. NAS storage system can be a bit expensive.

Example of the calculation: If you create a new storage pool with 3 disks of 4TB each, which gives me a total pool capacity of 12 TB. Now if you create a new storage space from this pool with the Parity resiliency type, you will get a maximum volume space of 8TB. Using the formula, (3-1)/3 x 3 = 11, which is wrong. This is because we should also consider the number of pools and also the pool fault tolerance. So based on the above information, 12 x 66.7% = 8. From this we will have 8GB for use and 4GB will be used for storing parity. It shows that in RAID-5, you will always lose 1 drive for parity storage.

Table 1 - Pool count and fault tolerance

Number of pools	Mirror type	Resiliency overhead	Pool fault tolerance (1)	System fault tolerance (2)
1	Two-way	50%	1 Disk	1 Disk
	Three-way	67%	2 Disks	2 Disks
2	Two-way	50%	1 Disk	2 Disks
	Three-way	67%	2 Disks	4 Disks
3	Two-way	50%	1 Disk	3 Disks
	Three-way	67%	2 Disks	6 Disks
4	Two-way	50%	1 Disk	4 Disks
	Three-way	67%	2 Disks	8 Disks

Now click on the 'Create Storage Space'.

o Once you complete the above steps, the RAID 5 storage
  will be created to start storing files with fault
  tolerance, and if one of the drives fails, all you need
  to do is to replace that drive and the parity of the
  other drives will be used to restore the lost data.

  Traditional HDDs can't be used for this type of RAID-5
  setup. You need to use special HDDs, like Seagate's
  Ironwolf or Western Digital Red.

AMD VS INTEL IN 2020

o The first decision you will need to make when choosing a motherboard is whether you want to go with the AMD or Intel for your CPU. Both offer processor options across a wide variety of different price points and performance levels whether you are putting together a low-cost build for light home use or something powerful enough 3D content creation or gaming & streaming at the same time.

o Since Ryzen has been around, Intel seems non-responsive, doesn't care and ignoring the current issues – these are some of the issues people, in general, have said. Now let's disuse how much of it is true?

o Considering the fact that INTEL has annual releases. Ryzen's release was not taken seriously in the beginning. Intel believed Ryzen to be another effect based processor that promised high core counts that just were very poor in IPC (inter-process communication In computer science, inter-process communication or inter-process communication (IPC) refers specifically to the mechanisms an operating system provides to allow the processes to manage shared data) and did not live up to the hype. Since 2016, AMD has promised a 50% improvement in IPC. They under promised and over delivered. Since then they continuously annually improved that IPC.

o Intel was not ready for such a competition and failed to release any newer improvements to compete with RYZEN.

o Ryzen has caught up to the point where Intel doesn't have anything ready to release as of the time, I'm writing this book.

o When AMD released the Ryzen 3rd Generation processor, with the processor increased to > 7nm. There was a drastic increase in single-core performance. This performance came in par or more with that of the Intel processor.

o Which runs hotter: AMD or INTEL? – As it turns out there are no industry standard ways, we can all agree on reporting the power consumption in terms of TDP of a computer processor. The thermal design power (TDP), sometimes called thermal design point, is the maximum amount of heat generated by a computer chip or component (often a CPU, GPU or system on a chip) that the cooling system in a computer is designed to dissipate under any workload.

LATEST NEWS: INTEL OPTANE MEMORY - POWERFUL OR POINTLESS?

o INTEL OPTANE MEMORY aims to accelerate the performance of your system by RAM caching bits and pieces of your most frequently used programmers so that your programs load faster.

o This is not a new technology by any means but a new hardware implementation, that is fast, affordable and adaptable.

o INTEL OPTANE is using the standard M.2 interface that is available in standard 16GB and 32GB capacities, inside of which is the Intel's new 3D XPOINT memory.

o It actively learns your usage habits and accelerates the low times of your programs that you use the most.

o Its algorithms are identical to Intel's older SSD CACHE technology.

o You can't select which programmers are accelerated.

o It doesn't have more features compared to its older technology SSD CACHE.

o It's around $44 and $77 respectively for 16GB and 32GB.

o Your motherboard having an M.2 slot doesn't mean it will support OPTANE memory. Only the z270 motherboard and a 7th GEN INTEL CPU to support this.

o Another drawback of this is that it will only accelerate your primary boot drive, where your OS is installed.

o Intel OPTANE aims to address the slow performance of spinning hard drives which enables for a cheaper option.

○ With the Intel OPTANE enabled, the PC boot timing is reduced to some extent.

○ Game loading time is significantly reduced. It closely matches that of the SSD.

○ Adobe Photoshop CC loading time is faster, closely similar to that of the SSD.

○ Primary concern: There is no way of knowing how much memory is occupied, caching o your more frequent programs.

○ Primary concern: Price is a big concern especially for the 32GB, $77 which is very high. With just a few dollars more and you can hose a much faster SSD.

MOTHERBOARD STAREDOWN

MSI Performance Gaming AMD Ryzen 1st and 2nd Gen AM4 M.2 USB 3 Crossfire ATX Motherboard (B450 Gaming PRO Carbon AC)

(Image Source: MSI)

B450 GAMING PRO CARBON AC

1	Flash BIOS Button
2	Intel Wireless / Bluetooth
3	Intel Gaming LAN
4	AMD Turbo USB 3.1 Gen2
5	Golden Audio Jacks with S/PDIF

6 Extended Heatsink Design

Leading heatsink design, extended for maximum cooling and performance

7 Gaming heatsinks with Carbon scheme

for maximum cooling and performance

8 DDR4 Boost

Optimized traces and isolated memory circuitry

9 M.2 Shield v2

Thermal enhancement for M.2 devices for best performance

10 2x M.2

NVMe support, up to 32 Gb/s using PCI-Express Gen3 x4, Supports STORE MI

11 PCI-E Steel Armor

Protecting VGA cards against bending and EMI

12 Audio Boost 4 with amplifier

Optimized gaming audio using best components, with Nahimic3

COMPONENTS REQUIRED TO BUILD BUDGET VIDEO EDITING PC 4K VIDEO EDITING

Most of the time, the blog or the different videos you watch doesn't completely add or mention the necessary components and accessories required to build the complete PC, like OS, Antivirus, Extra storage, sometimes even Graphics card, etc. Here I have included 99% of the items required. In a blog, these components cost
Under Rs 1,00,000/$1000.

1. MOTHERBOARD

MSI Performance Gaming AMD Ryzen 1st and 2nd Gen AM4 M.2 USB 3 Crossfire ATX Motherboard (B450 Gaming PRO Carbon AC) Rs 14,439/$149.97
https://amzn.to/2SYGJBV
[You can click/copy the link given to buy the product]

2. CPU

AMD Ryzen 7 2700X Desktop Processor 8 Cores up to 4.3GHz 20MB Cache AM4 Socket (YD270XBGAFBOX) Rs 19,199/$169.99
https://amzn.to/2IObVtX
[You can click/copy the link given to buy the product]

3. RAM

CORSAIR Vengeance LPX 16GB (1x16GB) DDR4 3200MHZ UDIMM C16 Desktop RAM Memory Module Rs 12,400/$156
https://amzn.to/2HT9n11

[You can click/copy the link given to buy the product]

4. NVMe SSD

Samsung 970 EVO Plus 500GB PCIe NVMe M.2 (2280) Internal Solid State Drive (SSD) (MZ-V7S500) Rs 10,799/$87.99
https://amzn.to/3c5IlkI
[You can click/copy the link given to buy the product]

5. GRAPHICS CARD

MSI RX 580 Armor 8G OC Gaming Radeon RX 580 GDDR5 8GB Crossfire VR Ready FinFET DirectX 12 Graphics Card Rs 15,700/$212.95
https://amzn.to/2veQfrp
[You can click/copy the link given to buy the product]

6. POWER SUPPLY

EVGA SuperNOVA 120-GP-0650-X1, 650 G+, 80 Plus Gold 650W, Fully Modular, FDB Fan, Includes Power ON Self Tester, Power Supply Rs 17,970.82/$98.99
This product was imported to my country from US, price includes:
Shipping & handling - Rs 4,234
Import Duty: Rs 5,134.82 (60%)
Actual Price: Rs 8,602/$98.99
[OR]
EVGA Supernova 650 G3, 80 Plus Gold 650W (Similar) Rs 19,739/$115.09
https://amzn.to/2Pj6HOH
[**You can click/copy the link given to buy the product**]
You can always check the required power for you PC in
https://in.msi.com/power-supply-calculator
Here you enter the details about the different components to be used.

7. CASE

NZXT H510 - Compact ATX Mid-Tower PC Gaming Case - Front I/O USB Type-C Port - Tempered Glass Side Panel - Cable Management System - Water-Cooling Ready - Steel Construction - Black Rs 6,445/$69.98
https://amzn.to/2HUPAyg
[You can click/copy the link given to buy the product]

8. MOLEX CABLE

CRJ 4-Pin Molex to 2 x 3-Pin 12V PC Case Fan Power Adapter Cable Rs 2,052/$4.99
https://amzn.to/391fAUn
[You can click/copy the link given to buy the product]

9. UPS

APC BX1100C-IN 1100VA/660W UPS System for Personal Computers and Home Entertainment System Rs 5,995/$84.11
https://amzn.to/37ZxzcD
[You can click/copy the link given to buy the product]

10. WINDOWS 10 HOME
10,972.82/$153.79

Go to the MICROSOFT.COM and download the operating system. I wouldn't suggest the OEM Product Key

11. BITDEFENDER TOTAL SECURITY
725/$10.13

https://amzn.to/3aftMcP
[3 YEARS - You can click/copy the link given to buy the product]
https://amzn.to/37VO5uc
[1 YEAR - You can click/copy the link given to buy the product]

12. STORAGE DEVICE [ADDITIONAL]

Western Digital WD10EZEX 1TB Internal Hard Drive for Desktop
(Blue) Rs 3,150/
https://amzn.to/2PpHdyK
[You can click/copy the link given to buy the product]

TOTAL = Rs $1246.88/1,19,847.64

COMPONENTS REQUIRED TO BUILD BUDGET VIDEO EDITING PC 1080P VIDEO EDITING (NOT GOOD FOR 4K)

Most of the time, the blog or the different videos you watch doesn't completely add or mention the necessary components and accessories required to build the complete PC, like OS, Antivirus, Extra storage, sometimes even Graphics card, etc. Here I have included 99% of the items required. In a blog, these components cost Under Rs 60,000/$600.

1. MOTHERBOARD

MSI Performance Gaming AMD Ryzen 1st and 2nd Gen AM4 M.2 USB 3 DDR4 DVI HDMI Crossfire ATX Motherboard (B450 Gaming Plus)
Rs 9,999/$104.99
https://amzn.to/3caH6Rq
[You can click/copy the link given to buy the product]

2. CPU

AMD Ryzen 5 3400G up to 4.2GHz 4 Core 8 Threads AM4 Socket 6MB Cache with Radeon RX Vega 11 Graphics Desktop Processor & Wraith Spire Thermal Solution (YD3400C5FHBOX) (YD2400C5FBBOX) Rs 13,080/$170.99
https://amzn.to/2TjWpOU
[You can click/copy the link given to buy the product]

3. RAM

2 x Corsair Vengeance LPX 8GB DDR4 3000 (PC4-24000) C16 PC
Memory (CMK8GX4M1D3000C16) Rs 6,950/$91.99
https://amzn.to/2PpD8up
[You can click/copy the link given to buy the product]

4. NVMe SSD

CRUCIAL P1 500GB 3D NAND NVMe PCIe M.2 SSD (CT500P1SSD8) Rs
5,750/$77.48
https://amzn.to/3caNR5N
[You can click/copy the link given to buy the product]

5. GRAPHICS CARD

Gigabyte GeForce GTX 1650 OC 4GB GDDR5 Graphics Card, 2X 80
mm Windforce Fans (GV-N1650OC-4GD) Rs 12,499/$149.99
https://amzn.to/2TdKkuE
[You can click/copy the link given to buy the product]

6. POWER SUPPLY

Corsair VS550 550W Active PFC 80 Plus Power Supply (Black)
Rs 3,498/$57.98
https://amzn.to/2VpBCvV
[You can click/copy the link given to buy the product]
You can always check the required power for you PC in
https://in.msi.com/power-supply-calculator

7. CASE

Corsair Carbide SPEC-05 Mid-Tower Gaming Case - Black Rs
2,999/$49.99
https://amzn.to/385KZ73
[You can click/copy the link given to buy the product]

8. MOLEX CABLE (OPTIONAL)

CRJ 4-Pin Molex to 2 x 3-Pin 12V PC Case Fan Power Adapter
Cable Rs 2,052/$4.99

https://amzn.to/391fAUn
[You can click/copy the link given to buy the product]

9. UPS

APC BX1100C-IN 1100VA/660W UPS System for Personal Computers and Home Entertainment System Rs 5,995/$84.11
https://amzn.to/37ZxzcD
[You can click/copy the link given to buy the product]

10. WINDOWS 10 HOME
10,972.82/$153.79

Go to the MICROSOFT.COM and download the operating system. I wouldn't suggest the OEM Product Key

11. BITDEFENDER TOTAL SECURITY
725/$10.13

https://amzn.to/3aftMcP
[3 YEARS - You can click/copy the link given to buy the product]
https://amzn.to/37VO5uc
[1 YEAR - You can click/copy the link given to buy the product]

12. STORAGE DEVICE [ADDITIONAL]

Western Digital WD10EZEX 1TB Internal Hard Drive for Desktop (Blue) Rs 3,150/$47.99
https://amzn.to/2PpHdyK
[You can click/copy the link given to buy the product]

TOTAL = Rs 75,617/$999.43

ENTRY LEVEL COMPONENTS REQUIRED TO BUILD BUDGET VIDEO EDITING PC 1080P VIDEO EDITING (NOT GOOD FOR 4K)

Most of the time, the blog or the different videos you watch doesn't completely add or mention the necessary components and accessories required to build the complete PC, like OS, Antivirus, Extra storage, sometimes even Graphics card, etc. Here I have included 99% of the items required. In a blog, these components cost Under Rs 50,000/$500.

1. MOTHERBOARD

ASRock MicroATX Motherboard (B450M PRO4) Rs 7,999/$75
https://amzn.to/2ThBig5
[You can click/copy the link given to buy the product]

2. CPU

AMD Ryzen 5 1600 Desktop Processor 6 Cores up to 3.6GHz 19MB Cache AM4 Socket (YD1600BBAEBOX) Rs 7,849/$85
https://amzn.to/2SZ0JUK
[You can click/copy the link given to buy the product]

3. RAM

2 x Corsair Vengeance LPX 8GB DDR4 3000 (PC4-24000) C16 PC Memory (CMK8GX4M1D3000C16) Rs 6,950/$91.99
https://amzn.to/2PpD8up
[You can click/copy the link given to buy the product]

4. NVMe SSD

CRUCIAL P1 500GB 3D NAND NVMe PCIe M.2 SSD (CT500P1SSD8) Rs 5,750/$77.48
https://amzn.to/3caNR5N
[You can click/copy the link given to buy the product]

5. GRAPHICS CARD

Gigabyte GTX 1650 OC 4GB GDDR5 Graphics Card, 2X 80 mm Windforce Fans (GV-N1650OC-4GD) Rs 12,499/$149.99
https://amzn.to/2TdKkuE
[You can click/copy the link given to buy the product]

6. POWER SUPPLY

Corsair VS550 550W Active PFC 80 Plus Power Supply (Black) Rs 3,498/$57.98
https://amzn.to/2VpBCvV
[You can click/copy the link given to buy the product]
You can always check the required power for you PC in
https://in.msi.com/power-supply-calculator

7. CASE

Corsair Carbide SPEC-05 Mid-Tower Gaming Case - Black Rs 2,999/$49.99
https://amzn.to/385KZ73
[You can click/copy the link given to buy the product]

8. MOLEX CABLE (OPTIONAL)

CRJ 4-Pin Molex to 2 x 3-Pin 12V PC Case Fan Power Adapter Cable Rs 2,052/$4.99
https://amzn.to/391fAUn
[You can click/copy the link given to buy the product]

9. UPS

APC BX1100C-IN 1100VA/660W UPS System for Personal Computers and Home Entertainment System Rs 5,995/$84.11
https://amzn.to/37ZxzcD
[You can click/copy the link given to buy the product]

10. **WINDOWS 10 HOME**
10,972.82/$153.79

Go to the MICROSOFT.COM and download the operating system. I wouldn't suggest the OEM Product Key

11. **BITDEFENDER TOTAL SECURITY**
725/$10.13

https://amzn.to/3aftMcP
[3 YEARS - You can click/copy the link given to buy the product]
https://amzn.to/37VO5uc
[1 YEAR - You can click/copy the link given to buy the product]

12. **STORAGE DEVICE [ADDITIONAL]**

Western Digital WD10EZEX 1TB Internal Hard Drive for Desktop (Blue) Rs 3,150/$47.99
https://amzn.to/2PpHdyK
[You can click/copy the link given to buy the product]

TOTAL = Rs 68,386.82/$883.45

ACCESSORIES REQUIRED TO BUILD PC

- Philips Screwdriver – Philips Magnetic

- Workspace: Wooden table covered with **ESD Sheet [https://amzn.to/3c7DDD7 – full set, Sheet with Wrist band]**, ESD Sheet further connected to the earth of a 3-PIN plug socket (Always check the earth of the 3-PIN plug if there is any electricity in the socket by using a tester screwdriver) & **Wrist band [above]** further connected to the ESD Sheet.

- ESD Gloves **[https://amzn.to/2TeuX5f]** – Some people might say, "Use it", others, "Don't use it". But I say," Use it". Don't take the risk, especially when it comes to your expensive PC components.

- Box opening Knife

- Pen Torch – Light source

- Scissor – To cut Zip Tie, etc

- Zip tie – It usually comes with the CASE **[https://amzn.to/390lapT]** This comes in an ESD pouch.

- 1 x 8-16GB Pen drive (1 – BIOS/UEFI, 2 – Windows 10 Pro), 8GB -> **[https://amzn.to/2T0dQ8s]** OR 16GB -> **[https://amzn.to/2VyIyHx]**

- Pen/Pencil

- Multiple metal cups (To keep the screws separate)

- Keyboard & Mouse Combo – Wired [https://amzn.to/3c0Hamy]

    - Screwdriver Tester – Stanley Black & Decker Spark Detecting Screwdriver 66-120, 100-500V AC – To check electrical leakage into the earth of the 3-PIN plug, where the ESD Sheet is connected to.

    - Mirror (Small standing) – To see the reflection of the I/O of the motherboard when inserted through the I/O Shield during motherboard installation **[https://amzn.to/2v5AWkV]**

    - Table Lamp (Can be adjusted and pointed)

WORK AREA PREPARATION

o Switch ON the air conditioner when you start building the PC if it's too humid and sweaty. As the sweaty hand and the dripping sweat can damage the circuit boards. A decent amount of humidity is good as it can minimize the static build-up in your body.

o Lay down ESD Sheets on the wooden table you will be building the PC. Wear an ESD wrist band and plug it to the ESD sheet. Connect the ESD sheet further to the earth of the 3-PIN plug connected to the wall socket with *the power switched off*. Make sure there is *no power leakage* to the earth of the 3-PIN plug by using a *tester screwdriver*.

o Keep small metallic magnetic bowls next to each component to sort out and keep screws, nut, standoffs, etc safe from losing.

  Wash hand thoroughly before starting to build your PC to remove dirt and oil from your hands.

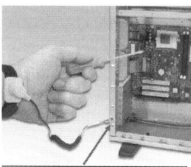

Connect to unpainted metal surface

ESD GLOVES

CASE UNBOXING
&
INSTALLATION

○ Unbox by cutting on top of the case box with a knife away from your side as a precaution.

○ Place the opened box upside down carefully without the case falling out. Hold the case with your hand while turning the box and keep it upside down on the table.

○ Now use the hands to grip on the groove on either lower side of the box. Lift the box shaking it gently to release the case from the box, on the table.

○ AVOID STATIC ELECTRICITY SHOCK from the plastic pouch covering the case as there will be static build upon it. This can be avoided by placing your elbow on the plastic cover to absorb the static electricity, which is painless.

○ Remove both the side panels from the case. If one side of the case is a glass panel. Gently remove it, without removing the protective plastic film covering the glass. This film protects the glass from scratches, dust, dirt, oil, and fingerprints. Remove it after the installation process is complete. ***Dispose of the plastic properly.***

○ Use the case carton box to dispose of waste if any.

○ Now go through the CASE layout. Study them. Compare the case manually with that of the case. Spend some time with just the case, planning your installation process.

○ Take the ***I/O shield*** from the motherboard box. Attach the I/O SHIELD to the back of the case. Be careful ***not to cut your hands*** as certain areas of the I/O shield can be sharp. You can use the bottom of the screwdriver to get the corners of the shield in place. Sometimes it is hard to reach with the hands. Push it all the way out till the shield is in place. If connecting the ESD wrist band to the CASE, make sure it is connected to the non-painted part of the CASE.

○ The metallic CASE can often be used to discharge static from your body by touching it.

Image Source: NZXT

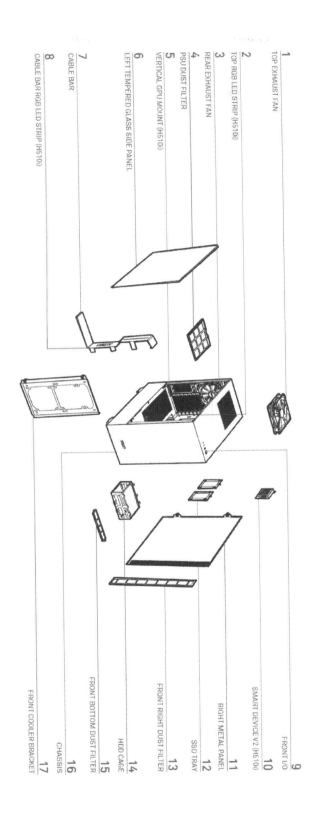

1 TOP EXHAUST FAN

2 TOP RGB LED STRIP (H510i)

3 REAR EXHAUST FAN

4 PSU DUST FILTER

5 VERTICAL GPU MOUNT (H510i)

6 LEFT TEMPERED GLASS SIDE PANEL

7 CABLE BAR

8 CABLE BAR RGB LED STRIP (H510i)

9 FRONT I/O

10 SMART DEVICE V2 (H510i)

11 RIGHT METAL PANEL

12 SSD TRAY

13 FRONT RIGHT DUST FILTER

14 HDD CAGE

15 FRONT BOTTOM DUST FILTER

16 CHASSIS

17 FRONT COOLER BRACKET

PANEL REMOVAL
EXTRACCIÓN DE PANEL
RETRAIT DU PANNEAU
BLENDE ENTFERNEN
RIMOZIONE DEL PANNELLO
REMOÇÃO DOS PAINÉIS
СНЯТИЕ ПАНЕЛИ
패널 제거
パネルの取り外し
卸下面板
移除面板

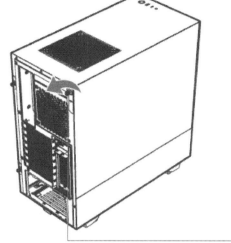

1 UNSCREW CAPTIVE THUMB SCREW

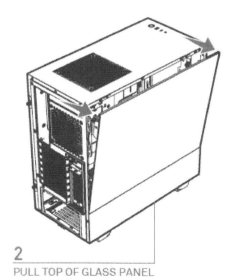

2 PULL TOP OF GLASS PANEL

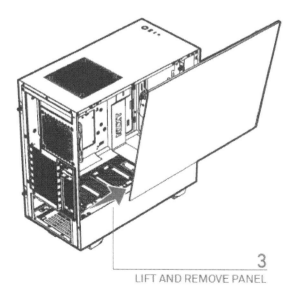

3 LIFT AND REMOVE PANEL

ACCESSORY BOX

CAJA DE ACCESORIOS
BOITE D'ACCESSOIRES
ZUBEHÖRSET
SCATOLA DEGLI ACCESSORI
CAIXA DE ACESSÓRIOS
КОРОБКА С ПРИНАДЛЕЖНОСТЯМИ
악세사리 박스
部品箱（説明書入り）
配件盒
零件盒

E Standoff 6-32 x 6.5+4mm
x1

A Hexagon screw 6-32 x 6mm
x4

F Standoff wrench
x1

B Screw 6-32 x 5mm
x21

G Cable tie
x10

C Screw M3 x 5mm
x12

H Breakout Cable
x1

D Screw KB5 x 10mm
x8

I 3.5mm Headset Audio Jack splitter
x1

CABLE MANAGEMENT SYSTEM
SISTEMA DE GESTIÓN DE CABLES
SYSTÈME DE CÂBLAGE
KABELMANAGEMENTSYSTEM
SISTEMA DI GESTIONE DEI CAVI
SISTEMA DE GERENCIAMENTO DE CABOS
СИСТЕМА ПРОКЛАДКИ КАБЕЛЕЙ
케이블 관리 시스템
ケーブルマネジメントシステム
理线管理系统
整線管理系統

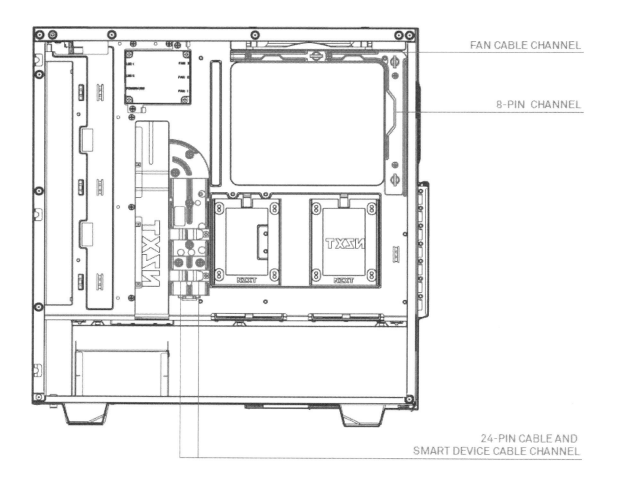

FAN CABLE CHANNEL

8-PIN CHANNEL

24-PIN CABLE AND
SMART DEVICE CABLE CHANNEL

MOTHERBOARD INSTALLATION

INSTALACIÓN DE LA PLACA BASE
INSTALLATION DE LA CARTE MÈRE
INSTALLATION DER HAUPTPLATINE
INSTALLAZIONE DELLA SCHEDA MADRE
INSTALAÇÃO DA PLACA PRINCIPAL
УСТАНОВКА СИСТЕМНОЙ ПЛАТЫ
마더보드 설치
マザーボードの装着
主板安装
主機板安裝

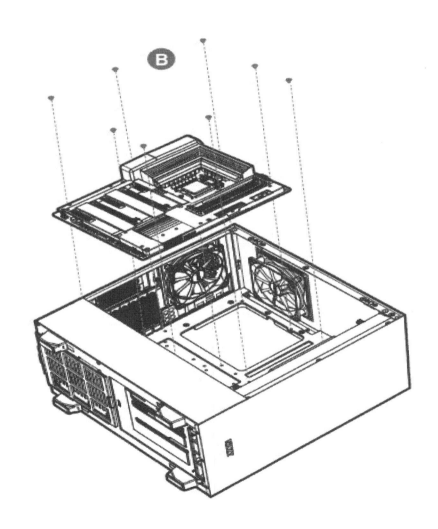

POWER SUPPLY INSTALLATION

INSTALACIÓN DE LA FUENTE DE ALIMENTACIÓN
INSTALLATION DE L'ALIMENTATION
INSTALLATION DER STROMVERSORGUNG
INSTALLAZIONE DELL'ALIMENTATORE
INSTALAÇÃO DA FONTE DE ALIMENTAÇÃO
УСТАНОВКА ИСТОЧНИКА ПИТАНИЯ
전원공급장치 설치
電源の装着
电源安装
電源安裝

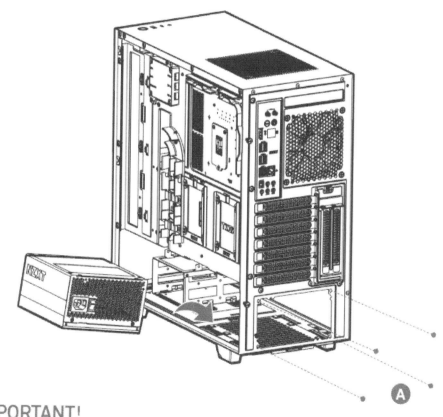

IMPORTANT!
Install the PSU with the fan facing down.

BUTTONS AND I/O

BOTONES Y E/S
BOUTONS ET E/S
TASTEN UND E/A
PULSANTI E I/O
BOTÕES E E/S
КНОПКИ И РАЗЪЕМЫ ВВОДА/ВЫВОДА
버튼 및 I/O
ボタンおよび I/O
按钮和 I/O
按鈕和 I/O

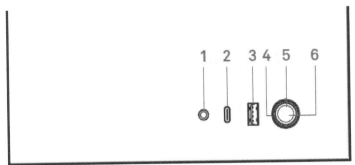

1. HD Audio Output	1. Uscita audio HD	1. HDオーディオ
2. USB 3.1 Gen2 Type-C	2. USB 3.1 Gen2 Type-C	2. USB 3.1 Gen2 Type-C
3. USB 3.1 Gen1 Type-A	3. USB 3.1 Gen1 Type-A	3. USB 3.1 Gen1 Type-A
4. HDD LED	4. LED HDD	4. HDD LED
5. Power LED	5. LED alimentazione	5. パワーLED
6. Power switch	6. Interruttore d'alimentazione	6. 電源スイッチ
1. Salida de audio HD	1. Saída de áudio HD	1. 高清音频输出
2. USB 3.1 Gen2 Type-C	2. USB 3.1 Gen2 Type-C	2. USB 3.1 Gen2 Type-C
3. USB 3.1 Gen1 Type-A	3. USB 3.1 Gen1 Type-A	3. USB 3.1 Gen1 Type-A
4. LED de unidad de disco duro	4. LED do HDD	4. HDD LED
5. LED de alimentación	5. LED de alimentação	5. 电源LED
6. Interruptor de encendido	6. Interruptor de alimentação	6. 电源开关
1. Sortie audio HD	1. Звуковой выход HD	1. 高清音頻輸出
2. USB 3.1 Gen2 Type-C	2. USB 3.1 Gen2 Type-C	2. USB 3.1 Gen2 Type-C
3. USB 3.1 Gen1 Type-A	3. USB 3.1 Gen1 Type-A	3. USB 3.1 Gen1 Type-A
4. Témoin disque dur	4. Индикатор жесткого диска	4. HDD LED
5. Témoin d'alimentation	5. Индикатор питания	5. 電源LED
6. Interrupteur marche/arrêt	6. Выключатель питания	6. 電源開關
1. HD-Audioausgang	1. HD 오디오 출력	
2. USB 3.1 Gen2 Type-C	2. USB 3.1 Gen2 Type-C	
3. USB 3.1 Gen1 Type-A	3. USB 3.1 Gen1 Type-A	
4. Festplatten-LED	4. HDD LED	
5. Betriebs-LED	5. 전원 LED	
6. Netzschalter	6. 전원 스위치	

EXPANSION CARD INSTALLATION

INSTALACIÓN DE LA TARJETA DE EXPANSIÓN
INSTALLATION DE LA CARTE D'EXTENSION
INSTALLATION DER ERWEITERUNGSKARTE
INSTALLAZIONE DELLA SCHEDA D'ESPANSIONE
INSTALAÇÃO DA PLACA DE EXPANSÃO
УСТАНОВКА ПЛАТЫ РАСШИРЕНИЯ
확장 카드 설치
拡張カードの装着
扩展卡安装
擴充卡安裝

UNSCREW THE THUMB SCREW

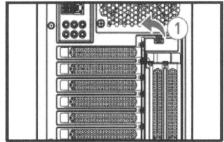

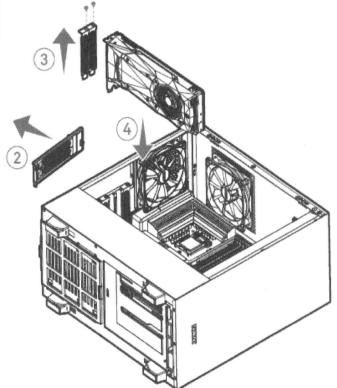

HORIZONTAL GPU MOUNT

FAN AND RADIATOR SUPPORT

COMPATIBILIDAD DE VENTILADORES Y RADIADORES
PRISE EN CHARGE DES RADIATEURS ET VENTILATEURS
LÜFTER- UND KÜHLER-UNTERSTÜTZUNG
SUPPORTO VENTOLE E RADIATORE
SUPORTE PARA VENTOINHA E A RADIADOR
СОВМЕСТИМЫЕ РАДИАТОР И ВЕНТИЛЯТОР
팬 및 라디에이터 지원
対応ファンおよびラジエータ
风扇和散热器支持
風扇和散熱排支援

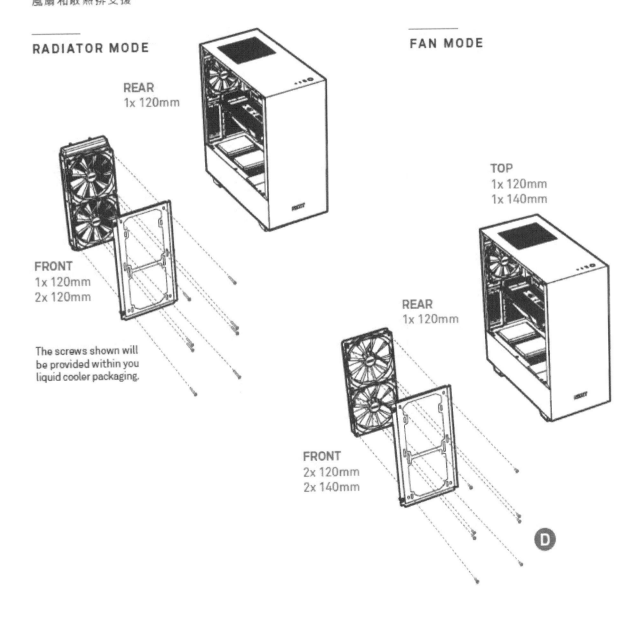

RADIATOR MODE

REAR
1x 120mm

FRONT
1x 120mm
2x 120mm

The screws shown will
be provided within you
liquid cooler packaging.

FAN MODE

TOP
1x 120mm
1x 140mm

REAR
1x 120mm

FRONT
2x 120mm
2x 140mm

D

CABLE CONNECTIONS

DISCO DE ADMINISTRACIÓN DE CABLES
CONNEXIONS DES CÂBLES
KABELVERBINDUNGEN
COLLEGAMENTI DEI CAVI
LIGAÇÕES DE CABOS
ПОДКЛЮЧЕНИЕ КАБЕЛЕЙ
케이블 연결
ケーブル接続
线缆连接
線路連接

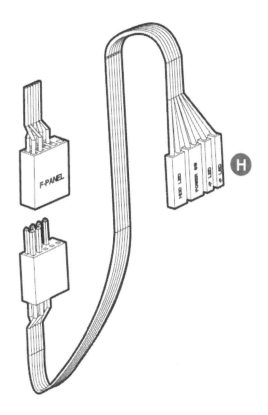

FOR INTEL STANDARD F_PANEL HEADER USE   FOR NON-INTEL STANDARD F_PANEL HEADER USE

POWER SUPPLY INSTALLATION

INSTALACIÓN DE LA FUENTE DE ALIMENTACIÓN
INSTALLATION DE L'ALIMENTATION
INSTALLATION DER STROMVERSORGUNG
INSTALLAZIONE DELL'ALIMENTATORE
INSTALAÇÃO DA FONTE DE ALIMENTAÇÃO
УСТАНОВКА ИСТОЧНИКА ПИТАНИЯ
전원공급장치 설치
電源の装着
电源安装
電源安裝

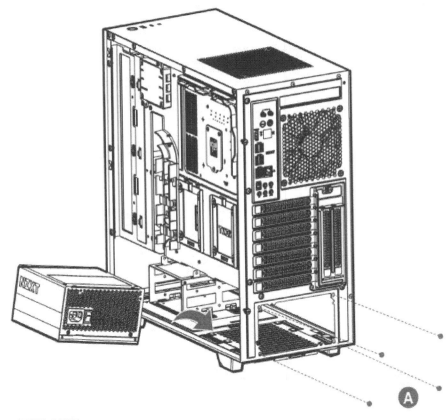

IMPORTANT!
Install the PSU with the fan facing down.

EVGA POWER SUPPLY:

- ○ Observe & study the motherboard layouts, about various connections, plan where, how many and how to connect these cables to the motherboard.

- ○ In this step, we are going to unbox the EVGA power supply. Connect the appropriate wire before testing it. This applies to a completely modular power supply.

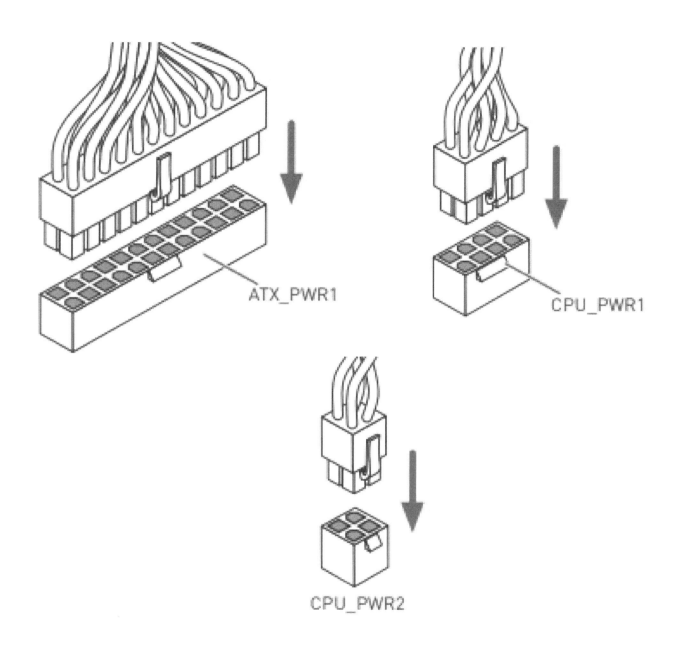

ATX_PWR1

CPU_PWR1

CPU_PWR2

Based on the motherboard cables to connect (provided) to the power supply are:

1) *Motherboard Cable/ ATX Cable (24 pin connector)*

- The first cable to install on your power supply will be the **Motherboard cable (24 pin connector)**. MB is inscribed on the panel next to the modular ports, short for 'Motherboard'.
- Comes with 2 headed cable on one side, which will be connected to the power supply and a single-headed 24-pin to the motherboard.
- Now line up to attach the Motherboard cable to the modular port. The port comes with 2 sections complementary to the 2 heads of the provided appropriate cable.
- Put the cable management name tag on the cable.

2) *CPU Cable/EPS Cable (8 pins to 2 x 4 pins)*

- Attach the **8-pin cable to CPU_PWR1 (Motherboard Header)**
- Name tag the cable.

3) *PCIe/VGA Cable*

- This cable connects PSU (Power supply unit) to the Graphics card.
- The cable is selected as per Graphics Card header. Comes as (i) 8-pin to 6+2 pin single cable (ii) 8-pin to 6+2 pin with a supplementary 6 pin.
- Select the **8-pin to 6+2 pin (Depends on the GPU power supply socket)**.
- Some extreme GPU requires more power, this is where the 8 pin to 6 pin with supplementary 6 pin is connected.
- Name tag the cable

4) *SATA Power Cable*

- This cable supply power from PSU to Hard disk (HDD), solid state drive (SSD) and optical drives.
- Check how many drives you will be connecting and take a cable for each. [1 x power supply cable & 1 x data cable for each]
- If you are planning to add more drives, pre-attach cables in advance.
- SATA power cable —> SATA1-6 on the motherboard.
- A second SATA data cable is connected between the drive and the motherboard.
- *IMPORTANT: Don't fold the data cable as this may lead to loss of data.*

5) *Molex Connection*

- SATA cable (Female 4 Pin) from the PSU sometimes branches to SATA power cable and Molex connectors.

Connect the Molex (female) power cable to a separate Molex (male) cable to power fan controllers, LED lights, etc.

To test the power supply unit (PSU) is working (Only applicable if ECO MODE present in EVGA power supply)

a. Switch off the power supply button indicated by 'o' for OFF & '|' for ON.

   |

b. Now use the 'power supply tester' piece that comes with the box. This is a cap to cover the motherboard cable end that is connected to the power supply to protect from accidentally touching the end of the motherboard cable. Line up the tester piece with the motherboard cable 24 pin connector and press to each other. The connection is closed now.

c. Now connect the power supply to the AC power. Switch on both the AC power and the power supply switch.

d. If the fan is running smooth. The test is completed and passed.

e. This works only if the EVGA power supply comes with ECO MODE. If not, this test cannot be performed.

f. I ran the test this without the Eco mode (220V in my country) and performed it to success. Since in

g. US its 110V, it's should either be 50% or more to run the test successfully or can be done with ECO Mode.

HDD/SSD INSTALLATION

- o Different CASE is designed differently and their way to install Hard disk (HDD) as well. So always go through the product manual before installation.

- o I will give an example of how to install HDD in NZXT H510 model CASE, as depicted in the pictures below.

- o The newer version is slightly different. The HDD trays are screwed to the bottom of the case.

- o Place the Case sideways to expose the bottom of the case. Remove the screws attaching the HDD trays to the case. Take the HDD tray outside.

- o Now insert the HDD into the tray. Screw the HDD firmly to the tray.

- o Put the tray back to the same place. Screw it back to the case tightly.

- o Keep the case straight and check if the tray and HDD are safely secured.

PLEASE REFER TO THE IMAGES BELOW FOR HDD/SSD INSTALLATION

HDD DRIVE INSTALLATION

INSTALACIÓN DE LA UNIDAD DE DISCO DURO
INSTALLATION DE LECTEUR HDD
HDD-LAUFWERKSINSTALLATION
INSTALLAZIONE DELL'UNITÀ HDD
INSTALAÇÀO DA PLACA DE EXPANSÀO
УСТАНОВКА ЖЕСТКОГО ДИСКА
HDD 드라이브 설치
HDD装着
HDD 驱动器安装
硬碟安装

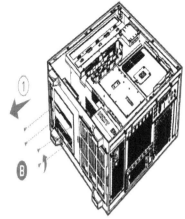

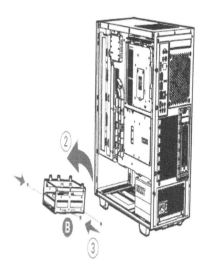

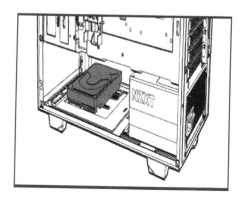

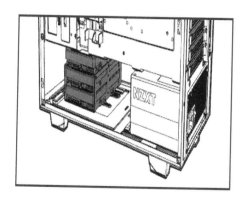

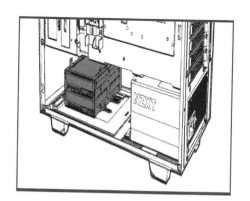

SSD DRIVE INSTALLATION

INSTALACIÓN DE LA UNIDAD DE DISCO DE ESTADO SÓLIDO
INSTALLATION DU DISQUE SSD
SSD-LAUFWERKSINSTALLATION
INSTALLAZIONE DELL'UNITÀ SDD
INSTALAÇÃO DA PLACA DE EXPANSÃO
УСТАНОВКА ТВЕРДОТЕЛЬНОГО НАКОПИТЕЛЯ
SSD 드라이브 설치
SSD 装着
SSD 驱动器安装
SSD 安裝

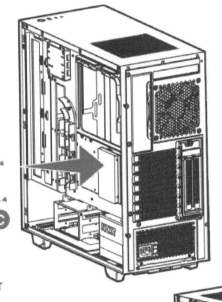

VERTICAL MOUNT

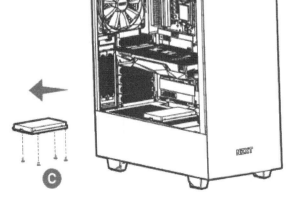

HORIZONTAL MOUNT

UNBOXING THE COMPONENTS

GRAPHICS CARD:

- ○ Don't remove it from the ESD bag.
- ○ Last one to install.
- ○ Don't forget to remove all the protective plastic film on the graphics card before installation.
- ○ Fan facing down – For installation.
- ○ Type of PCIe cable required – 8-PIN. The second picture indicates the type of PIN required.

M.2 NVMe SSD CARD:

- o Get the small screw you get from the motherboard box. The nut which is required for this screw either comes in the motherboard box or it is attached to the motherboard next to the M.2 Slot.
- o Keep the screw close to the SSD CARD to be installed.
- o The image below shows SAMSUNG 970 EVO PLUS M.2 NVMe 500GB SSD Card.

(Image Source: Samsung)

MEMORY (RAM):

o Keep it aside after unboxing.

(Image Source: Corsair)

MOTHERBOARD:

- Wear ESD gloves when unboxing.

- Keep it aside on the ESD sheet laid out on the wooden table work area.

- Keep the product registration card aside. Write the serial number (S/N, available on the product box or on the motherboard) on the registration card.

- The MSI manufacturer's website will show how to find the serial number.

- Write the names of the different connecting cables on the 'cable management sticker' for better management.

- Stick the case badge sticker available in the motherboard box later.

- Case STANDOFF notification available in the motherboard box - READ WELL

- Take the SATA data cables needed and keep the rest in the box.

- Keep the I/O shield next to the motherboard (If not already installed)

- Keep the Wi-Fi Antennas aside.

- RGB lighting cable [Read about it in the manual].

- Place the M.2 screw that comes in the motherboard box, next to the SSD card.

- Remove all the plastic pouches from the components. Save them for later use.

Use ESD gloves for removing components from their respective pouch.

Image Courtesy: MSI

Case stand-off notification

Before installing the motherboard into the case, install first the **necessary** mounting stand-off required for a motherboard on the mounting plate in the case.

To prevent damage to the motherboard, any contact/ **unnecessary** mounting stand-off between the motherboard circuitry and the computer case is **prohibited**. Especially for **unnecessary** mounting stand-off installation, the **Case standoff keep out zone** signs will be marked on the backside of motherboard (as shown below) to serve as a warning to user.

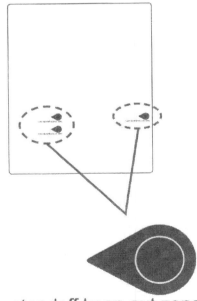

Case standoff keep out zone

MOTHERBOARD PREPARATION

1. _M.2 NVMe SSD CARD INSTALLATION_:

o Keep the M.2 screw & nut from the motherboard box ready. The nut can either be present along with the screw in the motherboard box or attached to the motherboard itself.

o Remove the HEAT SINK SHIELD by removing the screw attached to it.

o Now screw the M.2 nut on the bottom area of the shield on the motherboard. [This applies to M.2 SSD without HEATSINK or longer M.2 SSD cards]. SAMSUNG 970 EVO PLUS M.2 NVMe 500GB SSD Card doesn't require this.

o IMPORTANT: Align the notch of the M.2 SSD card with that of the motherboard socket (M.2 Slot) at a 30° angle and insert it. Now lower the SSD card.

o Tighten the M.2 screw on the M.2 nut. [This applies to M.2 SSD without HEATSINK or longer M.2 SSD cards]. SAMSUNG 970 EVO PLUS M.2 NVMe 500GB SSD Card doesn't require this.

o Remove the protective film and round rubber from underneath the shield. Now lower the Shield.

o Tighten the Heat Sink back on the motherboard with the provided screw, thus securing it.

Remove the protective plastic film covering the top of the heat sink shield.

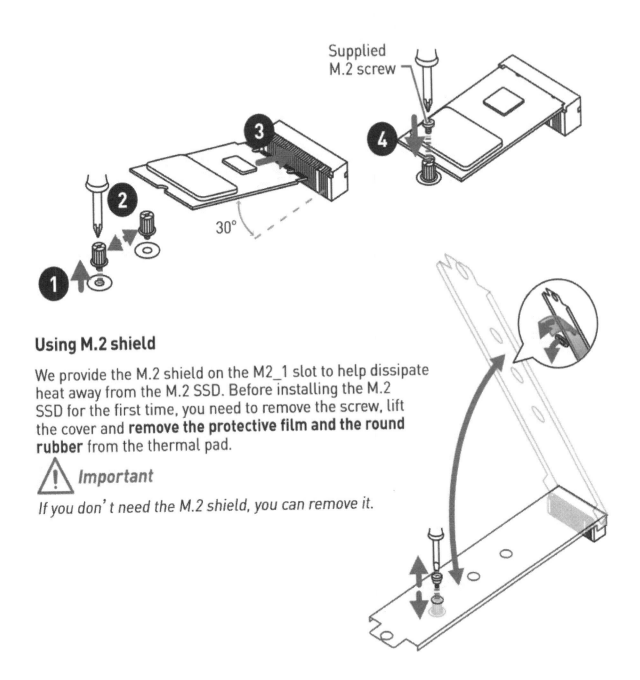

Using M.2 shield

We provide the M.2 shield on the M2_1 slot to help dissipate heat away from the M.2 SSD. Before installing the M.2 SSD for the first time, you need to remove the screw, lift the cover and **remove the protective film and the round rubber** from the thermal pad.

⚠️ Important

If you don't need the M.2 shield, you can remove it.

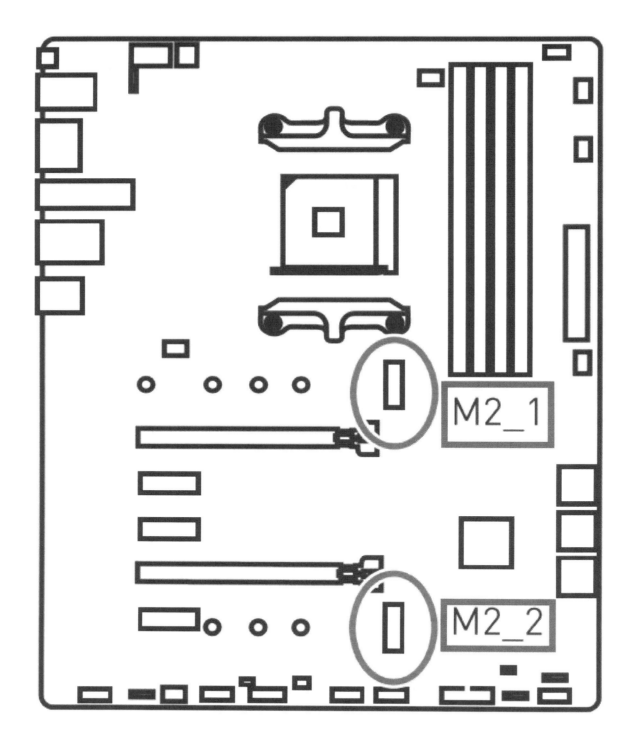

2. _MEMORY CARD INSTALLATION (RAM)_:

o IMPORTANT: Always insert the memory card in the **DIMMA2** slot first.

o Thus, installing RAM before CPU COOLER FAN makes the unobstructed installation of the later and viz.

o Read the motherboard manual to confirm what slot to install the RAM in.

o A small picture depiction next to the slots on the motherboard is also there to confirm what slots to insert.

o Read the manual on which side should the RAM face while you insert it into the slots. It can also be confirmed by placing the RAM at the slot without inserting and see if the notch of the RAM is coinciding with that of the slot.

o Open the latches found on either side of the RAM slot. In some cases, only one side latches can be opened usually the right-sided latch, other ones remain fixed.

o Line up the notch at the bottom of the RAM cards with that of the motherboard slots before pushing them gently into the slots with a click of affirmation at the end.

o IMPORTANT: If both the **RAM cards are on the same level** means they are **installed properly**.

Refer to the pictures below for more details.

DIMM Slots

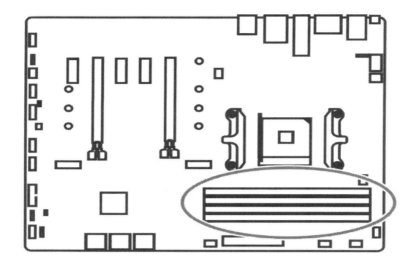

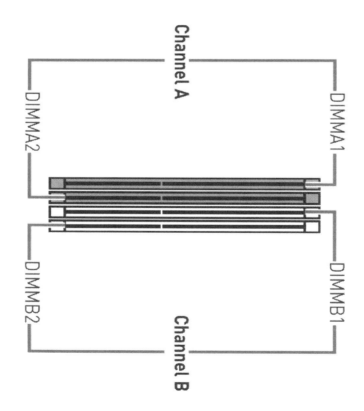

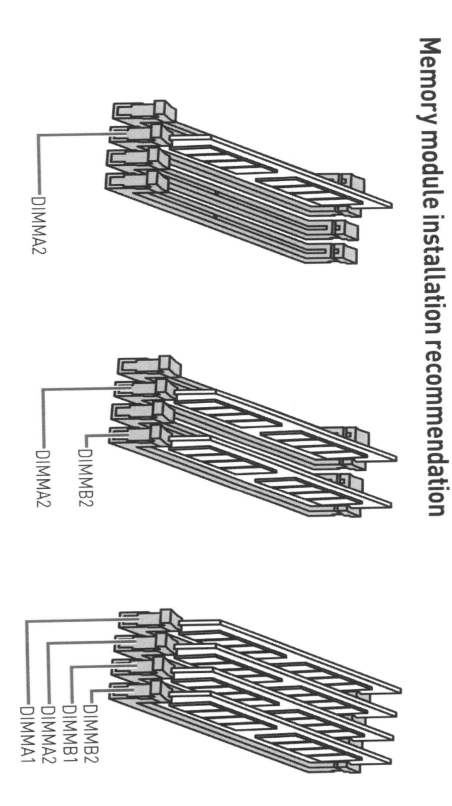

Memory module installation recommendation

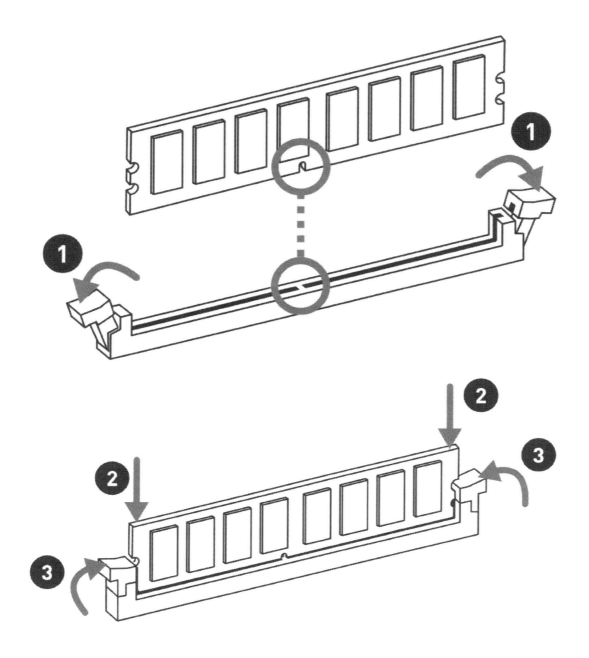

MOTHERBOARD PREPARATION

3. *CPU UNBOXING & INSTALLATION:*

o If the CPU COOLER FAN is the traditional screwing type. Remove the *off-market CPU cooler mounts* by the side of the CPU socket with the backplate intact. Gently remove the mounts and keep them safe in the motherboard box. This mount can come in handy for a wide variety of off-market fan coolers.

o Wear ESD gloves before removing the CPU as this prevents rubbing off oil and dirt from your hands to the CPU surface which can affect its performance.

o If you don't want to use the ESD gloves, make sure to hold only by the sides of the CPU.

o Caution: Don't touch on the metallic surface and the bottom of the CPU.

o Only the CPU unit is removed.

o CPU cooler fan is kept untouched in the box. This will be dealt with later in the process.

o Comes with Ryzen 7 CPU & Wraith AMD FAN cooler. [I bought the AMD RYZEN 7 2700X CPU]
o Before inserting the CPU into the socket - Unlock the metallic arm tab beside the CPU socket by gently pushing to the side and lifting it up.

o Notice the golden triangle symbol on the corner of the CPU (Picture below). Coincide this with the embossed triangle on the motherboard.
o Now align the CPU into the CPU socket on the motherboard. The CPU should fall into the socket with ease as these sockets are ZIFF - Zero Insertion Force sockets.

o Very gently wiggle or vibrate the CPU between the fingers to make the CPU fall in place if it didn't fall into place. Don't do anything drastic.

o Caution: Don't force the CPU on to the CPU sockets on the motherboard by pressing it. The bottom pins of the CPU are very fragile.

Now lower the metallic arm tab and lock it, to place the CPU in position.

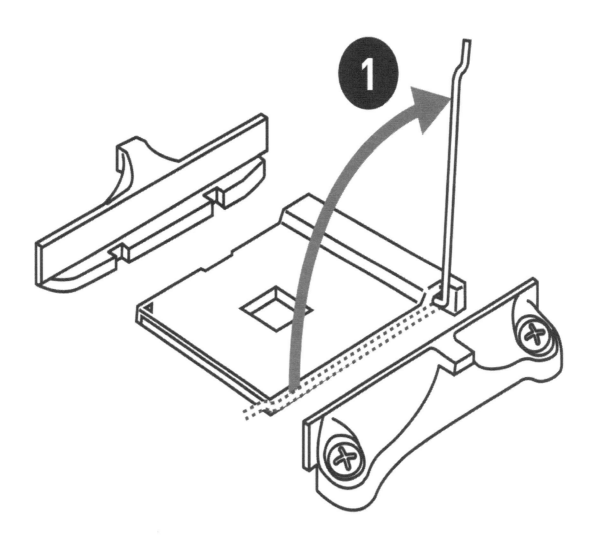

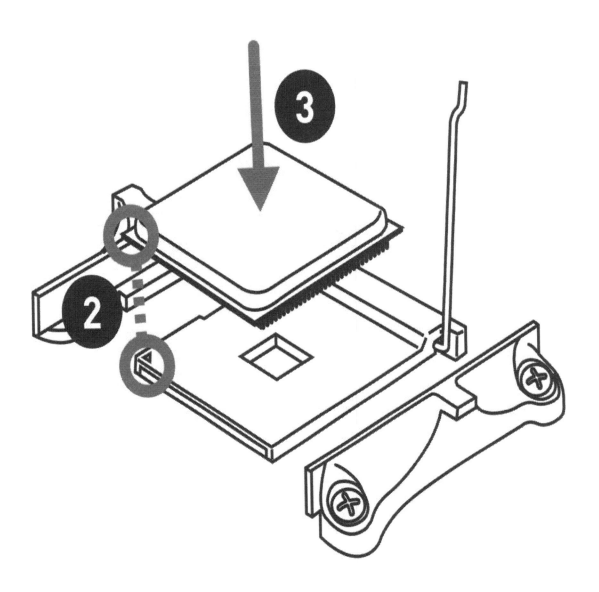

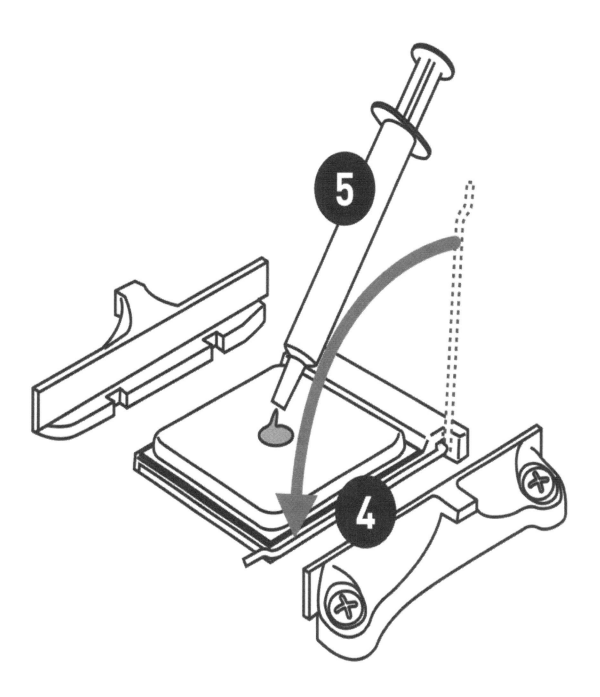

Processor Socket

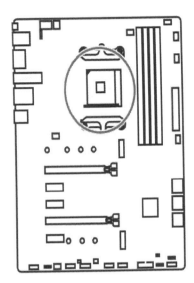

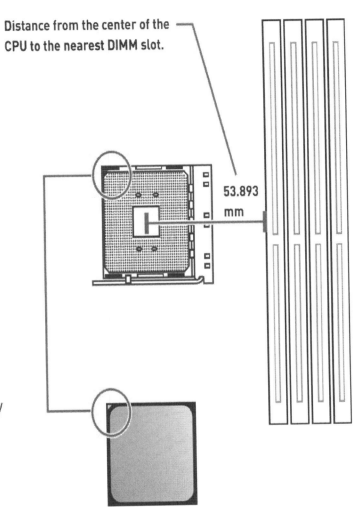

Distance from the center of the CPU to the nearest DIMM slot.

53.893 mm

Introduction to the AM4 CPU

The surface of the AM4 CPU has a yellow triangle to assist in correctly lining up the CPU for motherboard placement. The yellow triangle is the Pin 1 indicator.

4. *CPU COOLER FAN INSTALLATION*:

o You can now remove the off-market CPU COOLER FAN mount placed on either side of the CPU socket if you haven't already removed it (Read this complete section before removing it). Place them safe in the motherboard box. It can later be used if you are planning to buy an off-market CPU cooler fan. These mounts were screwed to the motherboard backplate. Keep the motherboard fixed in one position or the backplate will fall off from the motherboard. The CPU COOLER FAN will be attached to this backplate from the front of the motherboard using screws.

o Now remove the fan gently from inside the box.

o Important: Don't touch on the THERMO-PASTE at the bottom of the CPU COOLER FAN unit.

o Beware of the fan cable from touching the thermo-paste or any other parts of the motherboard while moving it around.

o Decide on the position to keep the fan on the motherboard. Take time for this process. The first time I did it and the AMD LOGO was upside down, but fortunately, everything panned out well.

o *NOTE*: Make sure the fan wire extends to the CPU FAN header on the motherboard (Labeled: CPU_FAN1)

o Now place the fan with four attached screws very gently into the standoffs, attached to the motherboard backplate.

o Tighten the screws gently starting at one corner a little by little moving into the next corner screw without finishing the previous screw. Move diagonally from one corner screw to others. This method will slowly lower the fan thermo-paste to the CPU metal surface evenly spreading it and leaving no space between them.

○ Now connect the fan cable to the motherboard (Labeled: CPU_FAN1).

○ Make sure the fan cable is tied & tucked in and not loose wire hanging out.

○ Now you can hold and lift the motherboard by the fan alone as it is tightly screwed to the motherboard. Nevertheless, it is always best to use 2 holding points for safety and less stress to the motherboard.

The new and high-end models of CPU come with CPU COOLER FAN which is a little different Example: AMD RYZEN 7 2700X CPU (Refer to the picture below).

○ These new high-end CPU COOLER FANS have a clip on either side. One clip has a lever and the other one doesn't have a lever. The Lever can be turned to tighten the CPU COOLER FAN against the CPU. These units have pre-applied thermo-paste.

○ There is no protective plastic film to be removed from the CPU COOLER FAN (If present).

○ Once the CPU is lowered into the socket and the metal arm latch locked.

○ Make sure the clip with the lever of the CPU COOLER FAN is *loose, easily moving up and down* before you lower the CPU COOLER FAN.

○ Decide on the position to keep the fan on the motherboard. Make sure the fan wire extends to the CPU FAN header (CPU_FAN1) on the motherboard. One way is to point the AMD logo on the FAN to the top left corner.

○ The CPU COOLER FAN UNIT is placed gently on the CPU covering it equally. Make sure both the clips are in line with the hooks of the metal CPU COOLER FAN mounts situated on either side of the CPU.

○ Now start with the clip that lacks lever. Use a small minus screwdriver, insert it into the gap just above the clip. Press and lower it carefully until the clip latches on to the hook of the metal CPU COOLER FAN mount.

o Now start with the next clip with the lever. Make sure the clip with the lever is latched on to the hook by manipulating the provided lever. Now turn the lever to the opposite side. This might need some force. Try gently pressing the CPU COOLER FAN down, with the lever turning to the opposite at the same time. This will press the FAN unit tightly against the CPU with the thermo-paste evenly spread, leaving no gap in between them.

o Now fix the CPU COOLER FAN cable to the CPU FAN header (Labeled: CPU_FAN1).

o CPU COOLER FAN comes with 2 separate cables, each for the different LED lights on the fan. To be installed after Graphics card wire installation. Not now.

If you find it difficult to fix it later, you can connect them to their respective motherboard headers now. For details refer to the 'FINAL TOUCH UP' chapter.

This picture below with the black arrow shows the CPU COOLER FANS with the LEVER CLIP. I'm currently using AMD RYZEN 7 2700X.

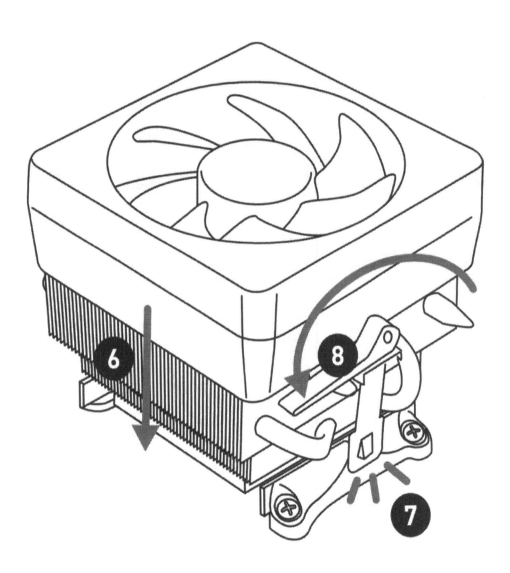

MOTHERBOARD INSTALLATION

o Remove the protective plastic film from the EXTENDED HEATSINK of the motherboard I/O units & the GAMING HEATSINK WITH CARBON SCHEME of the motherboard.

o Quickly check the different layouts of the Motherboard.

o Go through the various cable attaching headers on the motherboard.

o You can hold the fan to move the motherboard around if it's not too heavy. Preferable two holding points are always good to evenly distribute the force.

o Before installing the motherboard into the CASE. Install all the necessary mounting standoffs necessary for that particular motherboard or remove any that don't coincide with that of the motherboard.

o In some instances, there can be standoffs that don't coincide with the motherboard screw points. In such cases remove those particular standoffs. Always check the Case before installing motherboards.

o IMPORTANT: To prevent damage —> Any contact/ unnecessary between the motherboard and the mounting standoffs or with the PC case is prohibited. This can damage the circuits in the motherboard.

o Keep the 8 x standoffs (if not pre-installed), 8 x standoff screws (comes with the CASE) & the screw tightening nut (comes with the CASE) ready. The case comes with a pre-installed middle standoff which is usually raised and doesn't need to be screwed, acts as a guiding point to insert the motherboard.

o First Screw the standoffs complementary to the motherboard, to the CASE, if not already installed.

o Use the standoff tightening nut to tighten the standoffs, but not too tight as it can strip the tightening nut and make it useless.

o Keep the standoff tightening nut safely back in the motherboard box as it can be useful later to install/uninstall motherboard if you have to later.

o IMPORTANT: Now gently and carefully lower the motherboard at an angle so that the I/O of the motherboard pass through the I/O shield. Keep a mirror angles to see on the other side of the I/O shield and make sure the I/O of the motherboard passes through the appropriate entry points in the shield. TIP: The audio I/O pin is usually at the bottom row.

o Lower the other side to make the motherboard parallel to the case. Make sure the standoffs pass through the motherboard screw holes, all of them without touching the backside of the motherboard.

o IMPORTANT: Make sure not to touch or scrape the lower side of the motherboard with the standoffs. This can damage the circuit of the motherboard.

o Now gently tighten the motherboard screws to anchor the motherboard to the case. Not too tight as this can damage the motherboard.

o TIP: Hold the screw by keeping it attached to the magnetic screwdriver with the index finger. Now lower it to the screw points.

Please refer to the images on the next page.

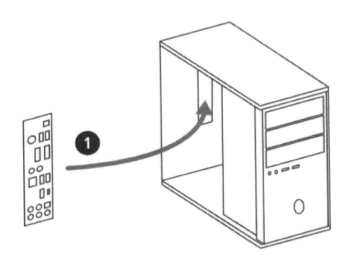

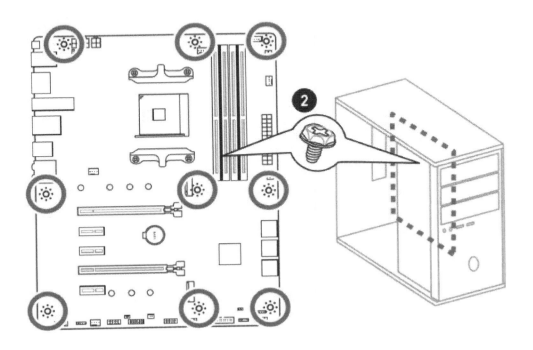

Overview of Components

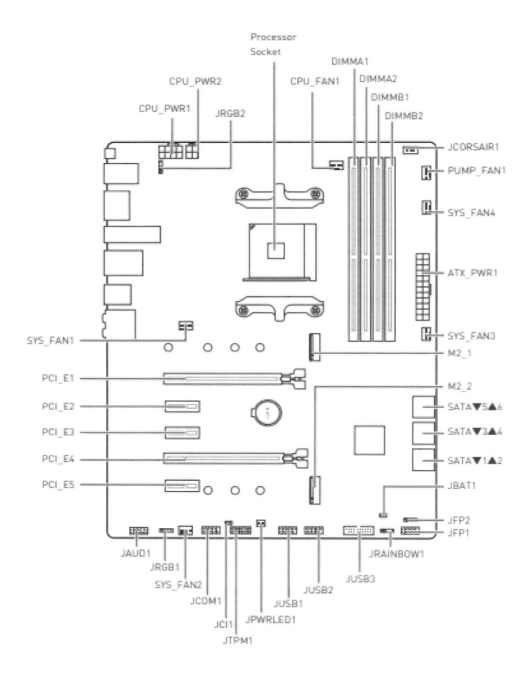

POWER SUPPLY INSTALLATION

o Remove the protective plastic film from above the fan.

o The back of the power supply unit (PSU) has the pin for the AC power cable. This part will be screwed to the posterior part of the case.

o And make sure the **fan is facing down**. This is another point to note to get the correct orientation of the PSU in the case.

o **PC CASE Scenario 1**: Remove the bracket from the back of the case, placed at the bottom.

o Now attach this bracket to the back of the PSU with the four screws that come along with the CASE/PSU.

o **PC CASE Scenario 2**: If there is no bracket at the lower backside of the case. The PSU has to be now inserted into the case through the lower gap on the side panel. Since the wires are all already connected to the PSU, the only thing for you to do now is to screw the backside of the PSU to the case with the four screws provided.

o Suggestion: It is ideal to install the Front Panel cables first before installing the PSU as the multiple wires from it can interfere with the front panel cables. Installing the front panel cables can be a bit tricky at times. It is easy if done patiently. Once it's out of the way, Installing the rest of the cables is as easy as a piece of the pie.

I suggest you install all the cables on the PSU and keep it aside to be installed after the front panel cables are connected.

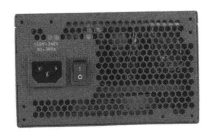

WIRE INSTALLATION REFERENCE GUIDE

o Different sets of wires, segregate them:

o Always read the MOTHERBOARD MANUAL thoroughly in advance to confirm the various cable header points. Refer to the picture under the title MOTHERBOARD PREPARATION for reference.

o Take a printout of the 'overview of the components' motherboard picture. Keep it close as this will help you in your wire's installation.

o Don't connect them yet. Below is the order to which cables will be installed. The list is to segregate them into batches.

o Headers are the pins on the motherboard where these cables will be connected. Each header is assigned a name which will be inscribed on the motherboard close to the header.

SET A: <u>**SETS OF FRONT PANEL WIRES**</u>: (This set of cables pass through the bottom lower gap of the motherboard)

o FRONT PANEL CABLE —> JFP1 (Header) Bottom left to right, Upper left to right header pins:

(i) HDD LED Lower left (+ -)
(ii) Reset Switch Lower right (- +)
(iii) Power LED Upper let (+ -)
(iv) Power Switch Upper right (+ -)
Please refer to the picture below for proper orientation of the pins.

o Higher-end model CASE comes with a single front panel cable but not compatible with the AMD motherboard yet. Waiting for the one that does. If not, the above description will help in the wire installation.

o My CASE NZXT H510 model comes with 2 types of Front panel connectors - For Intel standard Front Panel header & Non-Intel standard Front

Panel header. Hence, use the second option because you have an AMD motherboard. There is an adapter provided in the case to convert the Intel to a non-Intel header. Refer to the picture below.

2. USB3 (Cable) —> JUSB3 (Header)

3. HD AUDIO (Cable) —> JAUD1 (Header)

SET B: **PCIe/ VGA Cable** —> Graphics Card

- This cable passes through the gap the same as that of the front panel cable.

- This wire is connected after the graphics card installation.

SET C: **MOTHERBOARD, CPU & SATA CABLES:**

- ATX/Motherboard Cable, PSU —> ATX_PWR1 (Header)
- CPU CABLE, PSU —> CPU_PWR1 (Header)
- SATA Power cable, PSU —> HDD, If any
- SATA Power cable, PSU —> SSD, If any

- Connect (iii) & (iv) cables even if you don't have the drives for later use.

- Make sure to name tag all the wires & cables. segregate them well.

- Connect the system CASE FAN1 to the SYS_FAN1 header. Tie the excess wire with a zip tie and tuck in the remaining cable below the fan recess.

- Now connect the CASE FAN2 (NZXT H510 MODEL CASE - located at the top of the case) to SYS_ FAN3 or SYS_FAN4 header of the motherboard. This can vary and connect them appropriately.

- Now move to the opposite side of the CASE.

 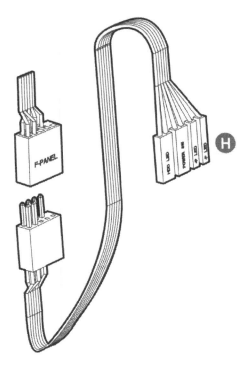

FOR INTEL STANDARD F_PANEL HEADER USE   FOR NON-INTEL STANDARD F_PANEL HEADER USE

<u>A</u>. FRONT PANEL CABLE INSTALLATION

○ Segregate FRONT PANEL cables, USB3 cable, HD AUDIO & PCIe Cable together as these cables will be taken through the same gap below the motherboard.

○ Now bring the *(A) & (B) SET* (Refer the previous page) cables from the gap below the motherboard.

○ Front panel cable attaching sites on the motherboard is at the lower end.

○ Cables are attached from right to left at the lower end of the motherboard.

○ <u>**SETS OF FRONT PANEL WIRES**</u>

○ FRONT PANEL CABLE —> JFP1 (Header) Bottom left to right, Upper left to right (If separate pins provided)

○ USB3 (Cable) —> JUSB3 (Header). This is a bigger cable. Try to loop it at the neck and zip tie it to the case, to prevent it from moving. *Refer to the image below.*

○ HD AUDIO (Cable) —> JAUD1 (Header).

<u>B</u>. PCIe/ VGA Cable (6+2 pin) —> Graphics Card

○ Connect the cables to the motherboard one by one in the same order as above, except the PCIe cable as it will be connected to the graphics card after it's installation.

o Extra fans can be connected to PUMP_FAN1 or
   SYS_FAN 3/4

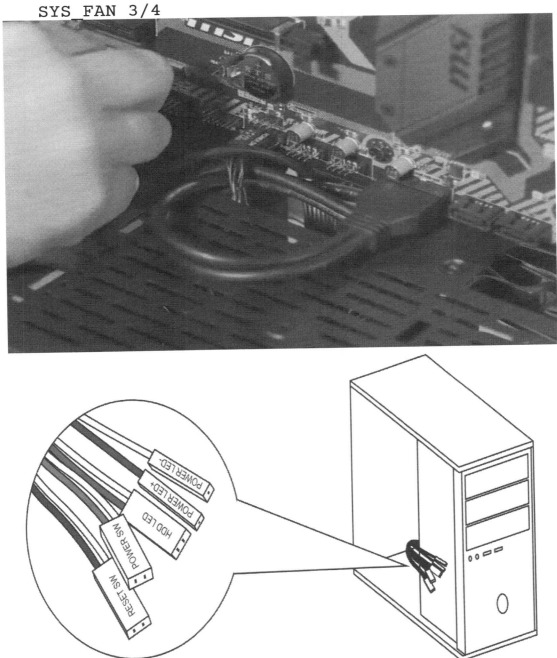

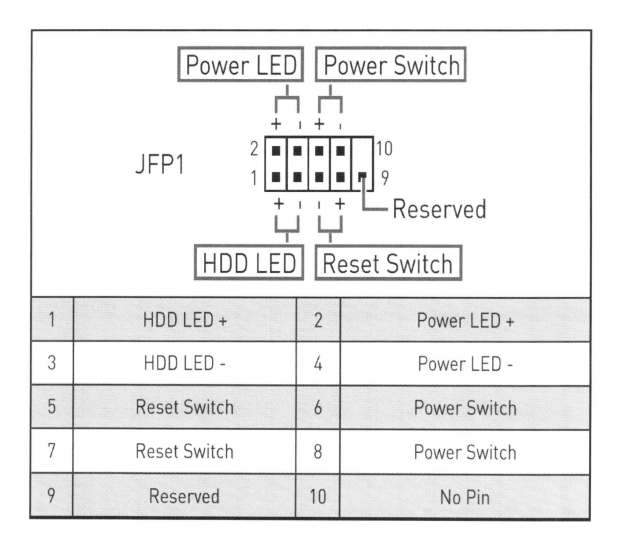

1	HDD LED +	2	Power LED +
3	HDD LED -	4	Power LED -
5	Reset Switch	6	Power Switch
7	Reset Switch	8	Power Switch
9	Reserved	10	No Pin

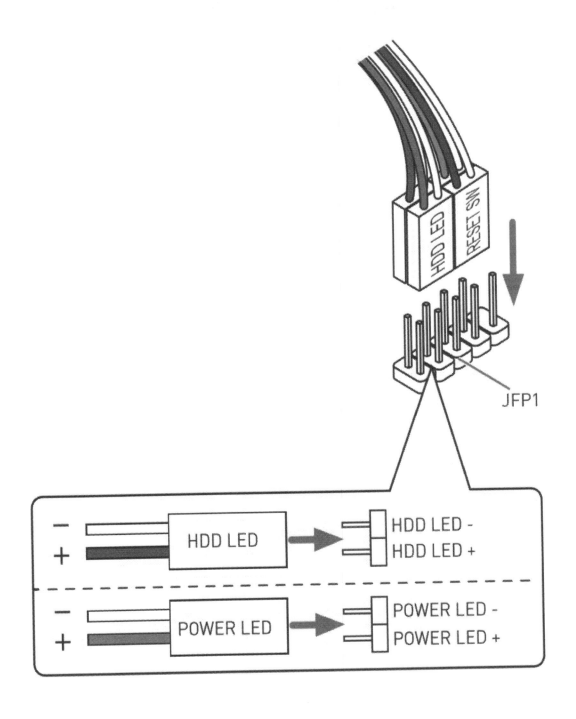

Component Contents

Port Name	Port Type	Page
CPU_FAN1, PUMP_FAN1, SYS_FAN1~4	Fan Connectors	37
CPU_PWR1~2, ATX_PWR1	Power Connectors	35
DIMMA1, DIMMA2, DIMMB1, DIMMB2	DIMM Slots	31
JAUD1	Front Audio Connector	37
JBAT1	Clear CMOS Jumper	39
JCI1	Chassis Intrusion Connector	38
JCOM1	Serial Port Connector	38
JCORSAIR1	CORSAIR Connector	41
JFP1, JFP2	Front Panel Connectors	34
JRGB1~2, JRAINBOW1	RGB LED connectors	40
JTPM1	TPM Module Connector	39
JUSB1~2	USB 2.0 Connectors	36
JUSB3	USB 3.1 Gen1 Connector	36
M2_1~2	M.2 Slots (Key M)	33
PCI_E1~5	PCIe Expansion Slots	32
Processor Socket	AM4 socket	30
SATA1~6	SATA 6Gb/s Connectors	34

The image above shows the motherboard header names and their attachments

CPU_FAN1, PUMP_FAN1, SYS_FAN1~4: Fan Connectors

Fan connectors can be classified as PWM (Pulse Width Modulation) Mode or DC Mode. PWM Mode fan connectors provide constant 12V output and adjust fan speed with speed control signal. DC Mode fan connectors control fan speed by changing voltage. When you plug a 3-pin (Non-PWM) fan to a fan connector in PWM mode, the fan speed will always maintain at 100%, which might create a lot of noise. You can follow the instruction below to adjust the fan connector to PWM or DC Mode. However, with auto-detection mode fan connectors, the system will auto detect the fan mode.

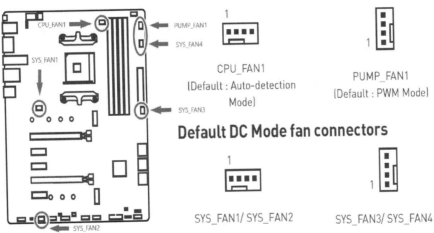

The image above shows various motherboard headers for FAN attachments.

JAUD1: Front Audio Connector

This connector allows you to connect audio jacks on the front panel.

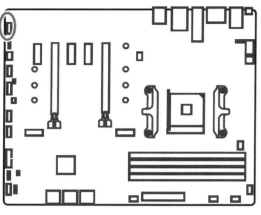

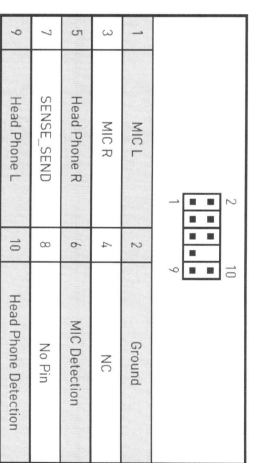

1	MIC L	2	Ground
3	MIC R	4	NC
5	Head Phone R	6	MIC Detection
7	SENSE_SEND	8	No Pin
9	Head Phone L	10	Head Phone Detection

MOTHERBOARD, CPU & SATA CABLES INSTALLATION

C. **MOTHERBOARD, CPU & SATA CABLES:**

  o ATX/Motherboard Cable (24-PIN) —> ATX_PWR1
    (Header)
- Bring the cable through the smart device cable channel (Refer CASE picture under CASE installation) and then through the gap in the middle part of the CASE, close to the ATX_PWR1 header on the motherboard.

  o CPU CABLE (8-PIN) —> CPU_PWR1 (Header)
- Bring this cable through the gap at the upper right corner of the back side-panel.

  o SATA Power cable (6-PIN) —> HDD, If any
- This cable is connected to the HDD and remains shortened and zip-tied at the bottom recess of the CASE.

  o SATA DATA CABLE, HDD —> SATA 1-6
- This data cable connects HDD to SATA 1-6 header on the motherboard. It's taken through the middle gap.

  o SATA Power cable (6-PIN) —> SSD, If any
- This cable is connected to the SSD, which is attached to the SSD tray at the back of the motherboard panel.

  o SATA DATA CABLE, SSD —> SATA 1-6
- This data cable connects SSD to SATA 1-6 header on the motherboard. It's taken through the middle gap.

- ○ Segregate the above cables together from other cables and connect them individually in the order as shown in the above list.
- ○ The above list shows the cable name and the header to connect the cable.
- ○ Connect (iii) & (v) cables even if you don't have the drives.

IMPORTANT: *Make sure to connect all the HDDs or SSDs only after the installation and setup of windows. Only the drive, in my case I used my NVMe M.2 SSD to install my OS, should be connected to the PC motherboard. Once the windows installation and update of all the drivers are done, shut down your PC. Now connect all the other drives to your motherboard and power supply. Start your PC.*

GRAPHICS CARD INSTALLATION

GRAPHICS CARD CABLE INSTALLATION

- Open the latch on the right side of the PCIe card slot.

- Now line up the graphics card to the PCI Express card slot without attaching it. This is to see what rear case brackets need to be removed before installing the graphics card to provide space for the I/O unit of the card.

- Release the screws to remove the bracket. Make sure that the screws and the bracket don't fall into the CASE.

- Release the latch on the side of the PCIe card slot of the motherboard, by pushing it toward the side.

- Now connect the graphics card to the PCIe slot (PCI_E1 header on the motherboard) by lining it up with the slot, make sure the notch on the graphics card line up with that on the PCIe slot on the motherboard and insert it by pressing the card towards the slot. The latch will automatically engage and lock the card in place.

- Put back the bracket screws to further keep the graphics card in position. Without this there can be excess stress on the PCI Expires card slots. There are instances where the Graphics card had fell out of its respective slot.

Attach the 8-PIN PCIe cable placed before at the base of the motherboard to the Graphics card. [This cable is based on the socket on the Graphics card]

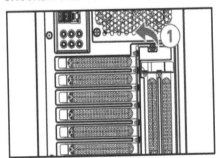

UNSCREW THE THUMB SCREW

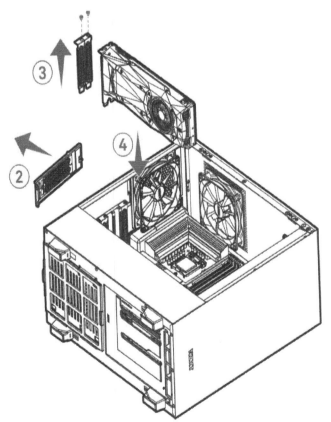

HORIZONTAL GPU MOUNT

UNSCREW THE THUMB SCREW

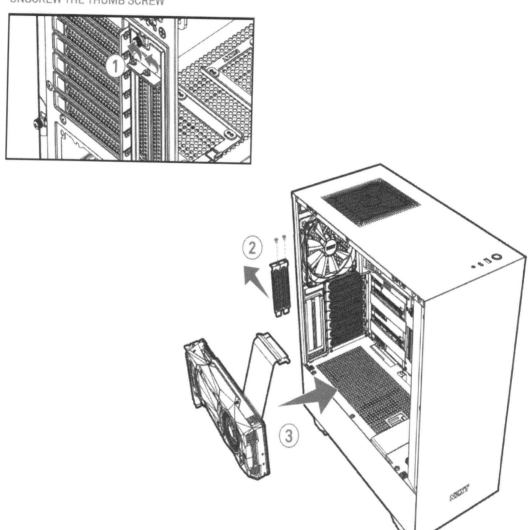

VERTICAL GPU MOUNT

FINAL TOUCH UP

CPU COOLER FAN CABLE INSTALLATION

o CPU COOLER FAN comes with 2 separate cables, each for the different LED lights on the fan.

o Now remove the rubber doors covering the 2 ports on the FAN.

o Attach the USB wire first. The small pin end goes into the right 3-PIN port of the FAN. Connect the other end to the USB 2.0 (JUSB1) header on the lower end of the motherboard.

o **OPTIONAL:** Now attach the RGB cable. Attach the small pin end of the cable to the 4-PIN port on the CPU COOLER FAN. The other end goes to the JRGB1 header on the lower end of the motherboard.

o **IMPORTANT:** Don't connect this cable if you are planning to control the CPU COOLER FAN LED lights with the 'COOLER MASTER WRAITH PRISM' software.

o NOTE: *The RGB cable can also be connected to the JRGB2 situated right below the CPU_PWR1 header,* whichever is closer. This step can be done right after the CPU COOLER FAN installation.

If you are confused about the position to fix the cable on the header. There is an embossed arrow at the bottom of the 4-PIN cable end which goes to the motherboard header. This arrow indicates the left side PIN which as it turns out to hold +12V (Positive). Point the arrow to the first left PIN before inserting it to the header. Refer to the motherboard manual.

FINAL TOUCH UP

o Zip-tie all the cables on the front and back side panels. Sort them. Rearrange and make it neat. Arrange the cables without any free cables disrupting the airflow inside the PC.

o Install the WIFI Antennas.

o Remove all the plastic protective sheets from all the components in the PC like HEATSINKS, GRAPHICS CARD, POWER SUPPLY, etc.

o Remove the protective plastic film from the glass side panel before installing it.

o IMPORTANT: Get the UPS connected to the AC power.

o Now connect the power cable from the UPS to the PSU of the PC. Switch ON the main power. Once the UPS is ON. Switch on the PC. If the lighting is blinking inside, it is a good sign.

o If not turning on, check if the FRONT PANEL CABLE is connected properly to the motherboard.

Stick the CASE badge you got with the motherboard.

PC SOFTWARE UPDATE
&
INSTALLATION

THINGS NEEDED:

- o Pendrive - 2 x 8-16GB, FAT32 Formatted. Make sure to securely remove the device using the windows extract function from your computer once the windows 10 and other drivers are copied.

- o Keyboard - Wired

- o Mouse - Wired

- o Ethernet Cable - If your newly build PC doesn't have a Wi-Fi connection.

USB FORMATING

- o If you are using Windows 10, Go to the devices and drives.

- o Select the USB drive.

- o Right-click the USB drive and select FORMAT.

- o Under FILE SYSTEM, select FAT32. FAT32 formatting is only applicable to USB size below 32GB.

- o securely remove the USB device using the windows extract device from your computer.

- o Keep separate USB drives for the BIOS setup and the WINDOWS INSTALLATION. Let us name it USB-1 for BIOS setup and USB-2 for WINDOWS installation.

MAKING OF WINDOWS INSTALLATION MEDIA

o Insert FAT32 formatted USB-2 to your working PC.

o Go to the Microsoft website to download Windows 10. Go to Microsoft.com > Software Download > Windows 10 > Download tool

o Click on the **download tool now.**

o Double click and install the downloaded file - MEDIA CREATION TOOL.

o Select "Create installation media"

o Change, Language: English US, Edition: Windows, Architecture: 64-bit. Select - Use the recommended option for this PC.

o Select the USB FLASH DRIVE. Make sure this USB is FAT32 formatted before downloading a copy of the windows to it.

o Make sure the file is downloaded to the appropriate USB drive.

BIOS & DRIVERS DOWNLOAD

- o Insert FAT32 formatted USB-1 drive to your working PC.

- o Go to the Motherboard manufacturing website. Go to your motherboard section.

- o Click support > Download the latest a) BIOS. Preferable directly into the USB-1. The old BIOS might not be able to detect the new BIOS setup file if it is deep in some folder during the BIOS setup through M-FLASH. After extracting the BIOS setup file into the USB-1, delete the zip file and rename the folder containing the BIOS setup file to BIOS UEFI.

- o Now go to Support > Driver > Windows 10 64 > LAN Drivers > Download a) Bluetooth Driver b) Intel Network Driver c) Intel Wi-Fi Driver.

- o Open the same USB drive. Create a new folder, name it after your motherboard. Mine is [MSI B450 GAMING PRO CARBON AC].

- o Copy the Drivers to the newly created folder.

- o Rename these folders to names like INTEL WIFI, INTEL NETWORK, etc. If you can recognize the files, this won't be necessary.

I never had to do this as the windows 10 recognized all the components in my newly built PC and installed drivers for them during the windows installation process.

UEFI/BIOS - UPDATING & HARDWARE CHECK

- **CAUTION:** Make sure the *PC is connected to UPS for the uninterrupted power*. If the PC shutdown while the BIOS is being updated which is a serious issue. You will have to take it to the service center for specialized service. They will need to unplug the bios chip, update it again and hopefully, it will work after that.

- Connect the newly built PC to a monitor via HDMI cable.

- Make sure to connect the wired keyboard and mouse to the PC too.

- *Plug the USB with the Windows 10, Bios & Drivers to the USB ports on the back of the newly build PC.*

- Switch ON the PC.

- When the PC boots up for the first time, it's going to access the motherboard's UEFI/BIOS. The monitor shows a flash green tinge with the *motherboard logo*.

- Make sure to note the writing at the bottom. It will only stay for a second. You can take a picture of it with your phone to confirm.

- Press DELETE —> To enter the SETUP mode (UEFI/BIOS)
- Press F11 —> To enter BOOT menu (To Install Windows)
- Press CTRL + F5 —> To activate M-FLASH for BIOS update.

- As the system is booting up -> Keep pressing/tapping the DELETE button once every second or two. This will help us to access BIOS.

o MSI CLICK BIOS 5 - This was the name of the BIOS when I was updating.

o Now time for —> REALITY CHECK. Make sure everything you installed in the PC like Motherboard, CPU, RAM is working, if it is detected in the BIOS.

UPDATE BIOS VERSION USING M-FLASH

o New versions of BIOS come all the time. BIOS can always vary over time, so don't be surprised if you see a different order of things in the BIOS than the one you saw in any picture or videos. But the basic steps here remain the same. Go through BIOS patiently and figure it out by yourself. It's not difficult.

o Now Plug the USB-1 drive to the USB ports on the back of the newly built PC.

o Click M-FLASH in the BIOS.

o Select auto reboot. The system will auto reboot and enter M-FLASH mode.

o Make sure the system remains plugged on to the UPS.

o This mode reads the USB drive. Open and select the folder you created for BIOS. Click OK. BIOS will update now.

o Once the BIOS is done updating, the system will reboot on its own.

o Keep tapping DELETE to get back to the BIOS.

o Now double-check everything, make sure (i) the BIOS is of latest version (ii) CPU is running at an appropriate speed (iii) Check RAM speed.

o Select MEMORY on the left side of the BIOS
   screen. Memory automatically runs at a default
   speed of 3200MHz, speed of the RAM.

o If not running at the fastest speed, enable the
   XMP settings. Click ON the XMP button on the
   top screen. You can notice two XMP profiles
   below. Select the one with the fastest speed by
   clicking on the number 1 or 2 on either side of
   the XMP button. Here press 2 (stand for profile
   2), which has faster speed.

o Now select storage. Check device list, model,
   size and connection. Make sure the storage
   devices connected are listed here and their
   details correct.

o IMPORTANT: Under 'Storage On Board' current
   mode should be AHCI mode (by default).

o FAN INFO – Fan speed can be adjusted here if it
   is connected to the motherboard.

o After booting into BIOS, use the arrow key to
   navigate to the "Boot" tab. Under "Boot mode
   select", select UEFI (Windows 10 is supported
   by UEFI mode.)

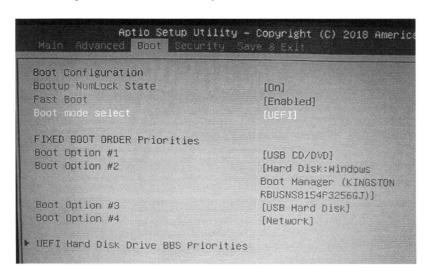

o Now insert the USB-2 drive to the back of the
   newly built PC.

o Press F10 to save, once all the changes are made [OR] Select ADVANCED MODE [F7] > Settings > Save changes and exit. This will reboot the PC.

o When the PC reboots, Press F11 to enter the boot menu. This will take you to a boot menu, where you can select the UEFI: USB DISK 2.0 PMAP, PARTITION 1. Now Select ENTER.

You will now enter into Windows 10 installation process.

WINDOWS 10 HOME INSTALLATION

o Enter all the details for the Windows 10 installation and click next.

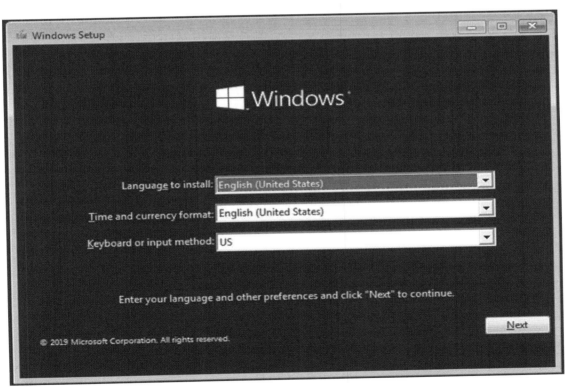

o Select INSTALL NOW.

o Windows will prompt for the product key. You have a choice to do it later after complete installation. If so, select I DON'T HAVE A PRODUCT KEY.

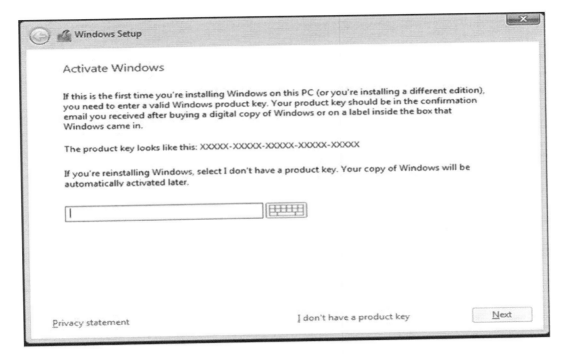

o Select Windows 10 Home/Pro.

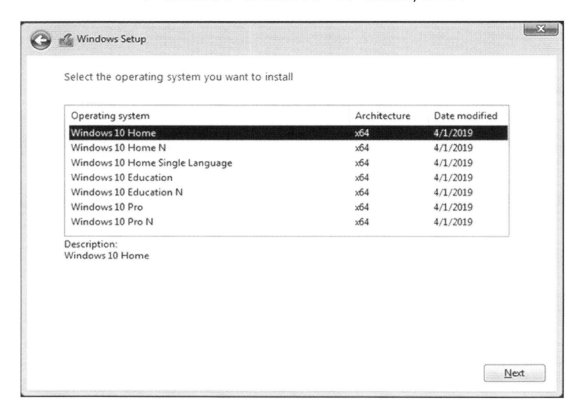

o Select *'Custom Install Windows Only (ADVANCED)'*.

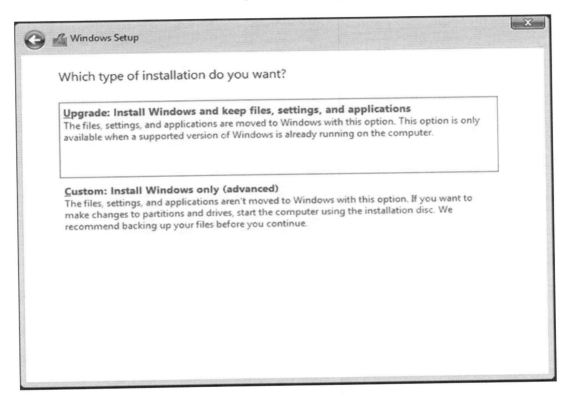

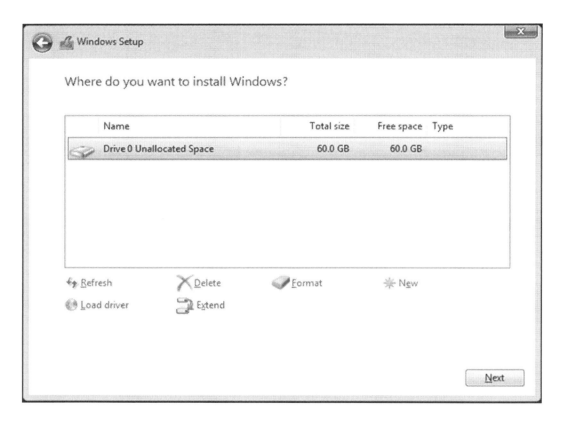

Where do you want to install Windows? – Select the
 UNALLOCATED SPACE and click next. But if you are
trying to install in a used previously partitioned
drive, it will show partitions, listed here. One by
one select and delete each partition all except the
 unallocated space. There should only be one
 allocated space to install the operating system
(OS). This is the reason why only the drive for OS
 is connected first. Now select the **unallocated
space** and click NEXT. (Other drives are connected
 post windows installation and drivers update)

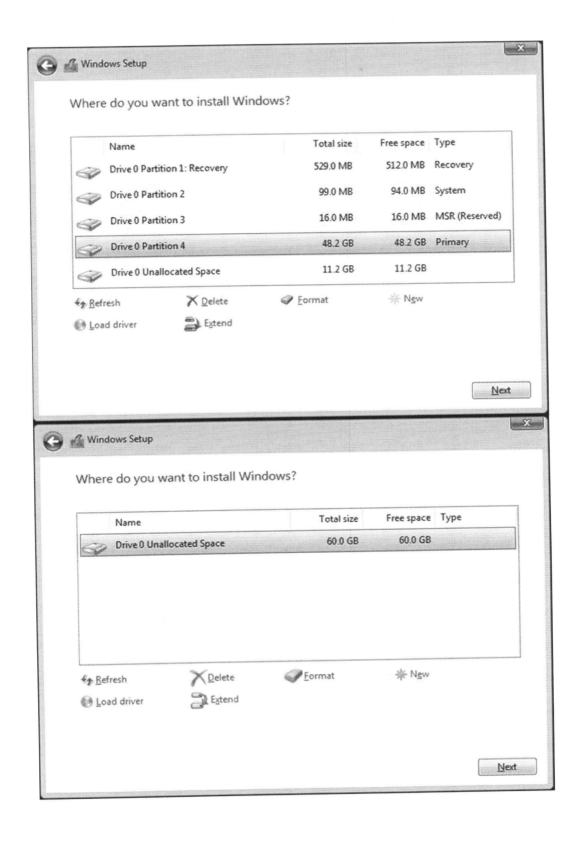

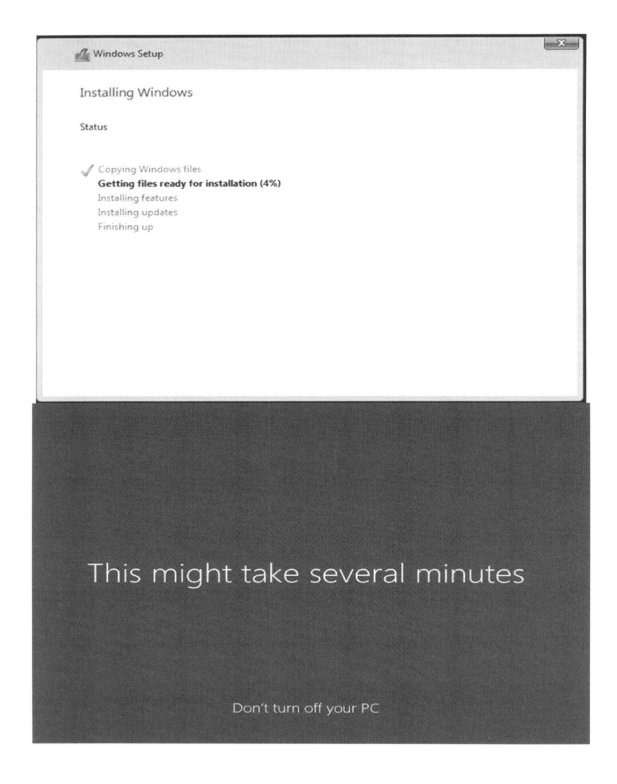

o Windows installation will start now. It takes around 8-15 min. After this PC automatically restarts.

o After quick restart > Select region > Keyboard layout: US > Second Keyboard Layout - Skip > Connect to NETWORK > Name your PC, Microsoft License attached to PC or yourself via Microsoft account > Create password > Make Cortana your personal assistant > Do more across devices with activity - No > Privacy setting - Read and choose > WINDOWS 10 HOME/PRO IS INSTALLED NOW.

SETTING UP WINDOWS

o Go to Windows Themes and Settings. Right-click on Desktop Screen > Personalize > Themes > Desktop Icon Settings > Select the Icon you want on the desktop screen > Click Apply.

o Open any FOLDER ICON > select VIEW > options > Open file explorer to > Select 'This PC' or Quick Access.

o Folder Ion > View > Folder Options > View

o Check Full path in the title bar
o Check Show hidden files and folders
o Uncheck Hide empty drivers
o Uncheck Hide extension for known file types.

o Move to the desktop screen. Right-click 'THIS PC' > Manage > Computer Management > Device Manager > Shows devices not recognized by the OS.

o Right-click TASKBAR > Uncheck Show people on the taskbar.

CONNECT TO INTERNET AND UPDATE

- If the windows don't recognize the driver for Wi-Fi in the PC > Restart PC > Tap/Press DELETE to enter into the BIOS > M-FLASH > Select Wi-Fi file > Click OK.

- Once connected to the Wi-Fi network > Go to NETWORKS > Click YES.

- Now to go to UPDATES, type updates in the web search at the bottom left on the desktop screen > CHECK FOR UPDATES > Windows updates automatically download and install updates.

- Manually restart PC once the update is complete.

- Repeat this cycle with going to windows updates. Repeat the cycle multiple times till the Windows shows "YOU ARE UP TO DATE".

- Download and install AMD RYZEN 7 2700X Driver (Windows 10 – 64-bit Edition) – AMD RYZEN MASTER from the AMD manufacturer website.

- Download and install AMD RYZEN WRAITH PRISM RGB LIGHTING CONTROL SOFTWARE from the COOLERMASTER website. This helps to control the LED lights of the CPU COOLER FAN.

INSTALLING GOOGLE CHROME

- Google > Download GOOGLE CHROME.

CONFIRM UPDATES

- Right- click THIS PC > Manage > Device Manager > Check if the windows recognize all the devices.

GRAPHICS CARD DRIVER INSTALLATION

Go to the MSI > Graphics card > MSI Radeon RX 580
ARMOR 8G OC > Support > Auto detect or Manual
driver download.

DRIVE PARTITION

<u>DRIVE PARTITION</u>

o Once the WINDOWS installation process is
   complete and all the drivers updated. It's time
   to connect all the other drives to the
   motherboard.

o Attach the SATA power cable from the PSU to
   their respective drives. The drives are in turn
   connected to the motherboard via SATA data
   cable. Close the CASE side panels.

   It's time to partition the drives. It might not
   even detect in the devices and drives under 'MY
                              PC'.

o Go to `MY PC` > Click on `Manage`.

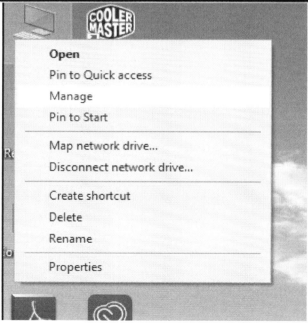

o You will enter `*Computer management*`.

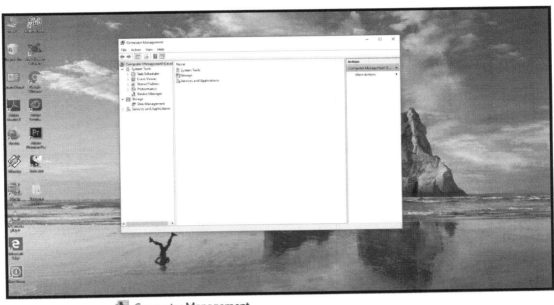

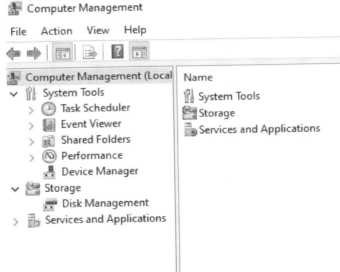

o Select **Disk Management** under **storage**.

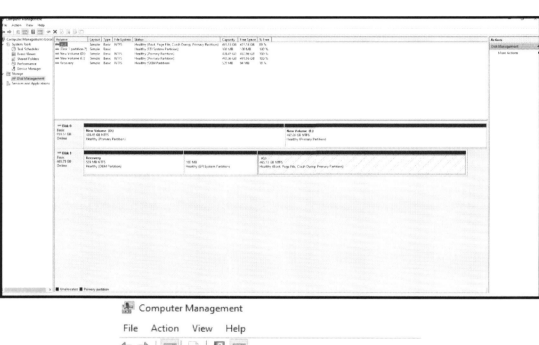

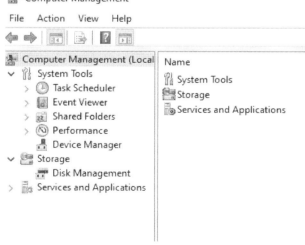

o Here you can see the different drives on your PC.

o Make sure which drive is the one that you are planning to do partition.

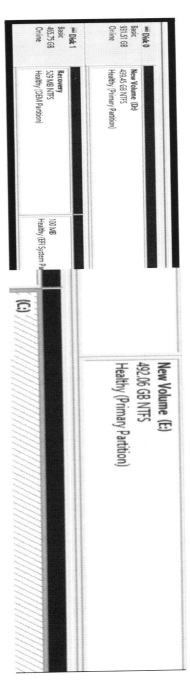

o Now right-click on that drive and select **'*Shrink Volume*'**.

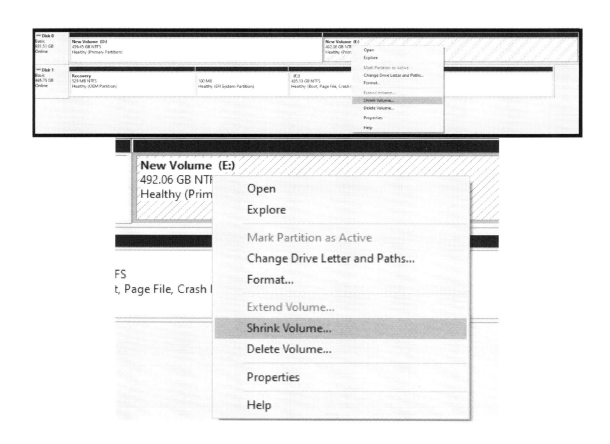

- o Here the total size of the drive is shown in MB (Megabytes).

- o If you are planning to divide the drive into 2 equal parts. Divide the total size by 2 in MB. Enter that amount into the **space to shrink in MB**. If 3 parts, divide by 3, so on and so forth.

If you want to have a certain specific storage size in mind, find out how much megabytes are a GB. It was 1024MB = 1GB. But different companies started using different values for their convenience. Sometimes it's 1000MB = 1GB. Here below in my case, 1026.2MB = 1GB. Calculate how much GB of the partition you need, now multiply that amount with the MB value for GB. If you want 5GB of partition, 5GB x 1026.2 = 5131MB. Enter this amount in the 'Space to shrink' section.

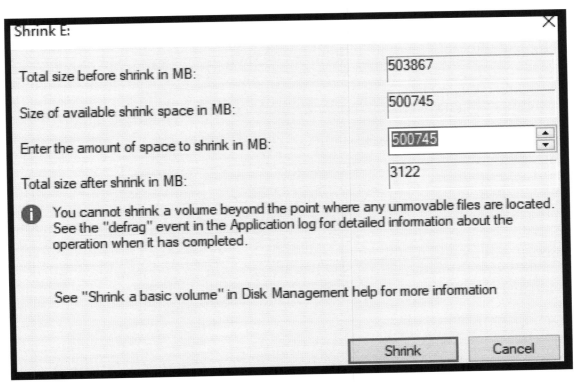

o In the below scenario, I had a total readable space of 491GB. I wanted to divide it into 2 equal half partition. Which means, 245.5GB X 1026.2 = 251933MB.

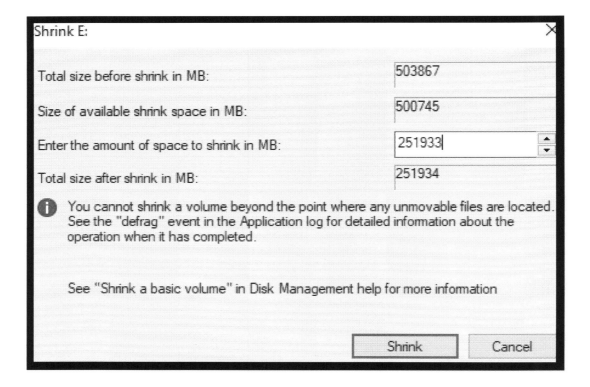

o The section to be partitioned appears as
  unallocated space as shown in the picture
  below.

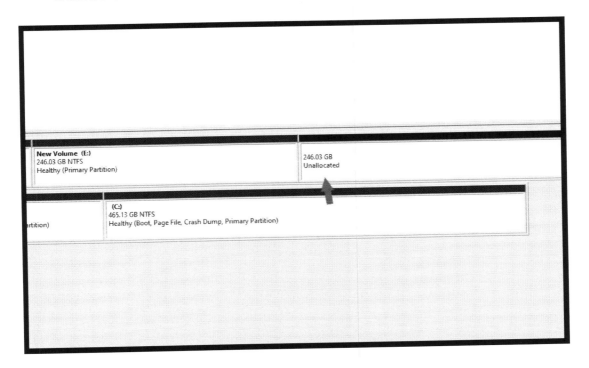

o Right-click on the unallocated drive and select
'*New simple volume*'.

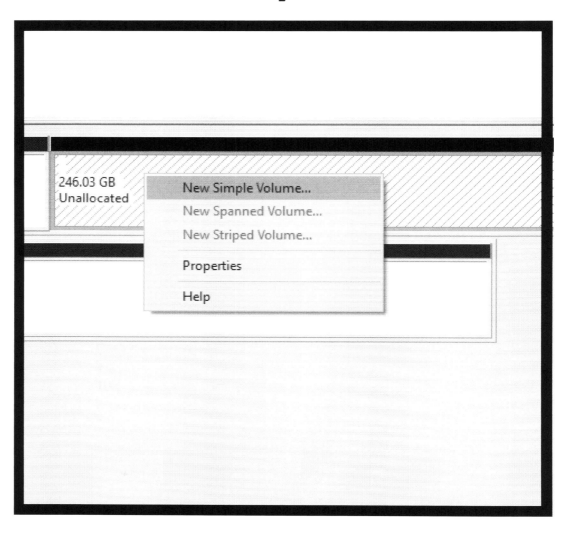

o A new simple volume wizard box appears. Click next to proceed.

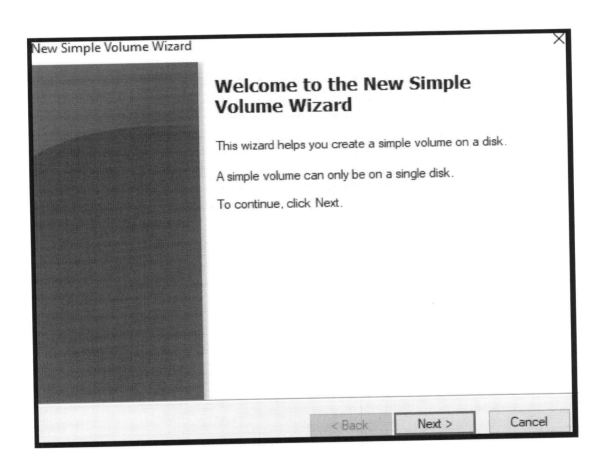

o This shows the size you want in your partition.

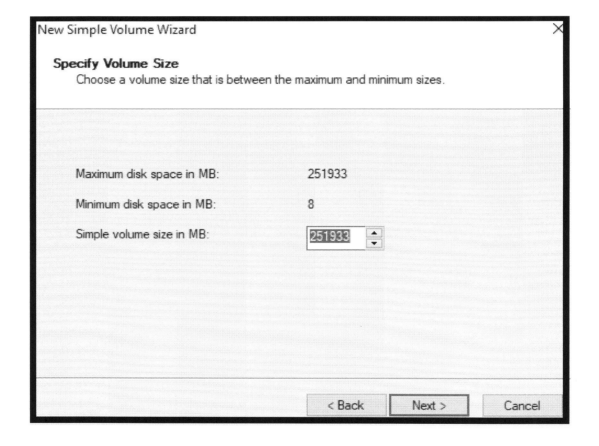

o Here you can assign any letter for your drive.

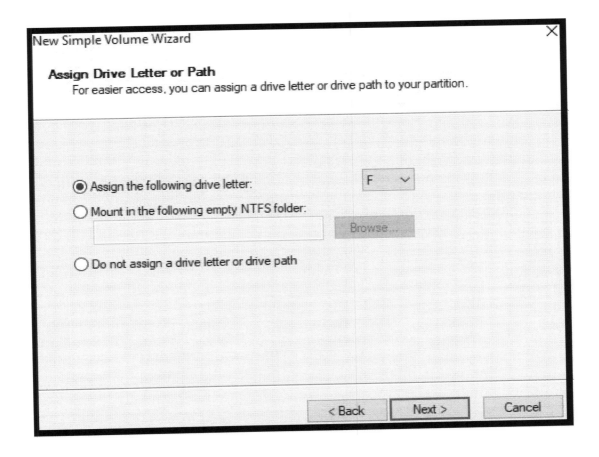

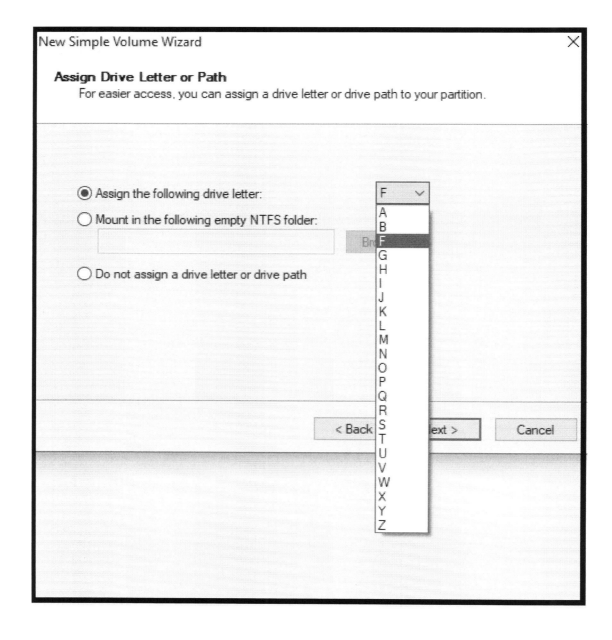

o Select 'Format with the following setting'
under which change the File system setting to
NTFS, Allocation unit size to 'Default'.

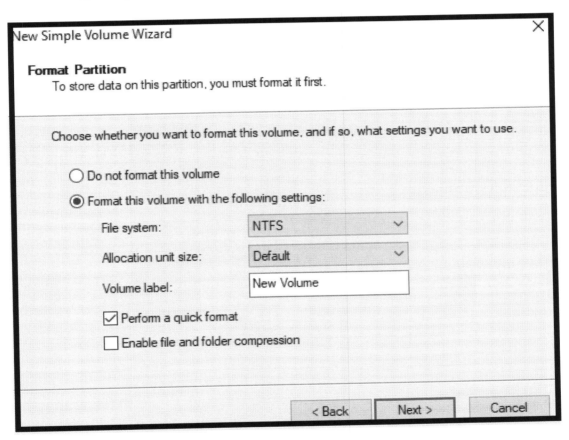

o Under the Volume label, you can assign a name for your partitioned drive.

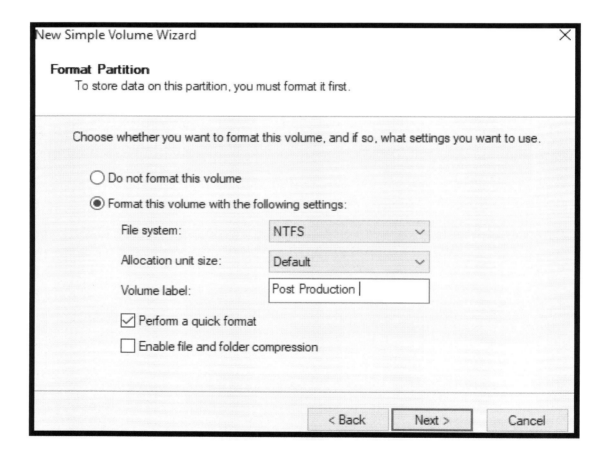

o Click 'Finish' to complete the New simple
volume wizard.

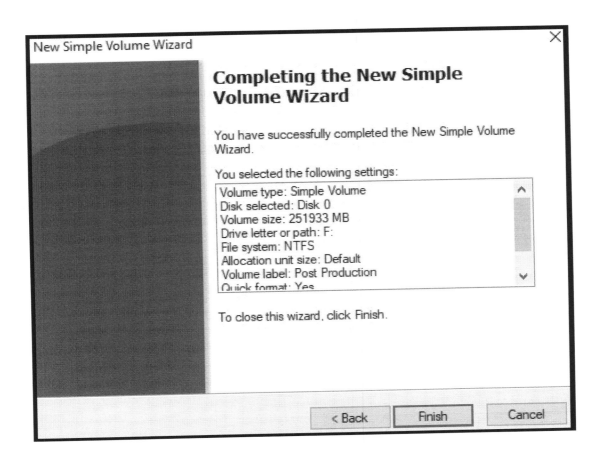

o As you can see a new drive has been created here.

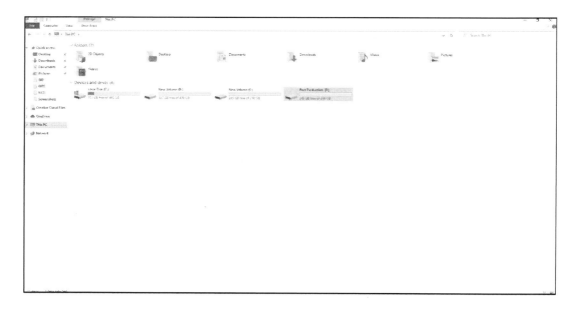

o **HOW TO REVERSE THE PARTITION?** - Now If you are not happy with your partition or want to change the partition size, you can always reverse the process immediately. If you are planning to do it later with some data inside the drive. Save it to a new location.

o Now to reverse the partition process. Right-click on the partitioned drive in the disk management section and select 'Delete Volume'.

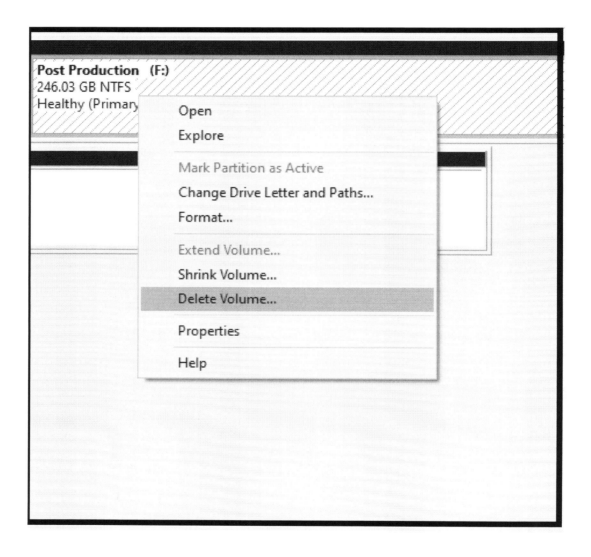

o Be sure the drive is empty and proceed by
clicking 'yes'.

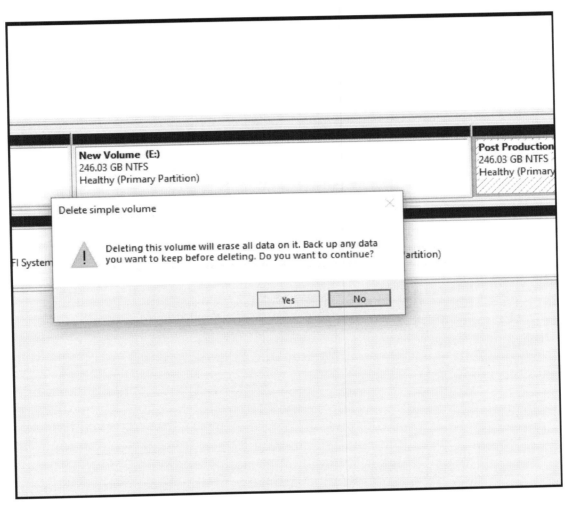

o The partitioned drive is now converted back to unallocated space.

New Volume (E:) 246.03 GB NTFS Healthy (Primary Partition)	246.03 GB Unallocated

	(C:) 465.13 GB NTFS Healthy (Boot, Page File, Crash Dump, Primary Partition)
n Partition)	

o Now right click on the original drive that was
  partitioned before. In this scenario, the 'E'
  was partitioned to create an 'F' drive. So
  right-click 'E' drive and select 'Extend
  Volume'.

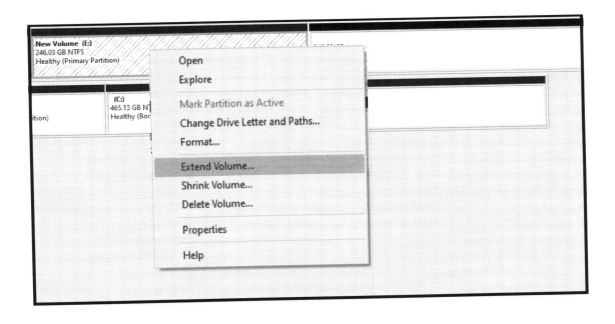

o You will enter the 'Extend Volume Wizard'.
Click next to proceed further.

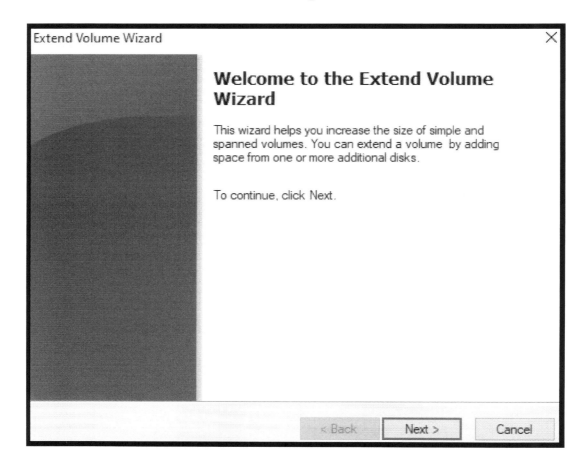

o This will show the size that will be added back
  to the original drive. Click next to proceed.

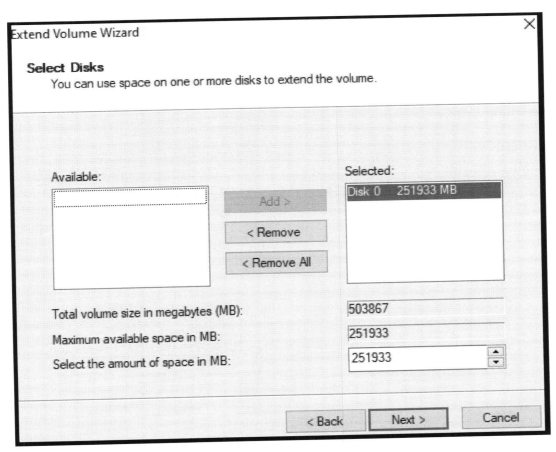

o Click 'Finish' to complete the Extend Volume
Wizard.

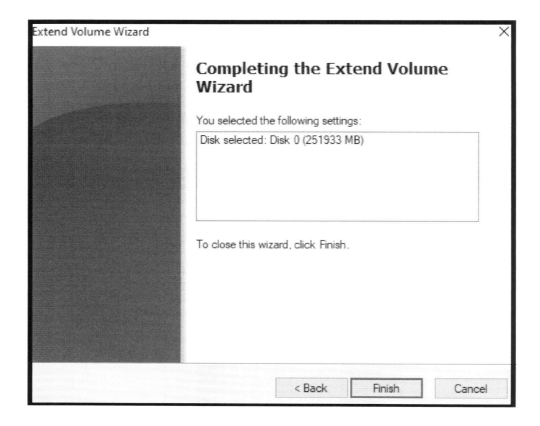

o The drive is now. extended back to its original space.

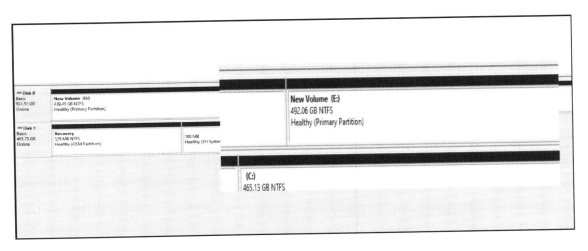

MOST COMMON PC BUILDING MISTAKES

o PCPARTPICKER - Go to the website, PCPARTPICKER.com. First select the motherboard or CPU are planning to buy, press ADD. This will create a list of components you can add to build your own PC. Now click on the component you are planning to buy. The website will show you the list of components in that particular category, CPU, RAM, PSU, GPU, etc that is compatible with the item/items already added. If you can't find the component in the list means the product is not compatible. One by one start adding the components. Add PSU in the end. Once you have done adding all the components, PCPARTPICKER will show you the required wattage in the right corner. Based on this value, choose the appropriate PSU.

o Don't cheap out on **PSU**. The parts in such cheap PSU are made up of cheap materials, which can, in turn, affect the other components in the PC. Go for branded ones. Discount is not a criterion here.

o If you want *multi-GPU (Graphics processing unit)* and the motherboard you picked has enough PCIe card slots. If you are going with **NVIDIA SLI**, the motherboard needs an SLI certification. Make sure it's mentioned on the motherboard box or under specifications. If you are choosing AMD, and if you want **CROSSFIRE**, you need only have the aforementioned PCI Express slots.

o Make sure there are **no loose screws** in the case, especially behind the motherboard. These loose screws can conduct electricity and can short or fry the motherboard by touching the circuits below it. Make sure to deal with these loose screws immediately. Motherboard STANDOFFS serves the purpose of minimizing this effect. Magnetic screwdrivers can be used to remove these free screws.

o You can use a **magnetic screwdriver** as the magnetic effect on these are very negligible.

o Many GPU especially higher-end models are **heavy** enough to put a significant amount of **stress on the PCI express slots** they are plugged into. You can avoid this simply by tightening the screws that attach the GPU on to the CASE. There are reinforced PCI express card slots available in the market which can be very expensive.

o **Front panel Headers** – It is not very uncommon to connect them wrong. Most of the time after assembling all the components and the PC is not switching on, the most common reason being front panel headers not connected properly. Please follow the motherboard manual diagram to avoid these mistakes. There is a diagram on the motherboard as well. They have + & – symbols indicated on the leads to further avoid mistakes. The colored wire is usually positive (+). There is also an embossed arrow below the leads indicating a positive pin. Even if you connect them wrong, it won't damage anything. Just turn it around and try again. Refer to the Front Panel header picture under the Wiring chapter.

o Tower Sized CPU COOLER FAN – Please pay close attention to your **CPU case specifications and compatibility**, as it will indicate the size of the fan. If bought appropriate size, the fan won't restrict the fixing of RAM on to the motherboard or closing the side panel of your PC CASE. Compatibility indicates the appropriate motherboard to be used. Make sure to note the RAM height mentioned in the RAM specification. Also, many CASE manufacturers indicate the maximum **CPU COOLER height**.

o **OVERCLOCKING (OC)** – Apart from having an unlocked/ OC processor, your motherboard chipset should also be able to support overclocking. Make sure it is mentioned on the motherboard.

- o **I/O SHIELD** - Make sure to attach them at the beginning of the PC assembly as most people tend to forget them, because they keep it aside to attach later, leaving the motherboard exposed at the I/O side to dust and other outside factors, which can affect other components as well. *Some I/O SHIELD have metallic tabs that need to be bend while installing.* If not, trying to connect USB here will push the tab into the motherboard causing damage.

- o **CPU FAN COOLER PROTECTIVE PLASTIC FILM** - Peel them before installing them as they can cause heat buildup on the processor, causing the plastic to melt and to deal with them later resulting in a waste of time and thermal compound.

- o **What to expect when you switch on the newly build PC?** Press the power button —> The system powers up —> Fans start spinning —> Display in the monitor shows the motherboard logo. *If the computer doesn't show a logo or you get a series of beeps?* To effectively test the build errors, we need to disassemble the PC to it's basic. Remove everything that is not required for the basic functionality of the computer like graphics card, hard drives, RAM. Now remove the motherboard from the CASE. You keep the hard drive connected if the monitor is successfully showing a logo post and searching for a boot drive. If not, remove it from the motherboard.

- o **Not installing the STANDOFFS before installing the motherboard** - The conductive underside of the motherboard must be separated from the case by an insulating air gap by using a STANDOFFS or risers. This prevents the motherboard's conductive underside from coming in contact with the computer chassis and thereby shorting.

Always count the number of standoffs required for the proper installation of the motherboard. Any extra standoffs can come in contact with the backside of the motherboard and damage its circuits and short the motherboard. Too little and the motherboard will flex and touch the computer chassis which will further result in the shorting of the motherboard.

o **Not installing your motherboard header switches correctly** – This will not damage your computer, but your PC won't power up. Check the **power switch** with the pin connecting the header **first**, if not installed fully or in the correct position. Check if it's installed on the correct header.

o **Check if you have a faulty motherboard header** – Bridge the connection of the power switch header pins with a small screwdriver or paper clips. If the power gets switched ON, no problem with the motherboard.

o Make sure the **LED front panel** wires are connected positive to positive and negative to negative for it to work properly.

o Make sure the power is switch on both at the PSU and the wall main **power supply**.

o Not ensuring the cards are **seated firmly (RAM & GPU)** – Installing the graphics card outside along with the motherboard ensures the graphics have been installed properly. You want a flat connection into the slot you are installing. Installation after the motherboard in the case doesn't always guarantee the snug fit of the graphics card. This could be the reason your computer is not switching ON. The beginners always install the graphics card this way, which isn't a problem as long as you make sure the graphics card is seated perfectly into the PCI express slot and the side latch/holding tab is locked in position.

o Make sure your graphics card is *installed in the fasted PCI express card slot*, which is usually the closest one to the CPU. Speed is also mentioned on the side of the slot on the motherboard, PCIEx2, x4, x16, etc. The below picture shows the slots and the type of card to attach to them. Taken from the motherboard manual of MSI B450 GAMING PRO CARBON AC.

PCI_E1~5: PCIe Expansion Slots

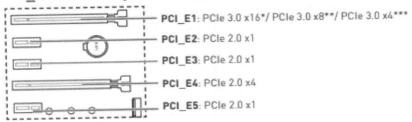

PCI_E1: PCIe 3.0 x16*/ PCIe 3.0 x8**/ PCIe 3.0 x4***

PCI_E2: PCIe 2.0 x1

PCI_E3: PCIe 2.0 x1

PCI_E4: PCIe 2.0 x4

PCI_E5: PCIe 2.0 x1

* For Ryzen™ 1st and 2nd Generation processors

o **RAM ALIGNMENT** – Make sure to line the RAM notch with that of the motherboard RAM slot and to hear a click sound along with the holding tab on the side locking when you push the RAM into the slot. Make sure to connect them to the assigned slot. Read the motherboard manual to get this info. There is a picture depicted next to the slot for verification. It's almost always on the DIMMA2 & DIMMB2. The first two slots and the second two are of different circuits hence you have to make sure to connect the RAM included in both the circuits especially if you have 2 memory cards. If only one, stick it in DIMMA2, the first one.

o RAM MEMORY – Also make sure to check the RAM MEMORY if they are compatible with the motherboard.

o **Not installing your CPU correctly** – This will result in bend damaged CPU pins resulting in the PC monitor not showing anything. Always hold the CPU by the sides and not under or below. Never touch the bottom of the top side of the CPU.

o ***Connecting the graphics card output into the motherboard in place of a dedicated GPU – FANS SPINNING BUT NO DISPLAY ERROR*** – Motherboard will default to an aftermarket graphics card unless explicitly told not to. So, no output is generated from your motherboard connection which you are connected to. This can be prevented by simply shifting the display output connection from your motherboard to your graphics card.

o ***Not installing additional CPU power connectors*** – If the CPU supplementary 8-PIN power cable not appropriately connected to the CPU power header, CPU_PWR1 depicted on the motherboard by the side of the header. Don't confuse them with the 8-PIN graphics card power supply. An alternative error is the cable is not connected to the CPU power header is that the system will go into a boot loop of around 3 seconds pairing ON and OFF. Photo Courtesy: MSI motherboard manual

o ***MOTHERBOARD (24 PIN)*** – Also don't forget to check if the 24-pin motherboard connector is seated correctly.

o ***Not installing additional Graphics card power connectors*** – Graphics card comes with a power supply like (i) 8 pin to 6+2 pin single cable (ii) 8 pin to 6+2 with a supplementary 6 pin. Make sure what PCIe cable is needed first for that particular graphics card and select the appropriate power cable from the PSU, during the PSU wiring and installation.

o Not using ***THERMAL PASTE*** – Air is a poor medium for heat dissipation. Thermal paste ensures even contact, thus even heat distribution between the CPU and HEATSINK surface, resulting in effective heat dissipation, if fixed appropriately. Most branded CPU FAN COOLER comes with thermal paste. Most aftermarket CPU COOLER FANS don't come with it and needs to be applied while fixing it to the CPU. If this step is omitted can result in excessive heating up of the CPU resulting in a not working PC.

o **NO CPU FAN CONNECTED** – The result is the same as that of not using the thermal paste, resulting in excessive heating up of the CPU. Make sure the fan is connected to the CPU_FAN header on the motherboard.

o **UNDERRATED PSU** – An underrated power supply unit may have thermal load problems. In times of high thermal load, PC is also demanding a high amount of power for the task at hand, when this is not supplied result in power OFF, restart or unable to power to your graphics card resulting in unreliable operation. Suggested power in a gaming PC, 4K video editing PC should be nothing less than 500W. The latest GPU requires about 150W typical and 280-300 at peak.

o **BALANCING YOUR BUILD** – This means you are choosing components that complement each other. The best way to do this is to go to the website WWW.PCPARTPICKER.COM, where you can compare the compatibility between all the components you are going to use to build a PC. Example: If you buy a cheap CPU, don't put it along with a powerful graphics card. The CPU will act as a bottleneck preventing the graphics card from its full potential. Or buying a high watt PSU for a single graphics card setup. Or installing a 64 GB RAM for watching INTERNET videos. Always build PC and select the components based on the necessity or the intention.

o Always **manage your cable** – Sort out the cables into groups. Use zip ties to secure them. Keep the inside of the case less messy so that it will be easy for you later if you have to disassemble the PC for some repairs or replacements. The excess unsorted messy cable can mess with the airflow inside, thus heating the PC. It is also a perfect magnet for dust.

o Connect HDMI cable of the **monitor to the Graphics card** - If you have a well efficient graphics card, it will be wise to connect the monitor to the graphics card to reap the full benefits of the card, especially when editing and watching 4K videos. Especially playing Games.

o Make sure your motherboard has a DUAL BIOS or a flashback. These motherboards have a backup BIOS in case something happens to the BIOS because of a sudden shutdown, power loss. This damages the BIOS. If you don't have the dual BIOS, you will have a big headache to take the motherboard to the service center. So, I suggest you use the UPS (uninterrupted power supply) backup power to your PC.

o If you are using more than 2 FANS in your case, it's better to create positive air pressure inside the case by having **more fans as intakes** and slightly fewer exhaust fans. This setup will reduce the dust build up inside of your case. This also allows you to run your fan at a lower speed resulting in a quieter environment.

o **POSITIVE VS NEGATIVE AIR PRESSURE** - Heart transfer relies on 2 main things for the best effectiveness: (i) A lower ambient temperature, how hot the air is around the HEATSINK (ii) Air movement. Living in a colder place and room air conditioner helps a lot. Since the components of the PC are enclosed in a CASE, the air use to cool these components can be considerably hotter than the rest of the room impeding cooling efficiency. The temperature inside the room itself can increase over time because of this. This is one of the methods, where the fan is useful to move the air inside faster. The drawbacks include - Noise, dust which can easily accumulate on the fans reducing their effectiveness, they also do plugs up the kinks of the HEATSINKS thus reducing their effectiveness. Adding more fans increases this unless done responsibly.

o So How to practice SAFE COOLING? - The answer to this problem is a BALANCED AIRFLOW. The fan can be configured in two ways: (i) If all the fans act as an exhaust pulling the air out from inside, these fans act against each other reducing their efficiency. This movement of air only outside creates a negative air pressure inside. The result is air is pulled inside from all the nooks and corners of the case. This can result in dust build up in these areas and are pulled into the CASE.

o If all the fans on the CASE are only pulling air inside, it has a similar issue as fans pulling air outside but dust doesn't accumulate in the nooks and corners of the CASE because of the POSITIVE PRESSURE inside because of which the air is pushed out through them. This doesn't help if you don't have filters in these nooks and corners of your CASE. So, the ideal way is to have filters on the fans for intake and extra filters in the nooks and corners of the CASE. If you don't have filters on your PC CASE, Cover the PC with a used pantyhose seems to do the trick. In the long run check for dust accumulation in the mesh panels and areas around the optical drive base. If present, time to make some adjustments in fan's intake/outtake ratios of your PC. There are options to adjust your FAN SPEED in your BIOS. Play around with it.

o If you have an equal number of fans and exhaust, having them at a higher level is the best way to expel the heat because hot air expands and rises which will be removed by these exhaust fans. [2 FANS IN THE FRONT & 2 EXHAUST IN THE BACK] o If you are using a tower-style CPU COOLER FANS, be careful when you handle the fins of these coolers as they can be sharp.

o If you go with water coolers - Make sure to buy components of the same metal as they can cause chemical reactions over time if mixed. Example: If you buy a copper CPU block but buy an aluminum radiator and put them in the same loop. The metals start eroding due to chemical reactions. This can result in water leakage and damaging other components of your PC.

o Try to build most of your components outside the case like motherboard, SSD, RAM, CPU with CPU COOLER FANS before attaching the motherboard inside the case. This reduces most of the hassle of connecting these components inside the case as there are limited space and light. Thus, reducing most of the error that can happen while building them with an already attached motherboard.

o ***THERMAL-PASTE*** - This is applicable if you are planning to replace your CPU, CPU COOLER FAN or the motherboard. Thermal-paste is also needed when the CPU cooler doesn't come with a pre-applied thermal paste. This is also applicable when you have to put them all back together again. When applying them on the CPU, make a pea-sized paste deposit on the center of the CPU or make an 'X' along the top of the CPU metal surface. The pea-sized deposit is more effective. NOTE: Try not to use the excess amount as this paste can leak onto the surrounding circuits and damage them as there are metal elements added to the paste to make it more conductive. The non-conducting is available in the market but can be very unappealing to look at if the thermal-paste is leaking through the sides of the CPU. Too less of thermal-paste can cause heat build-up within the CPU resulting in the crashing of the PC.

o Make sure your motherboard has M.2 slots and that it supports NVMe technology before purchasing M.2 NVMe SSD.

o Make sure what BIOS is necessary for your particular motherboard as some motherboard requires you to install older versions of BIOS.

o Buy a branded PSU (Power Supply Unit). If not, don't be surprised when your cheap PSU blows up.

o Don't spend extra money on the wattage of your PSU unless necessary. There are several websites out there to calculate your wattage requirement of your PC based on your components used to build your PC. So, your PSU will be the last one to be purchase based on other component's wattage. **Check out the required power for you PC in:**
  Power Supply Calculators:
  Seasonic - https://lmg.gg/seasoniccalculator
  OuterVision - https://lmg.gg/outervision
  MSI - https://lmg.gg/msicalculator
  be quiet! - https://lmg.gg/bequeitcalculator

o Think twice before investing in a fancy water cooler even though water cooling is significantly more effective than traditional forced air-cooling. It doesn't give too much of an advantage unless you are overclocking. Perfect for gamers and professional video editors.

o If you are planning to install multiple FANS, be sure about the number of available fan headers on the motherboard. Modern motherboards can control the FANS in the BIOS. So ideally it is best to connect these fans to the motherboard rather than to the power supply. There is a physical fan controller that can adjust fan speed from outside of your case or use a case that comes with a fan speed control switch.

o Building the most expensive PC without giving any attention to the Monitor. The monitor is equally important in translating the high-quality graphics and video coming out from the PC. (Refer to the chapter, "How to choose the best monitor" for more details)

o Always buy a motherboard that comes with backup BIOS. This will help in not sending the motherboard to the service center if your existing BIOS is damaged. This could happen when the PC shutdown when the BIOS is being updated.

BIOS FLASH BUTTON

<u>HOW TO USE BIOS FLASH BUTTON?</u>

- o The question is – How to recover my BIOS/BIOS UPDATE?
- o If the BIOS CRASHED – Do the following steps:
- o Put the latest BIOS from the manufacturer's website into FAT32 formatted USB Pendrive.
- o Change the BIOS filename to MSI.ROM. Click YES to renaming.
- o Plug-in power supply to your motherboard.
- o Check FLASH BIOS BUTTON PORT LOCATION in the motherboard manual.
- o Plug the above USB Pendrive into the Flash BIOS Button port.
- o Now press the FLASH BIOS BUTTON.
- o Wait for 5 seconds. The red light will start flashing next to the BIOS FLASH BUTTON to indicate the BIOS update is in process.
- o BIOS update process will take around 5 minutes.
- o The red light will stop flashing to indicate the FLASH BIOS Button process is finished.
- o The BIOS is now restored.

YOUTUBE CHANNEL RECOMMENDATION FOR VIDEOS

SOME YOUTUBE CHANNEL RECOMMENDATION

These are some of the best YouTube channels to help you in building your own PC:

- https://www.youtube.com/user/WhoIsMatt [✔✔Good Channel]

- https://www.youtube.com/user/KingstonTechMemory

- https://www.youtube.com/user/Techquickie [✔✔✔Excellent Channel]

- https://www.youtube.com/channel/UCmbkRUS_4Efdt5 UIhwNqtcw (Greg Salazar)

- https://www.youtube.com/user/msihowtochannel

- https://www.youtube.com/user/MSIGamingGlobal

- https://www.youtube.com/user/paulshardware [✔✔✔Excellent Channel]

- https://www.youtube.com/user/newegg [✔✔✔Excellent Channel]

- https://www.youtube.com/channel/UC05v8PDbY1pdVQ _SvbJik1g (GamingScan) [✔✔✔✔Excellent]

- https://www.youtube.com/channel/UCJQJ4GjTiq5lmn 8czf8oo0Q (PowerCert Animated Videos)

- https://www.youtube.com/channel/UCXuqSBlHAE6Xw-yeJA0Tunw (Linus Tech Tips) [✔✔✔Excellent]

- https://www.youtube.com/user/Jayztwocents (JayzTwoCents) [✔✔Good Channel]

<u>SOME YOUTUBE VIDEO RECOMMENDATION</u>

- https://youtu.be/Tdoys_HDZYU
(Build a Budget 4K Video Editing PC for $700 in 2019! | Ryzen Computer Guide)

- https://youtu.be/7-s04b5zel8
(How To Build A Video Editing Computer | $850 Ryzen PC Beginners Build Guide | 2017)

- https://youtu.be/-1FBs3W_lp0
($3000 4K Video Editing PC for Adobe Premiere Pro | Complete Parts List)

- https://youtu.be/Bah1Nv3W0QA
(Build a Budget 4K Video Editing PC for $650 in 2020! | AMD Ryzen Build)

- https://youtu.be/yKHI4eeVgFE
(PC Build - 4k Video Editing PC Build 2019 - $1000 Budget - DIY in 5 Ep 108)

- https://youtu.be/gHY6ygHj80c
(How To Build a Gaming PC in 2019! Part 1 - Hardware Basics, 3 Parts) - Very Useful

- https://youtu.be/5FtkzSY7mT8
(MSI B450 Gaming Pro Carbon AC Unboxing & Overview)

- https://youtu.be/D-1sP5Sn998
(MSI Armor RX 580 OC Unboxing - Bye Bye GTX 1060/ RX 480)

- https://youtu.be/iTkXunUAriE
(MSI - HOW TO use Flash BIOS Button)

- https://youtu.be/I2ARhJ7E5Fk
(ESD MAT, HOW WHAT WHY) - Very Useful

- https://youtu.be/kMGS7Deg_HY
(How to format a USB Stick to FAT32 on Windows 10)

- https://youtu.be/kx0ynC8Thlw
(All SSD Types EXPLAINED)

- https://youtu.be/JYwHB2P6GmM
(How to apply Thermal Paste) - Very Useful

- https://youtu.be/gejkP3PhrCo
(Building the $900 Gaming PC that Everyone Should Build!)

- https://youtu.be/w_HKRUPN1Mk
(4K Video Editing PC on a BUDGET)

- https://youtu.be/dYUgEZXboP8
(How to Install AMD Wraith Prism RGB CPU Cooler [Ryzen 3700x] Beginner Friendly)

- https://youtu.be/-plesrt8ZCs
(Avoiding Common PC Building Traps - Episode 1 - 6 Parts) - Very Useful

- https://youtu.be/g8EN3K-eaVA
(Positive vs Negative Air Pressure as Fast as Possible)

- https://youtu.be/Tay4Pz-PQDc
(Why is Water Cooling Better?)

- https://youtu.be/TbGjYumO_aw
(How to choose a motherboard: Your 2020 buying guide)

- https://youtu.be/ORwQL6dojXY
(Single Channel vs Dual Channel vs Quad Channel Memory (2020))

- https://youtu.be/u7O7UvUAJEQ
(AMD Wraith Prism RGB Fix)

o Thank You for Taking This Journey with Me...

Printed in Great Britain
by Amazon